The Growing Life

The Growing Life

A Daily Plan to Develop Your Spiritual Roots

Audley B. Lyon

MULTNOMAH PRESS
PORTLAND, OREGON 97266

© 1970 by Alverda E. Hertzler
Published by Multnomah Press
Printed in the United States of America

Third Printing 1982

The Library of Congress Cataloged the First Printing of this Title as Folllows:

Lyon, Audley B
  The growing life; devotionals for the young in Christ, by Audley B. Lyon. Portland, Or., Multnomah Press [c1970]
  255 p. 23 cm.

  1. Youth—Prayer-books and devotions—English.   I. Title.
BV4850.L9   148'.83   76-146252
                         MARC

ISBN 0-930014-07-3

DEDICATION

To those young people

who want joy in their hearts,

safety on their paths,

victory in their lives,

and a glorious future,

this book is dedicated.

PART I
KNOWING GOD

PART II
LIVING IN CHRIST

Foreword

To you who read . . .

If you want to grow in the most important part of your personality, your inner life, this book of daily devotional readings will help you. It will give you some of the great teachings of the Bible and lead you into reading it for yourself. Through your reading of the Bible you can come to know your heavenly Father, God, and your Savior, Jesus Christ. You will come to understand how to live the life that counts—the Christian life—and to grow in it.

The Growing Life has two sections: Part I, "Knowing God," tells you why we believe the Bible is from God and what it teaches about the purpose of Christ's coming to earth. "Living in Christ," Part II, tells you how the Holy Spirit, who dwells in your heart when you belong to Christ, will enable you to live the Christian life.

The Growing Life is designed for you to use in a daily devotional time. Ask the Lord to help you set a definite time and to keep it every day. Even ten or fifteen minutes with Him can make a great difference in your whole day. Plan to read a page every day with the Bible references and questions. If you should miss doing so, do not skip ahead. Just continue from where you read last because one day's reading is often related to a previous one.

Some of the readings may interest you more than others. However, each day you can find some thought or Scripture verse to carry with you through the day. The "For Thinking and Doing" questions and suggestions are important to help you think about the Bible verses as you read them and to do something about the things they teach you. This is the way of growing in your inner life.

Make your Bible your very own by underlining favorite verses or promises. (A fine ball point pen and a small plastic ruler will help.) Your marked Bible will become a treasured possession as you realize God's promises are for you. Memorizing them and other favorite verses will become increasingly easy and make the Bible living to you. You can learn to locate the books of the Bible more quickly by memorizing their order or by keeping a reference chart with the page numbers in your Bible.

The Growing Life can be valuable for your family to use for a family devotional time, with each one taking turns in reading, looking up Scripture verses, and sharing in discussion together.

As you faithfully read day by day what God has to say to us in His Word, may you find that life of true fulfillment for which everyone searches—that exciting great adventure for which we were created: knowing God and our Savior, Jesus Christ.

Editor's Note

Young people today are searching for realities in life, but many are searching in the wrong directions. However, Billy Graham and other evangelists are amazed at the great number of young people who are turning to Christ, who said, "I am the Way, the Truth, and the Life" (John 14:6). Young people who have found Him have realized new joy, inner satisfaction, and a deep purpose for the future as they have entered into a new quality of life—life that is eternal (John 17:3).

The Growing Life was written to help young people find in Christ this new life for themselves. Some of the greatest truths of the Bible and deepest experiences of the Christian life are presented through the daily readings and Scripture verses. The author, Mrs. Audley Lyon, was a teacher of young people, frail in body but strong in her spiritual life as reflected in these pages. She had planned to write readings for a full year, but failing health made this impossible. However, these which she completed cover some of the most important things to be learned about knowing God as Creator, the truth of God's Word, Christ's saving work, the Holy Spirit, and practical problems of Christian living.

The "For Thinking and Doing" sections I have added to Mrs. Lyon's manuscript at the suggestion of Rev. Norman Jerome of the American Sunday School Union, who gave valuable assistance in editing the manuscript. These sections will involve young people not only in reading, but also in thinking about what they have read and then applying it to their daily lives. This kind of personal involvement has been a secret which many members of Bible Study Fellowship classes have found so valuable in their Bible study. The questions about Bible passages are similar, although simpler, to those used in these classes for Bible study, personal thought and discussion. Such study has proved of blessing to hundreds and hundreds of members.

The material in *The Growing Life* has been experimentally used by some of these Bible Study Fellowship members in a family devotional period, as well as by their young people individually. The response has been enthusiastic, especially where the family discussed the questions and teachings of the Bible together.

I trust that as these readings are published, great numbers of young people may find through them a better knowledge of the

Bible and that life in Christ which alone can fulfill His purposes for them.

Alverda E. Hertzler
Member, Board of Directors
Bible Study Fellowship

God Lives

"He (God) exists" (Hebrews 11:6).

God lives; God cares for us. Believing these two great truths can make a wonderful difference in your life. Some people live as if God did not exist. A recent book expressed the idea "God is dead," but the Bible teaches us that God lives. A bumper sticker of a car commented in these words, "Your God is dead? Sorry about that; mine is living."

Not only is God living now, but back through millions and billions of years and even before that time He was living. He never had a beginning, and even before a person or a thing was made, God was. Not only in that strange, mysterious past God always was, but also He always will be in the future, in that endlessness which lies ahead. God will live on and on forever. The Bible tells us that His life is an everlasting life. "The Lord God, who is and who was and who is to come," "the living God" (Revelation 1:8, Psalm 42:2).

Perhaps you wonder how one can be sure that there was, and is, and always will be this living God. How do other people know that you are alive? Or how can we be sure that Thomas Edison or George Washington ever lived? We know they lived because there are certain things to prove it. Just so, there are countless things which prove that God lives and was living in the past.

This wonderful, almighty God wants you to know Him, and it is the most wonderful thing in all the world to have Him for a loving helper and a strong, wise friend. We can know God even though He is so marvelous and glorious that we cannot fully understand Him. All around us there are many things we cannot understand which yet are very real; we believe in them because we make use of them day after day.

Nothing is more real than God. His promise is, "Then shall we know, if we follow on to know the Lord" (Hosea 6:3, KJV). This devotional book with its short bit of reading for each day is to challenge you and is here to help you to reach out beyond the things you now understand about God and to come to know Him.

Whatever life will bring to you,
God will be true to you:

Friend by your side,
Light on your path;
Joy in your heart,
In your ears music,
In your heart songs.
Whatever life will bring to you,
God will prove true to you.

—Charles Herbert

For Thinking and Doing:

1. Read Isaiah 44:6, Psalm 63:1, 3.
2. What are your own reasons for believing in God?
3. What do you think would help you to come to know God better?
4. Decide on a plan to make sure you spend time each day to read the devotional portion and Scripture verses for the day.

2nd Day

Knowing God

"Come ye near unto Me." "Acquaint now thyself with Him . . . thereby good shall come unto thee" (Isaiah 48:16, Job 22:21, KJV).

Yesterday we read that we shall know the Lord if "we follow on to know" Him. Everything hangs on that word "if," doesn't it? It all depends on you.

You can always make friends if you go about it the right way. But you would not expect to get to know the boy down the street if you barely spoke to him in passing or only stopped long enough to ask a favor. Nor would you hope to win the friendship of that attractive girl next door if you never wanted to be with her or showed any interest in what she did or said. Yet we treat God in that way and wonder why we do not know Him.

14

There are a number of ways of learning about God, but it is through His Book, the Bible, that we first come to really know Him. In it God tells us about Himself. There, too, He speaks of the wonderful and thrilling things He will give to those who trust Him.

We must also speak to God, that is, pray. There is nothing we cannot pray about for He says, "In everything by prayer . . . with thanksgiving let your requests (your wants) be made known to God" (Phillippians 4:6). "Draw near to God, and He will draw near to you" (James 4:8). Thank Him for His love to you and for the good things you enjoy. Tell Him of all that troubles you; ask Him to keep you safe, to lead you in the right way, and to help you. He also wants you to talk to Him about those you love in order that He can help them too.

Of course you may draw near to God at any time, but the best time is when you first awake in the morning, before other people and things come crowding in. It is then, also, that the whole day lies ahead. It is best to begin it by putting yourself into God's keeping, for then the whole day will be better. He knows what the hours will bring, can guard you against harm and evil, and can help you with your problems. He will care for you and make things work for good if you will put yourself into His strong and loving hands.

It isn't always easy to pull ourselves out of bed a little earlier than usual in order to spend time with God. Often we don't feel like reading or praying, but if you do your part—draw near—the Lord will always do His part and will reward you in wonderful ways.

"Be ready in the morning, and come up in the morning . . . and present yourself there to Me" (Exodus 34:2).

> I am sure I know the secret,
> Learned through many a troubled way.
> If you seek Him in the morning,
> He'll be with you through the day.
> —Selected and adapted

For Thinking and Doing:

1. Read Isaiah 48:17, Job 22:25-28.

2. How can having a Bible of your own help you to come to know God?

3. Become familiar with the books of the Bible and their order so you can find verses easily.

4. Pray, asking God to help you keep a devotional time with Him each day.

God Speaks Through Creation

"A living God who made the heaven and the earth and the sea and all that is in them . . . He did not leave Himself without witness" (Acts 14:15, 17).

Have you ever acted as a witness? If so you may have told or shown what you knew, or had seen, or had heard. For instance, you may have been called to court to tell what you knew about an auto accident, or perhaps you were asked to repeat something you heard someone say.

We are all witnesses of one kind or another, for we give witness concerning other people by what we say of them. We each have silent witnesses, also, for without a word being spoken the things that we do tell to all around us whether we are kind or mean, true or insincere.

There is still another kind of witness that is like the huge jet plane, the beautiful violin, or the useful radio. All these show forth the knowledge and skill of the ones who made them.

In the same ways God has witnesses that speak of Him. Not only does He tell us of Himself, but those who know Him speak of Him also. There are silent witnesses which show Him forth. These silent ones are the things God has made, which are always truthfully telling about Him. Above us, around us and within us there are countless "voices" speaking to our eyes, ears and hearts and telling thrilling and wonderful things about our marvelous God. Every star and flower, each rock and tree, colors, light, sounds, ocean tides, winds and storms, birds and creeping things— all these witness in their own special way about the Almighty One who planned, made and keeps them.

As you listen, what do they say? "All Thy works shall praise Thee, O Lord" (Psalm 145:10, KJV). "It will be a sign and a witness to the Lord" (Isaiah 19:20). "But ask the beasts, and they will teach you; the birds of the air, and they will tell you; or the plants of the earth, and they will teach you; and the fish of the sea will declare to you. Who among all these does not know that the hand of the Lord has done this?" (Job 12:7-9).

This is my Father's world.
He shines in all that's fair.

16

In the rustling grass I hear Him pass.
He speaks to me everywhere.
—Maltbie Babcock

For Thinking and Doing:

1. Read Psalm 145:1-5, 10-12; Psalm 146:5, 6.

2. Think of the ways a watch witnesses to the skill of a watchmaker. Could it come into being by itself, or could our earth do the same without a Creator?

3. Give reasons why you think the things God has created tell us there is a Creator.

4. Thank Him today for something which speaks to you of His creative power.

4th Day

Seeing God in the Skies

"Our Lord . . . Who hast set Thy glory above the heavens" (Psalm 8:1, KJV).

Many hundreds of years ago in the land of Palestine lived a teen-age boy named David. His father raised sheep and David spent much time in the fields caring for the flock. As David lay down beside the sleeping sheep he must often have looked into the evening sky and watched the stars shine more and more clearly in the gathering darkness. Like tiny pinpoints of light they sparkled and glowed in pale blue, white or yellow brilliance. And the moon shined so beautiful, so silvery clear.

As David gazed he probably wondered about them. Who made them? They could not have made themselves. As David looked and wondered, the stars, moon and sun spoke plainly to his heart. They told him of the knowledge, power and glory of the One who made them all.

So David wrote this and we believe it to be true: "The heavens are telling the glory of God; and the firmament (and sky) proclaims His handiwork. Day to day pours forth speech, and night to night declares knowledge. There is no speech, nor are there words; their voice is not heard; yet their voice goes out through all the earth, and their words to the end of the world" (Psalm 19:1-4).

How amazed David would have been to learn some of the things that we of the space age know about the sun, moon and stars. In his time no man could have even dreamed of orbiting in a

17

space craft around the moon or of seeing photographs of the surface of the moon. The limitless reaches of space in our universe would have been completely unbelievable to him.

On Christmas Eve, 1968, millions of people heard the majestic Genesis story of creation over their radio and television sets. As three United States astronauts circled the moon, its expanse of nothingness reminded them of the day of creation when the earth was "without form and void" (Genesis 1:2). While they telecast to the world a view of the lunar landscape, they read the opening verses of the first chapter of Genesis from 69 miles above the moon. "In the beginning God created the heavens and the earth." How different was the witness of these men, all members of Christian churches, from that of the Russian astronauts who observed that they did not see God on their flight into space.

The United States astronauts and David had something in common—they saw the beauty and wonders of the stars and sky and gave honor to God as their Creator.

For Thinking and Doing:
1. Read Psalm 148:1-4, 11-13; Psalm 63:3, 4.
2. Where have you seen God in His creation?
3. What has spoken to you of His power?
4. What else did David praise God for in Psalm 63:3, 4?

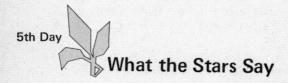

5th Day

What the Stars Say

"Great is our Lord, and abundant in power; His understanding is beyond measure. He determines the number of the stars, He gives to all of them their names" (Psalm 147:4, 5).

In David's time there were no telescopes through which he could discover what lay far out in space. He did not know, as we do, that the sun is a huge star 93 million miles away from the earth. Clustered around this great star and never leaving it, there are smaller heavenly bodies. The sun moves at the rate of 100 million miles a year. All these followers move with it in perfect order.

But the sun with all its followers is only a small part of an immense star group in which there are millions of millions, indeed billions, of other stars. Many of these stars are as large as our sun, while some are even larger and much brighter. When we use a telescope and look at this star group, the sky appears like a piece of dark velvet upon which stars have been sprinkled as numberless, glistening grains of salt. Among them, all the larger and nearer stars shine with dazzling splendor.

This great group of stars, or suns, is called a universe; it is like an island in a sea of space. How large is this island universe? If we could measure across the widest part of it we would find that light, traveling about 186,000 miles a second, takes about 100 thousand years to speed from edge to edge.

This isn't all. Billions of miles distant from our island group there are at least 100 million other island universes; all are quite as large as ours and stretch out into an immensity of space beyond what man can ever dream. So countless are the star groups that the astronomer James Jeans was led to say, "All the universes between them must contain about as many stars as there are grains of sand on all the seashores of the world." Have you ever been on the seashore and lifting up a handful of sand let it sift slowly out through your fingers? How could you even count the grains in that one handful?

No, man cannot count the stars and our minds grow a bit dizzy at the thought of them all, but "Great is our Lord, and of great power." "For He commanded and they were created" (Psalm 147:5, Psalm 148:5, KJV).

You believe there are these countless stars in the sky although you cannot see them with your natural, unaided sight. Then dare to believe that there is a living God although you do not see Him.

For Thinking and Doing:
1. Read Psalm 139:17, 18; Psalm 148:3, 4; Psalm 9:1, 2.
2. How do the stars bear greater witness to God today than in David's day?
3. In what ways do you think God thinks of us? (Psalm 139:17, 18).
4. Name some of the ways God has provided for your needs. Do you think you could count them all?

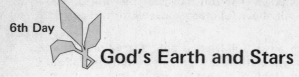

God's Earth and Stars

"Lift up your eyes on high and see: Who created these? He who brings out their host by number . . . by the greatness of His might, and because He is strong in power not one is missing" (Isaiah 40:26). *"He . . . hangeth the earth upon nothing"* (Job 26:7).

Let us again think of what the stars say about God. They seem quiet and unmoving, yet we know they are constantly moving at great speed. Every star follows its own orbit. Because this path is somewhat circular, after traveling many years or many thousands of years, the star arrives once more at its starting point, only to begin again and go on and on.

You remember that our earth follows the sun, moving in three ways at once as it travels. Think of the earth as a top spinning on the palm of your hand at one thousand miles an hour. Then move your hand in a circular direction as though around a central point (the sun). Now, with the top still spinning and your hand still moving in a circle, walk around the room. These are the three ways the earth travels as it follows in the orbit of the sun.

As the earth circles about, it is often moved a bit from its course by the pull of the moon and sometimes its speed is changed, but always the earth returns to its path and makes up the lost time. Thus it arrives at its starting point again on the split second, having lost not more than one thousandth of a second in one hundred years. How can this be?

Although the sun probably takes thousands of years to complete its orbit it, too, is never late. And what of the other countless millions of stars? Some travel much faster than others; some follow orbits of quite a different pattern and direction than do their neighbor stars. In all the boundless universe with its numberless hosts of heavenly bodies, no star falls behind; there is no confusion among any of them. How can this be?

No man can even guess the weight of all the stars, but it is known that our earth weighs millions of tons. That is rather heavy to be just hanging in space, isn't it? The sun weighs over a million times more than the earth. The star Betelgeuse is about 248 times the size of the sun, and many stars are much larger than that. How is it that these stars remain in the sky and do not fall?

As we consider the countless millions of enormous stars hurling through space at terrific speed—moving steadily, unfailingly and easily—we ask, "How?" God is the only possible answer.

For Thinking and Doing:

1. Read Psalm 8:3-5; Romans 1:19-21.
2. What speaks to you about God's creative power?
3. What do you think David was saying in Psalm 8:3-5?
4. Why does Paul say in Romans 1:19-21 that men who do not honor God are without excuse?

The Birds

"Look at the birds! They don't worry about what to eat . . . for your Heavenly Father feeds them. And you are far more valuable to Him than they are" (Matthew 6:26, LNT).

A young man who was studying the stars through a telescope was filled with awe as he thought of the mighty force which kept those countless and enormous worlds always moving onward. As he looked he felt that he was only a tiny speck in the limitless universe. The One who is the source of such power surely could not care for anything as small as he. Troubled, he turned from the study of the stars to a study of birds. As he saw how God had provided for them he realized that the same God had also wonderfully planned for him.

Just think about this: among the thousands of different birds, each is perfectly fitted for the kind of life it must live. There are meat-eaters with strong beaks for tearing flesh. Some birds feed upon seeds, bugs or worms; their bills are made to get this kind of food. Birds who live on land have feet and toes for hopping and running; those that swim have webs between their toes.

Why are flight birds able to mount up and fly about with so little effort? It is because of their streamlined bodies and their bones and feather quills which are hollow, yet very strong. Then too, while the body feathers are soft and sometimes small, the wing feathers are quite different. These are so large, flat and firm that the birds can easily remain in the air, gliding, flying swiftly, or poised and still.

21

Sometime look at a feather through a microscope. Examine the soft little spears that branch from each side of the quill and see how most of them are hooked to the next one to keep the feather firm, strong and flat. Think also of the many different colors and patterns of birds' warm, waterproof coverings, and most of them are so beautiful.

Have you ever examined birds' nests? Some are on mountain tops or in trees. Some are built behind and under waterfalls, under the eaves of a building, or on the ground. Some birds use sticks to build their nests, while others want mud, hair, feathers or grass. Some nests are sheltered and hard to find; others are easily seen. Each bird finds in its surroundings that which its nature needs to make a home.

Look at the birds. As you see how God has planned for each one, do you think He would have less care for man—for you and me? The marvelous provisions God has made for the needs of these small winged creatures are a silent witness to His love and care for us all.

In the days when Jesus taught his disciples He mentioned that five sparrows were worth two pennies. "Yet," He said, "God does not forget a single one of them. And He knows the number of hairs on your head! Never fear, you are far more valuable to Him" (Luke 12:6, 7, LNT).

For Thinking and Doing:

1. Read Psalm 106:1, 2; Psalm 104: 10-12, 16, 17, 24, 27.
2. How does Psalm 104:24 sum up the thought of today's reading?
3. What is the Lord saying to us in Matthew 6:26?
4. What does the thought in Luke 12:6, 7 mean to you?

8th Day

Growing Things

"Thus says the Lord, your Redeemer, Who formed you from the womb: 'I am the Lord, Who made all things, Who stretched out the heavens alone, Who spread out the earth—who was with Me?'" (Isaiah 44:24).

Look about you any day and you will see some of God's best witnesses and busiest workers, the plants.

Watch a plant grow. The little seed, dropped into the ground and covered with earth, lies quietly until at last a power not its own stirs it into life and action. The roots grow down or outward and the first little shoot pushes up through the darkness. Who tells that sprout it needs the light and guides it up?

The earth and the air hold certain substances man must have in order to live, yet we cannot eat earth or air. Plants take in some of these substances; we get them by eating the plants or animals which have eaten the grasses or plants. For instance, gas nitrogen is needed by all growing things. Human beings and animals need it to build protein, which is one of our necessary foods. Some of the grasses, plants and smaller growths gather in nitrogen from the earth and air, and we get part of our supply of it through them. Plants also draw into themselves the minerals our bodies need, iron, phosphorous, calcium, iodine, etc.

God arranged that most plants should receive their energy from the sun. You have probably noticed how cleverly the plant stem turns the leaves to keep them toward the light, for the leaves have many tiny storehouses in which to keep it. These little rooms also hold the water sent up to them by the roots and the carbon dioxide that has been taken in from the air. All the time, in some wonderful way, the carbon and oxygen are being separated; the oxygen is returned to the air and the carbon is manufactured into starch which turns into sugar.

These growing things also keep moisture in the air and ground. Their roots bind and hold the soil on the earth's surface. And then, who does not love the beauty of God's growing things, trees, grasses and plants.

Again, through all these things, we see a mighty Mind in action. "This is the Lord's doing, and it is marvelous in our eyes" (Matthew 21:42, KJV). "I am the Lord, Who made all things" (Isaiah 44:24).

For Thinking and Doing:

1. Read Nehemiah 9:6; Matthew 6:28, 29; Psalm 104:14; Psalm 147:7-11.

2. What is the thought you find in Matthew 6:28, 29?

3. Have you realized anew today some of the wonderful ways God has provided for us?

4. Thank Him today for something you have taken for granted before.

Upholding Power

"He is before all things, and by Him all things consist" (Colossians 1:17, KJV).

How many different kinds of things are around us? Some are living and growing; others like cloth, bricks or metal have no life. All such stuff is called dead matter although lately scientists have found that in one way dead matter is very lively indeed. It is made up of billions of invisible parts called molecules. Each molecule is made up of atoms, of which we hear so much these days. It is said that atoms are so small that a pile of them could not be seen through a microscope even if there were a million in the pile.

You probably know that each atom is really a group of unbelievably small particles: neutrons, protons, positrons, electrons, etc. The electrons with their electrical charge apparently swirl continually around the inner, central part of the atom in much the same way as the planets and satellites move about the sun.

Thus the things you see and use are not the quiet, unmoving things they seem to be. Energy is within each atom in every drop of water. Energy is also in the great star clusters that march across the heavens. Whether we think of a continuous flow of light, the ever-active electric currents, the upspringing and growth of plants or any part of the universe, we are faced with tremendous ceaseless power in action.

None of these things can create its own energy. Man cannot do it; he cannot even fully explain it. Energy comes from the almighty God whose power has been working since the creation of the universe. "Power belongs to God" (Psalm 62:11). Man can only make use of what God has already made.

Not only has God made all things, but He keeps them going. Even now He is "upholding the universe by His Word of power" (Hebrews 1:3). "In Him all things hold together" (Colossians 1:17). If for a brief moment the Almighty should cease to uphold the universe, there would be utter destruction; all things would break apart.

Let us read that verse again. "In Him all things hold together." That counts you in. It means that there is not a moment when you are not in the thought and plan of God. "The

Lord takes thought for me" (Psalm 40:17). "In Him we live and move and have our being" (Acts 17:28).

For Thinking and Doing:

1. Read Psalm 62:11; Psalm 40:17; Isaiah 25:1; Jeremiah 10:12.
2. What does it mean to you that God thinks of you?
3. Is He faithful to us even when we neglect Him?
4. Which verse in today's reading did you like best? Underline and memorize it.

Men Are Different

"God my Maker . . . teaches us more than the beasts of the earth, and makes us wiser than the birds of the air" (Job 35:10, 11).

We have listened to only a few of God's witnesses, but they all tell us that He is a person. Just exactly what is a person? Perhaps you answer, "I am alive and know it. I am conscious of my own self; I have physical life and a body in which I move and act. I have emotions: I feel love and anger, joy and sorrow. I can think, imagine and plan; I have a mind and a will by which I make decisions and act."

What great differences there are between human beings and all other creatures on earth. Let us notice a few of those differences. Animals, birds and insects have some remarkable abilities, but these are limited. Some spiders make clever traps to catch their food, but they make them after the same pattern. The beaver builds a comfortable lodge to live in, but all beavers make the same sort of houses. Birds of a certain kind usually make the same sort of nests. A fish lives exactly as do all the other members of its special fish family. It is by their instincts that animals are able to live in their own special ways. They can invent nothing and make no plans.

None of them have made anything on wheels, made clocks or boats, or planned a church or hospital. How different is man. He has imagination which leads him to paint pictures, write books, erect buildings, make missiles and orbit the earth.

However, the greatest difference between men and animals is that man has been given something which we call conscience. By

25

this he knows the difference between right and wrong and between good and evil. Man is the only creature on earth that shows any desire to know God and to pray to Him. He alone is able to worship Him and have fellowship with Him.

"There is a spirit in man: and the inspiration of the Almighty giveth them understanding" (Job 32:8, KJV). God has made you a person with wonderful possibilities, and His most precious gift to you is that you can come to know Him.

For Thinking and Doing:

1. Read Genesis 1:26, 27; Psalm 95:6, Proverbs 20:27; John 4:24.
2. Explain what Proverbs 20:27 means to you.
3. In what ways can we worship God?
4. How do you think we worship "in truth"?

11th Day

"How Great Thou Art"

"He who planted the ear, does He not hear? He who formed the eye, does He not see? . . . He who teaches men knowledge, the Lord, knows the thoughts of man, that they are but a breath" (Psalm 94:9-11).

It is hard for us to think of a person without thinking of the body as the most important and necessary part. But I know a young man who lost both arms and one leg in a war, yet he was still a person and a very brave and wonderful man. The real you, which makes you a person, is your inner self—your spirit and soul, which live within your body. No one has ever seen your soul or spirit, but you and others know they exist, for without them your body would be useless and you could not think, speak, feel or understand. So you are a spirit and a soul living in a body.

Come back now to the thought that God is a person. That does not mean He is the same kind of person that man is. He Himself tells us that "God is a Spirit" (John 4:24, KJV). That means He is a Spirit Being, a Person whose spirit does not need a physical body like ours in which to live.

How do we know that God is a person? We know it because of what He has done and is doing. For instance, all the billions of things that make up the vast universe could never have been here if

Someone had not willed or decided to make them. They would never have been made just as they are if Someone of great wisdom and knowledge had not first planned each part of every single thing. They could not have been made if that same Almighty One had not been able to make and keep all things as He had planned.

Above all else, only a Being who Himself is alive could possibly create living things and make anything as strange and wonderful as a spirit and a soul. God is indeed a living person, but one who is far, far greater than any other person in what He knows, in what He is, in what He does, and in what He has.

"The Lord . . . is the living God . . . It is He who made the earth by His power, Who established the world by His wisdom . . . For I am God, and there is no other" (Jeremiah 10:10, 12; Isaiah 45:22).

For Thinking and Doing:

1. Read Jeremiah 10:6, 10; Isaiah 45:18, 19; Psalm 86:8, 9; Psalm 48:14.
2. Count the words in the above verses from the Bible which prove that God is a living person.
3. What promise do you find in Psalm 48:14?
4. Try to learn that verse.

12th Day

God and You

"Don't be concerned about the outward beauty that depends on jewelry, or beautiful clothes, or hair arrangement. Be beautiful inside, in your hearts, with the lasting charm of a gentle and quiet spirit which is so precious to God" (I Peter 3:3, 4).

This question was asked in a magazine quiz, "What wild animal is most helpful to man?" The answer was, "The earthworm; it turns over the soil as it eats its way through the earth, thus increasing fertility of the land." What a surprise that a worm was called a wild animal, and what a surprise, also, that we owe so much to a little creature like a worm, which we tend to despise. Soundlessly there in the darkness and seen only by God, worms are faithfully doing their part in His plan of working for man.

It is often the same with human lives. Someone may start life in a poor or quiet place, unnoticed by others. But God sees, and He can pick up that one and make him great and useful.

George Washington Carver was born of poor Negro parents. While still a child he was stolen and traded for a horse. Everything seemed against him. He was just one small, black, lonely boy among thousands of other unnoticed and unimportant children. But God cared for him, and George Carver cared about God. Then in the Lord's own time things began to happen. Because he always asked the Lord for wisdom and sought to do God's will, George Carver became one of the world's noblest men and greatest scientists.

We often judge the importance of people by their appearance, by the things they have, or by what they wear. We are impressed by their popularity with others and sometimes by their talk. But aren't we foolish?

God's greatness and power are often shown in quiet things. A tiny seed is planted; there is no fanfare, yet by and by a beautiful, strong tree grows. Without a sound the rays of the sun do their work upon the earth. Noiselessly the moon controls the tides of the restless sea. Quietly the great cloud-ships of the air carry about their heavy cargo of water to pour upon the thirsty lands. These are God's ways, and He does not want you to measure the value and success of your life or others' lives by outward show or material things. Instead He wants you to learn of Him, listen to what He has to say to you, and trust Him. Then quietly and perhaps slowly, but very surely, He will work out in you and through you something more wonderful than you have ever dreamed.

"Thus says the Lord: 'Let not the wise man glory (boast) in his wisdom, let not the mighty man glory in his might, let not the rich man glory in his riches; but let him who glories glory (boast) in this, that he . . . knows Me.'" (Jeremiah 9:23, 24). "Humble yourselves before the Lord and He will exalt you" (James 4:10).

For Thinking and Doing:

1. Read Proverbs 3:1-6; I Corinthians 10:31.

2. Someone has said, "God has a plan for your life far greater than anything you have ever dreamed." What does this mean to you?

3. What is our part according to Proverbs 3:1?

28   4. Memorize the wonderful promise in Proverbs 3:5, 6.

God Has Plans for You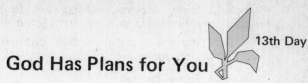

"Ah Lord God! It is Thou who hast made the heavens and the earth by Thy great power . . . Nothing is too hard for Thee" (Jeremiah 32:17).

As you think of all God's marvelous works do you suppose there is anything too hard for Him to do?

Not only do the things God has made speak of Him to us, but He also seems to speak to us through them. The Lord wants you to understand that He has planned for you just as carefully as He has planned the universe and that He, whose power is shown by every flower, bird and star, is able to do most wonderful things for you and through you.

The fruits and grains tell us that as God uses them to strengthen bodies, He can use you to help and strengthen others to do right. As a spreading tree gives welcome shade to hot and tired travelers, your life can give help to others who are discouraged. Like a strong wind, your life can be used of Him to influence and sway other lives. Like a mighty electric current, a power God gives you can work within your life. Then others will count themselves happy to have you as a friend. Like a star, your life can quietly shine for God.

Can God do all these things with us who are so weak and full of mistakes? "All things are possible with God" (Mark 10:27). To each of us the Lord God is saying, "Follow Me, and I will make you . . . " (Matthew 4:19). What will He make you? There is no limit to what He can do.

Perhaps you feel you don't amount to much—you are neither charming, clever, talented or popular. Perhaps you are poor or feel you could not achieve much. None of these things matter to the God of the impossible. The only ones God cannot help or use are those who are filled with pride and think that they are so clever, strong and wise that they have no need of God. But if you are willing to follow God, He can make your life count.

Will you say "Yes" to God's call to follow Him? To follow means to go somewhere, and to go somewhere means to leave certain things behind. When we follow the Lord we have to turn away from many things. What are these things? They may be unbelief, pride, laziness, wrong friendships, selfishness, or hatred—anything that keeps you from going His way.

Don't be afraid to follow. Step out and trust the Lord; He will not let you down.

For Thinking and Doing:

1. Read Psalm 86:10, 11; Jeremiah 29:11, 13.

2. Put David's prayer in Psalm 86:11 into your own words. Will you pray this today?

3. Jeremiah 29:11 in "Living Psalms and Proverbs" reads, "For I know the plans I have for you, says the Lord. They are plans for good and not for evil, to give you a future and a hope." What does this mean to you?

4. When does God say we will find Him according to Jeremiah 29:13?

14th Day

God Has Answers

"Behold, God is mighty . . . He is mighty in strength" (Job 36:5).

There are many questions that often bother us. Some of your questions may include the following.

1. Will the world always go on as it has in the past?

2. Is there anything beyond this life? If so, what and where?

3. Why is there so much trouble in the world, and why do mean, selfish people often seem to have the best of things?

4. Do we always just have to guess our way through life, or is each of us a part of a great plan?

5. What's life all about? Why are we here?

6. Nations, people and groups disagree as to what is right or wrong. Does anyone know for sure?

7. We are told such different things about God and religion. How can we tell the true from the false? Just Who and What is God?

Yes, we have many questions, but they can be answered by God through His Word. It is only Someone who knows all things that can give us truthful answers; no man can do it. "God . . . knows everything" (I John 3:20). "His understanding is beyond measure" (Psalm 147:5). "The Lord gives wisdom . . . knowledge and understanding" (Proverbs 2:6).

Not only do we need someone who can answer our questions, but we also need someone to whom we can take all our troubles: someone who knows all about us and who knows the other fellow or girl too. We want a friend who loves and cares, one who understands about our life today and also sees what lies before us in each hour of every day.

We wish for a helper who would know without being told when we are lonely, disappointed or discouraged and a friend who would know when we tried to do right and failed. How grand it would be to have a friend we could always trust and one ready and able to give us every kind of help we need.

We have such a friend in God. God can give us the help we need and He cares for us. He has given us great truths in the Bible to answer our questions, and He is a friend Who always understands and loves us.

"There is a friend who sticks closer than a brother" (Proverbs 18:24). He "is able to do far more abundantly than all we ask or think" (Ephesians 3:20). He who "is perfect in knowledge is with you" (Job 36:4). "He cares about you" (I Peter 5:7). Believe it. Say in your heart, "Almighty God cares for me!"

> Absolutely tender, absolutely true,
> Understanding all things, understanding you;
> Infinitely lovely, exquisitely near;
> This is God our Father—what have we to fear?
> —Selected

For Thinking and Doing:

1. Read Psalm 139:1, 2, 3, 6; Psalm 31:19; I Peter 5:7.
2. Which of the promises in today's reading meant the most to you?
3. Will you count on God's help to answer your questions and help solve your problems?
4. Memorize I Peter 5:7.

The Bible Reveals God  15th Day

"To whom will you compare Me, that I should be like him? says the Holy One. . . I am God, and there is no other; I am God, and there is none like Me. . . Before Me no god was formed" (Isaiah 40:25; 46:9; 43:10).

Let us think about yesterday's last question. People have such different ideas of God. How can we tell what is right and true?

There is only one Person in all the universe who knows all about God. That is God Himself. It is foolish and very dangerous for a person to trust his own thoughts about this Almighty One whom no man has ever seen. Nor will it help us to listen to others on this subject, for some say one thing and some say another. The more we listen to others' views the more puzzled we become. It is as though we were hearing the program of every station on our radio at the same time.

All thoughts of men about God can only be guesswork; some may be partly right and others be altogether wrong. Many think up some kind of a god to suit themselves and worship it. Thus there were the ancient gods of the Babylonians and Egyptians, those of the Greek myths, the gods of the Hindus, and many others. You can see that it is impossible for God to be all the different things which people have thought Him to be; some of them are really far off from His true nature.

Then can we ever know Him? Yes, for the Lord has told us about Himself in the Bible. "God has spoken" (Psalm 62:11). "Unto you . . . I call; and My voice is to the sons of man" (Proverbs 8:4, KJV). You say that you have never heard Him speak? Perhaps you do not know how to listen or just how you can hear His words.

People speak to us in a number of way. They talk to us face to face, over a telephone, through written words, by letters, or in books. In the past God has talked to men in different ways, but now He speaks to us in the Bible.

In this Book, God tells us of Himself and answers the questions no man can answer. From this Book we learn that God has glorious plans for man—for you—and that He is willing and able to carry them out. We have the Bible today because the Lord wants you to know the truth and to live in victory, joy and safety.

The surest way to hear God speak is to go to His Book and read what He says. "God speaks" (Job 33:14). "Let me hear what God the Lord will speak" (Psalm 85:8).

For Thinking and Doing:

1. Read Proverbs 8:6; Proverbs 14:12: Jeremiah 10:23; Psalm 119:133.

2. What ideas about God have you had which may not be true?

3. Is there some new thought about Him you have had since beginning your reading of His Word?

4. Will you pray today the prayer of Psalm 119:133?

Understanding the Bible

"O Lord; give me understanding according to Thy Word" (Psalm 119:169).

God gave us the Bible because He knows how important it is for us to have the truth, yet there are millions of people who do not read it or accept it as from God. Of course many people do believe the Bible and others that think those who do are rather odd and out of date.

If this Book really is God's message to man, why doesn't everyone accept it? There are a number of reasons. Some say, "Oh, we tried reading the Bible but it was so hard to understand that we gave it up." Yes, much of this Book is difficult to understand, especially when we read it for the first time.

However, we don't give up trying to learn arithmetic after the first attempt. Girls studying nursing or boys studying law or engineering do not give up because they cannot understand the whole subject all at once. How foolish that would be. Instead they press on, knowing that with further study it will become clear and plain. Let us treat the Bible in the same way. Ask God to help you to understand as you read. Psalm 119:130 promises, "The unfolding of Thy words gives light," and Job 32:8 (KJV) says, "The inspiration of the Almighty giveth them understanding."

There are also those who refuse to believe that this Book is the Word of God although they have never even read it through. There are thousands of people in India and in the jungles of Africa and South America who have never read the Constitution of the United States. If those jungle people said that there is no such thing as the Constitution, it would only prove their ignorance. The fact that some people say they cannot believe the Bible does not prove that it is not the Word of God. "He who is of God hears the words of God" (John 8:47). "He who rejects Me and does not receive My sayings has a judge; the word that I have spoken will be his judge on the last day" (John 12:48).

33

Some people just don't care. They may say, "Sure, maybe the Bible is God's Word, but what difference does it make? I'll get by all right, and for the present this world's good enough for me. I'm going to enjoy myself while I can." Of all such people God says, "Because I have called and you refused . . . you have ignored all My counsel . . . when distress and anguish come upon you. Then they will call upon Me, but I will not answer. . . Because they hated knowledge and did not choose . . . the Lord" (Proverbs 1:24, 25, 27-29).

For Thinking and Doing:

1. Read Psalm 100:5; Psalm 119:73, 125.

2. Is the fact that some parts of the Bible are difficult to understand a good reason not to read it, or could that just be an excuse?

3. Think of other things you have found hard to do at first. What has helped to make them easier?

4. Read Paul's prayer in Ephesians 1:17-19. Try to say in your own words the main thing for which he prayed.

17th Day

Unchanging Truth

"Heaven and earth will pass away, but My words will not pass away" (Luke 21:33).

Do you think it is strange and out of date to read and believe the Bible? None of us wish to be thought odd, so we usually just run with the crowd. But you had better make sure which way the crowd is running, for sometimes a whole school of fish swims trustingly into a waiting net.

Many years ago nearly all the educated people of the world believed the earth was flat, and they were so sure that the sun moved around the earth that Giordano Bruno was burned alive because he taught that the earth turns daily on its axis and revolves around the sun. Those who disagreed with him were up to date with what was believed at that time, but were they up to the truth? Which will you choose: to be right with those who trust the Bible, or wrong with many who don't? God says, "Blessed are they that hear the word of God, and keep it" (Luke 11:28, KJV).

34

There is another group which rejects God and His Book because they know the Bible condemns their sins. How utterly foolish to choose evil instead of good, death instead of life, and sin rather than God. They will not face the fact that some day, "each of us shall give account of himself to God" (Romans 14:12). "The fool hath said in his heart, There is no God" (Psalm 14:1, KJV).

Some people say they will not believe what they cannot understand; therefore, they turn away from the Book which tells them about God, miracles, angels, heaven and eternal life. These same people do not understand how it is that food entering the blood stream keeps within our bodies that mysterious thing called life, but they believe it and go right on eating. Very few know all about electricity, gravitation, chemistry, or what causes a little dry seed to spring up into life and grow. If they really believed only what they fully understood, they would not use a telephone or radio and they would never sow grain, plant a seed, or drive an automobile.

Let us not be so foolish, but gladly read God's wonderful Book and ask Him to help us know the meaning. "Open my eyes, that I may behold wondrous things out of thy law" (Psalm 119:18). "Then He opened their minds to understand the Scriptures" (Luke 24:45).

For Thinking and Doing:

1. Read Psalm 119:33, 34, 89, 105.
2. Can you think of ways in which the crowd can be wrong?
3. Put Psalm 119:105 into your own words.
4. Memorize Psalm 119:105.

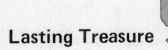

18th Day

Lasting Treasure

"No mere man has ever seen, heard or even imagined what wonderful things God has ready for those who love the Lord" (I Corinthians 2:9, LNT).

Near the ocean in the state in which I live there was a bare and ugly tract of land; it had no rivers, trees or farms. Years ago some small houses were built on this land and these became the homes of a group of poor, hard-working people.

One day a few men came to that quiet spot and began to dig deep into the hard, dark earth. Soon a derrick was raised and as it pumped, oil flowed out in almost unbelievable quantities. You can imagine the excitement.

Almost overnight everything seemed to change. Derricks were set up and started pumping away in back yards, front yards and all over the place. It was noisy with much coming and going. The lives of the people changed most of all. They were excited and happy; some moved to finer homes in town and some built larger houses. Now they were rich instead of poor; they were able to buy all sorts of costly, beautiful things.

The oil had been in the earth all the time, but the people had not been helped by it because they did not know that below the surface of their land lay buried wealth.

This true story is a picture of countless people who are poor, who could be rich. They do not know that God has laid up wonderful treasures for any who will have them—greater riches for this life and for the world to come than man could ever dream. God tells us of these riches in His Book.

All around us people are planning and working to make money. Why? Because with it they can get what they need and can have the things they think will keep them safe and happy. This is what God's riches do, they supply our needs, keep us safe, and make us happy. The riches of this world can be lost and the pleasures may pass away, but the things God gives are as sure and everlasting as the Lord Himself.

"I will give you the treasures . . . in secret places, that you may know that it is I, the Lord" (Isaiah 45:3). "Yes, if you cry out for insight and raise your voice for understanding, if you seek it like silver and search for it as for hidden treasures; then you will understand . . . and find the knowledge of God" and "will dwell secure" (Proverbs 2:3-5; 1:33).

All these treasures are for you, but you will have to dig deep into His Word to find them.

For Thinking and Doing:
1. Read I Timothy 6:17-19; Proverbs 10:22.
2. What are some of the dangers of trusting in earthly riches?
3. In your opinion what are the really valuable things in life?
4. Memorize Proverbs 10:22.

Sincere but Wrong

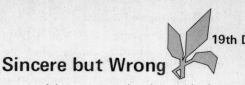

"There is a way which seems right to a man, but its end is the way to death" (Proverbs 14:12).

Often I have heard it said, "It doesn't matter what a person believes, just as long as he is sincere." What do you think of this?

At an intercollegiate football game I saw a brilliant player with the ball in his arm run swiftly toward the distant goal line. The men of his team tried to intercept him, but he dodged them all. Not until he was about one foot from the line did he realize he had been running toward the wrong goal. His great sincerity had only carried him all the faster and farther in the wrong direction. He was sincere, but wrong.

One day some babies were blinded for life because the hospital nurse put poison into their eyes, thinking it was eyewash. Numbers of people have died from eating toadstools which they mistook for mushrooms.

It is not enough to be sincere as we go through life; we must be sure we are also right. What you believe is of great importance, for it decides what you do. What and whom you believe can mean either life or death, joy or sorrow, success or failure. Even this moment what you sincerely believe is settling the future of your soul forever. So above all else we need to know the truth.

You have the Bible, a book that claims to have been given by God, to lead you into truth and to guide you through life. Suppose that it is all this and you refuse to believe it and obey it; what then? If it is God's Word we are in terrible danger if we pay no attention to its warnings. We are very foolish if we do not seek to learn of all the glorious things God has promised to those who trust and obey Him.

If this Book was given to us by the all-knowing, all-wise and all-powerful God and if you refuse to believe it, you are then acting as if what God says isn't true. Are you willing to do that?

God has given us proofs of the truth of His Word, and we should examine them carefully. Meanwhile let the prayer of your heart be, "Teach me . . . O Lord" (Psalm 27:11). Your prayer will surely be answered for the Lord has promised, "If any man will (or wills) to do His will, he shall know of the doctrine (teaching), whether it be of God" (John 7:17).

37

For Thinking and Doing:

1. Read Proverbs 23:23; Psalm 27:11.

2. Think of some times when you have been sincere, but sincerely wrong.

3. Can you sincerely pray with David his prayer of Psalm 27:11? What do you think are some of our "enemies"?

4. Will you ask God to help you make the Bible a guidebook for your life?

20th Day

The Wonder of the Word

"Thy testimonies are wonderful; therefore my soul keeps them" (Psalm 119:129).

God's Book was named "The Bible" centuries ago. The Latin word for it was "biblos" or "biblia" which means "The Books." In English it means "the Book made up of little books," for that is what it is.

Let us turn to the Bible's index. Most books list the subjects of the different chapters so that readers can know what the book is about. But in the Bible's index we find instead names of men and women, happenings, places and songs. The reason for this is that the Bible is not a single book, but is more like a small library bound into one volume. It is a library quite different from any other in the world.

Why is it so different? In the first place the men who wrote it claimed that, although they did the actual work, the real Author of all that they wrote was God. Do you know of any other library where all the books are said to have come from God?

Although this library contains some of the oldest writings known to man, yet it is the best seller of all the world's literature. Not only do the books of this library record the history of man from his beginning on earth, but in some instances they have also given history in advance, as they foretell of things to take place hundreds and thousands of years later.

These books, 66 in number, are for people of all languages, tribes and nations. They are for those who lived when the books were written, for us living now, and for people not yet born.

Most libraries contain the writings of many authors, but in this one there is only one. In an ordinary library we find that some authors write books on science only, other specialize in history, some write only fiction, and so on. But the one Author of the books within the Bible has written on all sorts of subjects: science, history, prophecy, biography, romance and adventure. This Author uses many ways to get His messages into men's hearts and minds, such as type, symbol, parable, poetry and prose. This library, the Bible, is a marvelous thing, and we should expect it to be so because "these are the words that the Lord spoke" (Jeremiah 30:4). Again and again throughout the Bible the men who wrote it made this claim.

For Thinking and Doing:

1. Read Psalm 119:129; Proverbs 19:20, 21; Proverbs 22:12, 17-19.

2. In what ways do you think the Bible is a remarkable Book?

3. Which verse of today's reading do you like best?

4. Will you thank God today that He has given us the Bible?

The Bible Is God's Word

"The whole Bible was given to us by inspiration from God and is useful to teach us what is true and to make us realize what is wrong in our lives; it straightens us out and helps us do what is right" (II Timothy 3:16, LNT).

The Bible is inspired by God. That is, the Lord led the men who wrote it to put down just what He wanted them to say.

Sometimes He caused them to write of people they knew or of happenings which they knew about. Some of the men wrote about themselves, the happenings of their lives, and their experiences with God. At other times these writers were inspired to put down what had been revealed to them by God. To "reveal" is to show forth something that has not been seen or known before. The Bible is full of what men could never know unless the Lord revealed it to them: things about God Himself, heaven, hell, life after death, angels, demons and other secret things. "There is a God in heaven that revealeth secrets" (Daniel 2:28, KJV).

You can see that, although all the writings of Scripture are inspired, they are not all revealings, or revelations, from God. For instance, when these God-chosen men wrote of what was going on at the time or of what they knew had happened before, they were

39

inspired simply to write it down as history. But when they were inspired to write of things which were to take place many years later, then of course they were telling what had been shown to them only by direct revelation from God.

Many people refuse to believe the Bible is inspired because it tells of very evil things and wicked men. Certainly the Holy God does not approve of any evil, but He knows that we all need to be warned against sinning and to be shown that to leave God out of our thoughts and lives can only end in sorrow.

You may wonder how we can say that God is the author of the Bible when it was written by men. Suppose you are visiting away from home and you receive a type-written letter from your dad. In it he explains that he has a sprained right wrist so he is dictating the letter to his stenographer. Who would be the real author of that letter?

Thank God, we need not stumble through life as a blind person walking along an unknown road, for "God has revealed (His truth) to us through the Spirit" (I Corinthians 2:10). Where has He done this? It is in the Bible.

For Thinking and Doing:

1. Read Psalm 100; II Timothy 3:14-15.
2. When you read the Bible who is really speaking to you?
3. What four things does the opening verse in today's reading say the Bible will do for us?
4. Will you ask God today that His Word will do these things for you?

22nd Day

The God of Power and Love

"And we also thank God constantly for this, that when you received the Word of God which you heard from us, you accepted it not as the word of men but as what it really is, the Word of God" (I Thessalonians 2:13).

The tireless work of scientists has opened up before us marvels which have been here all the time, but which were neither seen nor heard by our dull eyes and ears. If we carefully examine the Bible we shall discover that the Scriptures were inspired by God.

The Bible does not start by telling us that it is God's Word and then go on to give the proof of this. Rather we have to study it, and as we do more and more truths and proofs unfold. We cannot know the flavor of any food until we taste it for ourselves. A musician cannot prove the melody contained in the written notes until he plays it on an instrument. In the same way the Bible proves itself to us most surely as we study it.

Let us first examine the witness of some of the men who wrote God's Word for Him. They believed and said that what they spoke or wrote was given to them by the Lord. David said, "The Lord spoke by me." Isaiah said, "This is the word that the Lord has spoken," and Jeremiah said, "The word of God came to Jeremiah." Indeed, such phrases as "The Lord said," "Thus says the Lord," etc., are found some 2,000 times throughout the Scriptures. Sometimes people say one thing while they mean another, and so we cannot trust them. But the writers of the Bible wanted it made clear that God was speaking through them.

Moses states that God said to him, "I will be with your mouth and teach you what you shall speak" (Exodus 4:12). "Moses wrote all the words of the Lord" (Exodus 24:4). Samuel tells us, "The Spirit of the Lord speaks by me, and His word is upon my tongue" (II Samuel 23:2). The apostle Paul said of his message, "We have even used the very words given us by the Holy Spirit, not words that we as men might choose" (I Corinthians 2:13, LNT). "It really is, the word of God" (I Thessalonians 2:13).

If God cares anything for man, we should expect to have a book like the Bible. If God could tell us what we need to know, but wouldn't, then He would be cruel. If He wished to, but couldn't, then He would not be a God of power. But we have a God of love and power, and so we have His Book.

For Thinking and Doing:

1. Read Daniel 2:19-22; Deuteronomy 29:29.

2. What thought in today's reading seems most important to you?

3. What difference can it make in our lives if we accept the Bible as God's Word?

4. Besides accepting it as His Word, what must we also do?

God Has Spoken

"Then you shall know that I, the Lord, have spoken, and I have done it, says the Lord" (Ezekiel 37:14).

"The word of God came to..." "The Lord spoke unto..." Think of what it would mean if the mighty Creator should break through the invisible curtain which hides Him from men's eyes and ears and speak to you. What a thrilling, awesome experience that would be.

In different ways God gave His Word and message to those He chose to write His Book; these chosen ones were men who had listening hearts as well as ears. Sometimes the Lord's voice was heard in the stillness of night, as when He "...came and stood and called" to the child Samuel. With one as faithful as Moses, God "talked...face to face." At other times God spoke to His servants "in a vision...in a dream."

We are not told just how the Lord made it known that He was speaking, but in whatever form the message came there was no mistaking it. Those who received it were sure it was from God. Though at times God's servants were afraid to give out His Word and though often they did not understand the full meaning of what they were told to write or say, yet they were forced on by a strong power within.

Scripture says, "No prophecy ever came by the impulse of man, but men moved by the Holy Spirit spoke from God" (II Peter 1:21). How do you move anything? That is the meaning in this verse of the word "moved." These men did not write their own thoughts, but were carried along and kept going under the control of the Spirit of God. This is what the writers themselves tell us.

Perhaps you say, "How do we know they were telling the truth? Maybe they only said the Lord spoke to them to win followers or to make a name for themselves." That idea is not valid. Many of these men suffered great persecutions and even death because they dared to give out God's Word. Men do not suffer or die because of what they know is false.

Either God was the Author of the Bible, or it was authored by men. If it can be shown that the entire Scriptures could not be the work of men, we will have to admit it is from God. There is no other choice. "Then you shall know that I, the Lord, have spoken, and I have done it, says the Lord" (Ezekiel 37:14).

For Thinking and Doing:

1. Read I Samuel 3:1-18.
2. What do you think it means to have a "listening heart, as well as ears"?
3. Do you have to fully understand the Bible in order to believe it?
4. What do you think our part is? What will God do for us if we ask Him to?

Only One Author

"The good man . . . brings forth good, the evil man . . . brings forth evil" (Matthew 12:35).

Someone has said, "As nothing is easier than to think, so nothing is more difficult than to think well." As you read now, please think well. Either God through the Holy Spirit was the Author of the Bible, or it was only the writing of men. If men were the authors, they were either good men or bad men.

We have laws in our country which rule that murderers and thieves are responsible for their crimes and must be punished. Do you think that these laws were made by thieves and murderers? Certainly not; evil men don't make laws which work against themselves.

Throughout all the Bible we are told of God's hatred of every kind of sin and are warned of the judgment that some day is sure to come upon those who persist in choosing sin rather than God and right ways of living. Would bad men have written a book by which they constantly condemned themselves? Or course they would not.

You may say, "It could have been written by good men." Let us see. Even the good men who were writers of various books of the Bible were not perfect. Besides this, in all the times in which they wrote, they were surrounded by all kinds of impurity, false teaching and idolatry. Yet the Bible contains perfect moral teachings and the most beautiful thoughts that men have ever known. Could even good men have been the authors of such

43

perfect teachings and thoughts? How were they kept from including the false teachings of their day?

Most writers of Scripture state that they wrote the truth and wrote as God commanded them. Would good men have said this if it were not true? Would good men have tried to put over on mankind such a fraud? What must we decide? If bad men would not have written a book by which their lives were condemned and good men claimed they wrote as God directed, who is the Author? There can be only one answer: God is the Author. "God who never lies" (Titus 1:2). "Blessed are those who have not seen and yet believe" (John 20:29).

If the Author of the Bible is God, it should make a great difference to us. Of course a book full of good teachings written by men would be valuable to us, but when we believe the Author of the Bible is God, the Bible is put into a place above all other books. No other book is known which has this place. Since God is the Author we should know more about this Book. This is the reason you should set aside a special time each day when you listen with the "ears" of your heart to what God has to say to you in His Book.

For Thinking and Doing:

1. Read Proverbs 30:5; Psalm 119:97-104.
2. Can you put the thought of today's lesson into your own words?
3. What verse in Psalm 119:97-104 do you like best?
4. Will you memorize it?

25th Day

The Best Seller

"Search . . . in the book of the records" (Ezra 4:15).

If you one day should ask the librarian in a library to give you a short list of some of the very oldest pieces of literature, she would probably tell you about Homer, the Greek who wrote about 900 B.C., and about Confucius, the wise Chinese man who lived 551-478 B.C. She would also mention the Vedas, those ancient religious writings of the Hindus.

Those books are indeed old, for they were written more than 2,500 years ago. Yet there are others still older, for the first five books of the Bible and the Book of Job are among the most ancient of any writings known to man.

You may be sure that not all libraries contain the writings of Confucius and the Vedas. Outside the countries in which they were written few people know these ancient volumes. You certainly couldn't call them popular. But then, how many books in the English language have remained popular for as long as even 100 years? Shakespeare's plays are still well known, but even the best sellers of ten years ago are not best sellers today.

Scientific books and many others often have to be rewritten and brought up to date to keep up with new discoveries and changing times. However, the Bible forever stands as it was written; it is always up to date.

Here is a Book that breaks all rules. It was written many centuries ago, yet it is the best seller of all time. In 1933 the British Museum bought from Russia an old copy of the New Testament for $510,000, a very large price to be paid for a book.

Today the Bible is the most widely-read piece of literature. Into the darkness and ignorance of pagen lands and to the distant islands of the seas this Book has gone. People of more than 1,150 different dialects and languages read the Scriptures or some part of them in their native speech. Why do millions of people want this ancient Book? "It really is, the word of God" (I Thessalonians 2:13). "Good news of a great joy which will come to all the people." (Luke 2:10).

For Thinking and Doing:

1. Read Psalm 119:18, 34; I Thessalonians 2:13.
2. What new information about the Bible did you find in today's reading?
3. What thought meant most to you?
4. Why do you think the Bible helps people of today as well as in other times?

26th Day

A Book for All People

"For ever, O Lord, Thy word is firmly fixed in the heavens" (Psalm 119:89).

The more we learn about how the Bible was written the more we realize it is a miracle Book, beyond the power of man to write.

45

Think of the kind of men who wrote it. This was to be a book which should last for all time and reach all races and kinds of people. It was for those who lived in the so-called Dark Ages as well as for our modern, scientific age. If you or I had planned such a book, we would search out the best-known and best-educated men in all the world to do the writing. But God did not do this.

Of the men who wrote His Book all but one were Hebrew Orientals. In their early history these people seemed to show no special interest in the writing or reading of books. Perhaps we would think that they were somewhat narrow-minded, for their training and interests separated them from other nations. Among these writers Moses and Saul of Tarsus were well-educated men, as were Isaiah and a few others. Solomon was a great and very wise king; Luke was a physician; David had been a shepherd and a soldier before he was a king in Israel. The rest were a mixed group including a farm hand, a king's cupbearer and an Arab sheik.

Some of the writers were farmers, ranchers or owners of cattle or sheep. Matthew was a tax-gatherer and Peter was a fisherman. We might describe some of them as ignorant or maybe even a bit crude. Yet these men wrote a Book which is unlike all others. No other book contains such beautiful language or noble teachings, yet it is so written that some of it can be understood by a little child.

Most of us like books which were originally written in our own language and show an understanding of our ways and thoughts. But whether the Bible is translated into the language spoken by the Dyacks of Borneo, the Chinese or the Americans, the boys and girls who read it in their own language feel that it belongs to them. Why is this? It is because the Author of the Book knows what is in the heart of everyone in every land and nation. His loving message is for all; it is for you. "This is the word which the Lord spoke" (Isaiah 16:13). "Let your ear receive the word of His mouth" (Jeremiah 9:20).

For Thinking and Doing:

1. Read I Corinthians 1:26, 27; Psalm 65:4; John 15:15.
2. Put Psalm 65:4 into your own words.
3. What point about the men who wrote the Bible seems the most remarkable?
4. Ask God to make the Bible meaningful to you as you read it.

A Master Plan

"Thy Word is true from the beginning" (Psalm 119:160, KJV).

The United States has built many powerful planes and missiles. They are made of many materials and of thousands of pieces of different sizes and shapes. Hundreds of men worked on these different pieces.

Now suppose that these men had lived in different parts of the country. Suppose that instead of being given a pattern to follow, each man was allowed to make his part of the plane after a plan of his own, in any size or shape he chose. Finally all the finished pieces must be sent to one central place and fitted together. But would they fit together? No. The engine would not be the right shape and it might be too weak to do its job. The instrument board and wings would not be the proper size; the body perhaps would be too small. The whole thing would be a useless mess.

However, even with the thousands of parts and the hundreds of builders, no United States ship is a mess. Why? Because each is built according to a plan. Someone has designed each part so that all will fit together perfectly.

Carry this thought over to the making of God's Word. It contains 66 books and in these books we find many different kinds of teaching. There is symbol, type, history and prophecy. We read of things of this world and of another world. At least 40 men wrote the Bible. Few of these men could have known each other, for it was written over a period of about 1,500 years. Many of the writers died before the others were born.

Then too, most of these men lived miles apart. Some wrote in Arabia, Syria, Babylon, Palestine, Rome or Greece. Some of the books were written in a prison, in a palace, in the desert, or by the seaside. Remember that in those days there were no radios or newspapers. People were not in close touch with one another as we are now. Yet as the various parts of Scripture were written and added to the other parts, it was found that the teachings of each book fit in with the teachings of all the others.

This perfectness of the whole Book could not have come about by chance. There had to be a Master Mind. "The . . . Lord has done this" (Job 12:9). He planned the whole and gave to each man the part he was to write. "God . . . spake in time past" (Hebrews 1:1, KJV). "Thy Word is true from the beginning" (Psalm 119:160, KJV).

For Thinking and Doing:

1. Read Deuteronomy 3:24; Psalm 119:111, 127, 128.

2. What thought in today's reading would you like to remember about the Bible?

3. Put Psalm 119:111 into your own words.

4. If the Bible is truly an inheritance, what should we be doing with it?

28th Day

The Bible Changes Lives

"God's message (the Word) is alive and full of power in action . . . passing judgment on the thoughts and purposes of the heart" (Hebrews 4:12, Williams).

Think of several things that have great power and name them. Did you count "words" in your list? Words have tremendous power. Wicked leaders have used words to stir up nations and people to hate, kill and torture thousands of their fellow men. Unbelievers have written lying words about God and millions have lived and died without Him because they believed these lying words.

Words have a strong influence in your life too. They can make you sad or glad, angry or kind. All through the years you will go on making choices because of words you read or hear. If the words of human beings have such force, how much greater power must the words of God have! The Lord has said, "The words that I have spoken to you are spirit and life" (John 6:63). It is because God's words have a living force that the Bible changes lives as no other book can do. And all lives need changing.

Some people believe that men can be wholly changed by education. Knowledge of the world and its affairs and of oneself is often helpful, but it only improves minds. It cannot change natures. For example, a young man committed murder in a horrible way. In prison he was so violent he was called "the tiger boy." There in his cell he heard the Scriptures. As he let the words of the Lord enter his heart, he turned from his evil ways to God. His life completely changed.

48

Countless times the Bible has done its glorious work with just such sinful people. Could books on science, history, sports or mathematics work such miracles? Indeed not.

Whether or not your reading of the Bible has made any changes in your life, only you know. It certainly has had an influence in your life, for if you lived where neither the Bible nor its influence had reached, there would be no churches, hospitals or many other good things. If you had been born in a heathen family, your mother might have drowned you when you were born or thrown you to the wild animals when you were still a tiny baby. Why? It would have been to please her gods.

"God's message (the Word) is alive and full of power in action . . . passing judgment on the thoughts and purposes of the heart" (Hebrews 4:12, Williams). No man can do what God has done and will yet do with words.

For Thinking and Doing:

1. Read Colossians 3:16, 17; John 6:63.

2. Give an example or two of your own concerning the power of words.

3. Can you think of ways the Bible has an influence in our lives today?

4. What changes would you like made in your life? Are you willing to have them made?

The Power of the Word

"Blessed are they that hear the word of God, and keep it" (Luke 11:28, KJV).

Picture a scene in World War II. A small object is floating in the South Pacific. Something moves. Could it possibly be . . . ? Yes, it was men. Three men were drifting on a tiny raft with the current which carried them toward one of the Solomon Islands. For many hours after their bomber was shot down, they had been unprotected from the cold night and the scorching heat of the day. They had no water or food and were in constant danger. Yet upon that strip of land toward which they drifted lurked even greater dangers. The enemy was there waiting to destroy them, and the natives of the island were reported to be fierce man-eaters.

At last they reached the land and went ashore, weary and full of fear. The stealthy, deadly enemy was there, but no cannibals. Instead the chief and his tribesmen came to meet them with Bibles in their hands and showed them every kindness. At the risk of their own lives they protected the stranded fliers and then sent them safely on their way.

What power had changed the native savages into Christians? Missionaries had been in that land, and from them the islanders had learned the power of the words of the "Miracle Book." "The word of the Lord . . . prevailed" (Acts 19:20).

Picture another scene. It is Easter time in Russia and hundreds of godless men and women pack Moscow's leading theater. The object of the play is to make fun of God and His eternal Son. On the stage a church altar is being used as a bar. Actresses dressed as nuns sit on the floor gambling. Coarse, noisy actor "priests" are drinking vodka at the altar bar.

To wild applause a matinee idol strides upon the scene. He is to read two verses from the New Testament held in his hands, then throwing off his robe will join the others in their drunken orgy.

Loudly, slowly, Alexander Rostovzev read two verses from Matthew chapter 5. For a moment he paused as if paralyzed. A violent trembling seized him. He finished the entire chapter and then a bitter, longing cry rang out, "Jesus, remember me when Thou comest into Thy kingdom!" Quickly the curtains of the stage were dropped to hide him. Rostovzev was ill the stage director said.

Was that the truth? No. The impossible had happened. Through the Word this Russian actor had met his Lord. God's Word had won another heart. "For whatever God says to us is full of living power" (Hebrews 4:12, LNT).

For Thinking and Doing:

1. Read Proverbs 22:17-21; Romans 10:17.
2. Since "blessed" means "happy," why would you think Luke 11:28 is true?
3. How would you explain Romans 10:17 to a friend?
4. Memorize this short verse and think about what it says to

you.

The Indestructible Book

"Heaven and earth will pass away, but My words will not pass away" (Matthew 24:35).

In the early Christian times men hated the Bible because it showed up their wickedness. The flame of their hatred spread like a prairie fire. The Book was forbidden; it was burned and torn to shreds until it seemed that not one copy remained. Even the people who loved the Bible and tried to protect it were imprisoned and persecuted; some were tortured and others burned to death.

However, the Book only seemed to be lost, for out from the hiding places—simple cottages, cracks in rocks, and under piles of dirt—copies of the Scriptures were brought out again. They came as a tiny stream that was some day to flood the earth in spite of all that men could do to stop it.

In 325 A.D. the Emperor Constantine proclaimed to his people that the Bible was man's one, sure source of truth. However, Constantine's proclamation did not change men's hearts, and thus again and again evil men have persecuted Christians and sought to destroy the Scriptures. Yet always the Book has remained. Another method of destruction was used: the unbelievers decided not to try to destroy the Book itself, but to show that what it said and taught was false.

Atheists tried to prove that the Bible was full of mistakes and that the men who wrote it lied about God, history, the universe and men. They sneered at those who still believed. Voltaire, a Frenchman, boasted that in 100 years the Bible would be gone. But in less than 100 years the very press he used to print his bold words was used to print thousands of copies of the Scriptures, and his home became a storage house for Bibles.

"He who sits in the heavens laughs; the Lord has them in derision" (Psalm 2:4). Where are those unbelievers now? Where are Voltaire and others of God's enemies? His enemies perish, but the Book lives on, increasing in number year by year. It will always live, for the Lord has said, "Heaven and earth will pass away, but My words will not pass away" (Matthew 24:35). Men might just as well use a cup of water to try to quench the blazing surface of the sun as to attempt to destroy the Scriptures!

For Thinking and Doing:

1. Read I Peter 1:24, 25; 2:2, 3.

2. How does the story of the preservation of the Bible speak of divine authorship?

3. In what ways today do some people try to get rid of the Bible and its influence?

4. Why does I Peter 2:2 say we should desire or "long for" the Word of God?

31st Day

Prophecy About Tyre

"Has He said, and will He not do it?" (Numbers 23:19).

Look at a new five-dollar bill under a magnifying glass sometime. You will see many hair-like threads woven through the paper. Only real bills have these threads; they are not in counterfeit money. Running all through the Bible are certain things which show it to be God's true Word, and not a counterfeit. These are the thousands of prophecies by which the Lord told in advance what would happen later. "I am the Lord . . . Behold . . . new things I now declare; before they spring forth I tell you of them" (Isaiah 42:8, 9).

Let us consider the ancient town of Tyre in Phoenicia. It was a busy, beautiful place in that day more than 2,500 years ago. The markets were filled with rare and valuable things brought in from other countries: ivory, ebony, gold, precious stones, fine linen, gorgeous clothing, mules, lambs, choice spices, and delicious foods.

How the people of Tyre gloried in their riches! Most of their merchants were princes, and was not Ithobaal, their king, a god? Had not their own power conquered and made slaves of other nations? They were strong and safe. So, too, they seemed to the rest of the world, but not to God. Because He saw a city full of boundless evil and worshipers of idols, He pronounced a punishment upon Tyre.

"Therefore thus says the Lord God: Behold, I am against you, O Tyre, and will bring up many nations against you, as the sea brings up its waves. They shall destroy the walls of Tyre, and break down her towers, and I will scrape her soil from her, and make her a bare rock. She shall be in the midst of the sea a place

52

for the spreading of nets . . . and she shall become a spoil to the nations . . . I will bring upon Tyre from the north Nebuchadrezzar king of Babylon . . . and a host of many soldiers. He will slay with the sword . . . he will set up a siege wall against you . . . and with his axes he will break down your towers . . . they will break down your walls . . . your stones and timber and soil they will cast into the midst of the waters. Then all the princes of (the lands of) the sea will step down from their thrones . . . they will . . . tremble. I will bring you to a dreadful end" (Ezekiel 26:3-12, 16, 21).

Tomorrow we shall see whether or not these things really did come true.

For Thinking and Doing:

1. Read Isaiah 42:8; Ezekiel 14:3.
2. What reason do you find in Isaiah 42:8 for God's purpose in destroying Tyre?
3. What else was wrong with the people of Tyre?
4. Do we worship any idols today? What are they?

32nd Day

Tyre Destroyed

"But I the Lord will speak . . . and it will be performed" (Ezekiel 12:25).

Some years after Ezekiel's prophecy of the destruction of Tyre, the things he told about began to happen. Nebuchadnezzar, king of Babylon, came against Tyre. He had no ships so he did not attack the island part of the town. But again and again his armies battered the walls of the old city until finally, about 13 years later, Tyre was conquered. Many of its people were killed, much valuable loot was carried away, and the place came under the rule of the Babylonians. Meanwhile the high-walled city on the island continued to be rich, powerful and proud.

More than 200 years passed and still not all of Ezekiel's words had come true. Stones of the ancient wall lay as they had fallen; timbers and rubble of the old city had not been removed. Still the island was safe and envied by other peoples and princes. How the people of Tyre may have laughed at the old prophet who had predicted their destruction!

But wait. One day Alexander the Great and his Greek army began their world conquest. Eventually they came to the island city of Tyre. There were no guns, cannons or planes then. The narrow strip of land stretching from shore to island was too narrow to hold an army, and with no navy, how could soldiers reach the town? Quickly timbers, rocks and rubble were gathered from what remained of old Tyre, and with these the Greeks built a wide runway through the water to the island wall. There the battle raged with war machines, burning oil and sulphur, but Tyre stood. However, the Greeks were clever. They put war engines and soldiers onto rafts, and floating them around the city, they were able to take the city, killing many and selling others into slavery. So terrible was the destruction that neighboring peoples, trembling with fear lest they should share in Tyre's fate, surrendered to Alexander's army without a struggle.

Although the town was rebuilt years later and was in use during Jesus' time on earth, it was again overthrown and became empty of all inhabitants. It became only a heap of rocks where fishermen dried their nets. Finally even the stones were taken to build other cities, and so Ezekiel's words came true. Later a few people returned, but Tyre is now only a tiny place clinging to one side of the broken island.

How could the prophet look centuries ahead and see what would happen? He could not. It was God who looked forward through the years and told His servant what to write.

"But I the Lord will speak the word which I will speak, and it will be performed. It will no longer be delayed, but in your days, O rebellious house, I will speak the word and perform it, says the Lord God" (Ezekiel 12:25).

For Thinking and Doing:

1. Read Romans 15:4, 13; I Corinthians 10:11.
2. What has impressed you most about the story of Tyre?
3. Was there some detail in the prophecy as it was fulfilled which seems remarkable to you?
4. What does I Corinthians 10:11 give as the reason for prophecies in the Bible?

Prophecy About Babylon

"Because you sinned ... this thing has come upon you" *(Jeremiah 40:3).*

Today let us think about Babylon, capital of Chaldea in the year 700 B.C. Travelling slowly down the Euphrates River we would see before us the high and massive walls of this largest, most fortified city of that time. Its safety lay in the two sets of walls which surrounded it and the deep, wide moat which was always filled with water around the base of the outer wall. The Euphrates ran through the town, and the only gates into the city were built across the river where it flowed in at one side and out at the other.

Entering, we would see all around us signs of great riches and luxurious living with beautiful gardens and parks. Huge and colorful buildings would meet our gaze: the palaces of the king and the temples where the priests lived and carried on the evil forms of idol worship. We could find nothing to show that these people worshiped the one true God.

Like Tyre, Babylon was strong, feared because of her cruelty, and envied because of her riches. Although she had seen other peoples and places destroyed, Babylon went right on in terrible sin, godless and unafraid. While it was still a mighty city, God foretold the end of Babylon. He even gave the name of the yet-unborn king, Cyrus, who would conquer these people more than 100 years later.

This is what God said through the prophets Isaiah and Jeremiah: "Thus says the Lord to ... Cyrus, whose right hand I have grasped, to subdue nations before him ... to open doors before him that gates may not be closed!" (Isaiah 45:1). "Babylon, the glory of kingdoms ... It will never be inhabited ... no Arab shall pitch his tent there, no shepherds will make their flocks lie down there ... its houses shall be full of howling creatures" (Isaiah 13:19-21). "Out of the north a nation has come up against her, which shall make her land a desolation ... both man and beast shall flee away" (Jeremiah 50:3).

"Because of the wrath of the Lord ... her bulwarks have fallen, her walls are thrown down ... The noise of battle is in the land, and great destruction! ... Let nothing be left of her ... A drought upon her waters, that they may be dried up!" (Jeremiah 50:13, 15, 22, 26, 38). "The warriors of Babylon have ceased fighting . . . the soldiers are in panic . . . The broad wall of Babylon shall be levelled to the ground" (Jeremiah 51:30, 32, 58).

Tomorrow we shall see how this prophecy was fulfilled.

For Thinking and Doing:

1. Read Ecclesiastes 8:12; Jeremiah 7:23, 24; 50:24.

2. What reason is given in Jeremiah 50:24 for the fulfillment of the prophecy about Babylon?

3. What is included in the command God gave in Jeremiah 7:23?

4. What did the people do that we sometimes do? (Jeremiah 7:24).

34th Day

How Babylon Fell

"The Lord has brought it about, and has done as He said" (Jeremiah 40:3).

Cyrus, king of Persia, sent armies to capture Babylon, but they failed at first because of the great walls, heavy gates and deep moat. Today airplanes would drop bombs on a city, but then men used bows and arrows, spears and swords. They fought with battering-rams and with fire which they threw against or over the walls. Because Cyrus' soldiers were unable to conquer the city in these ways, they tried another way.

The records show that the attacking army drew back some distance up the Euphrates and there they dammed up the waters of the river and turned them into another channel.

With the enemy no longer battering their walls, the Babylonians thought the fight was over and spent the night feasting and drinking. Stealthily and in midnight darkness, the enemy hosts entered Babylon by the dried-up riverbed which lay under the gates. Inside they opened the great two-leaved gates, just as God had said they would do. No strong warriors met them; they were at the feast and the people were in their homes. Thus, about 539 B.C. Babylon fell without a struggle. Taking over the city, Cyrus had the massive walls destroyed.

There is more. Two other armies later came against the doomed spot; they showed no mercy, but swept on in fury. There was the awful sound of idols and great temples crashing and of huge and gorgeous palaces crumbling to the ground. There was the sight of treasures being carried away as priests and people were gone. Nothing remained but silent, broken stones. Babylon became desolate except for wild animals which made their homes upon its heaps. Through the centuries the city has not been rebuilt where it was, although a town is now taking shape. It is where Hillah, the slave town, once stood just outside Babylon's walls.

Only God can see future events as though they had already happened. "To whom will you liken Me . . . and compare Me? . . . For I am God, and there is no other . . .none like Me, declaring the end from the beginning and from ancient times things not yet done, saying, 'My counsel shall stand, and I will accomplish all My purpose'" (Isaiah 46:5, 9, 10).

God and His Word stand alone. We need to trust Him. He will always do as He has said, whether it be for judgment or for blessing. "Blessed rather are those who hear the word of God and keep it!" (Luke 11:28). "You shall therefore lay up these words of Mine in your heart" (Deuteronomy 11:18).

For Thinking and Doing:

1. Read Hebrews 2:1; Mark 14:38.

2. Do we need to "lay up God's Word in our hearts" before we can "keep" it? Are you hearing and laying it up in your heart?

3. What promise is given to us in Luke 11:28?

4. Put Mark 14:38 into your own words. What else does it tell us we need to do?

35th Day

Truth Confirmed

"Truth shall spring out of the earth" (Psalm 85:11, KJV).

Because the Bible is an ancient book, it speaks of ancient peoples, places and happenings. Since some of these things are not told about in any other books, many people have decided the Bible must be wrong.

Archaeologists have gone to the lands of which the Scriptures tell. They have taken picks and spades, hoping to uncover cities of ancient civilizations.

Much can happen to places and peoples during thousands of years. Sometimes tribes were driven from their homes by enemies; fear or famine often caused people to look for safer, better spots to live. Empty buildings, left for centuries to the sun and rain, crumbled and fell. Sometimes the people were unable to carry away their belongings, so these lay buried beneath the ruined walls and roofs. At times villages were smashed to the ground by conquering armies and many towns were wiped out by fire or flood. Often a new town would be built over the ruins of an old one. Sometimes these were ten strata (or villages) deep.

The old buildings were left as they had fallen until at last the desert winds completely covered them with sand. Sometimes they were hidden by stones piled up by overflowing rivers.

Many things have been found in such ruins, such as ornaments, jewelry, toilet articles, furniture and cooking utensils. Literature, beautiful works of art, clothing, weapons of war, great temples, musical instruments and countless other articles which are thousands of years old are now in museums around the world. These all show how the people of those days lived. They speak of riches and poverty, work and play, peace and war. We learn also of religions, evil idol worship, and horrible human sacrifices.

How exciting to bring back to life again these things that have slept so long in the dust and to have them tell us the true stories of centuries ago. Above all, to those of us who love God there comes an added thrill, for archaeologists have confirmed that the Bible speaks truly of peoples and places. God chose to preserve past civilizations to show up the ignorance of those who sometimes think they know more than the Lord Himself.

For Thinking and Doing:

1. Read Psalm 119:41-48; I Corinthians 1:27.

2. How would you explain to a friend how the introductory verse applies to the reading for today?

3. Why do you think those who trust in the Bible will not be "put to shame"? (Psalm 119:46).

4. For what reasons is it important to "meditate" or think about God's Word?

Where Our Confidence Belongs

"It is better to trust in the Lord than to put confidence in man" (Psalm 118:8, KJV).

About 2,000 B.C. "the Lord said to Abram, 'Go from your country . . . to the land that I will show you'" (Genesis 12:1). "Terah took Abram his son and Lot . . . and Sarai . . . and they went forth together from Ur" (Genesis 11:31). In recent times Bible "scholars" doubted that there was an Abram or city called "Ur."

Then down went the spades into a huge mound of earth near the Euphrates River and into the ruins of a very ancient buried town. Among the ruins were clay tablets giving the city's name—Ur of the Chaldees. Still downward went the spades until they uncovered another city which was probably the town of Abram.

If we could go back into the Ur of Abram's day, we could as it were walk the narrow streets between comfortable, two-story houses. We would meet well-dressed people. Certain men, bearing small clay tablets, would be mail carriers. Young people with clay "books" would be hurrying to school and others would be on their way to the temple library.

This temple of the Moon Goddess was a huge affair. Around it were grouped other buildings, and together they formed a sort of civic center much like those of our time. In this center there were government offices and houses for the idol goddess and its priests. There were palaces, a choir hall, a large kitchen, and workshops where women spun thread and wove fine cloth. Craftsmen made beautiful articles of silver, jewels, gold, marble, clay and alabaster.

Ur was a busy place and it may surprise us to find that the lives of the people were so much like our own. Some writing tablets show records of things bought and sold; others list the amount of work done in the factories and the number of hours the laborers spent at work. No, Abraham was not a wandering, untaught tribesman as many people have supposed; he grew up in a large, rich, civilized city. Rich? The spade says so, for it uncovered dining sets of solid gold. There were daggers, saws and spears of gold and beautiful ornaments and headdresses of gold and jewels. There were games, musical instruments, chariots and many other rare things.

Who is right: the Bible or those critics who doubted the existence of Abraham and Ur?

For Thinking and Doing:

1. Read Genesis 12:1-3; Psalm 118:8; Hebrews 11:8-10.
2. What was the most interesting to you in today's reading?
3. What does Hebrews 11:8-10 tell you was the secret of Abraham's life?
4. In what ways is God's Word important to your life?

37th Day

Some Facts Are Proven

"Moses wrote all the words of the Lord" (Exodus 24:4).

But some Bible critics have said, "Moses did nothing of the sort. He lived on earth more than 1,200 years before Christ was born, and in those days no one could read or write."

"Wait a minute," answers the archaeologist, "I have a few things to say about this. You know Moses spent forty years in Egypt, and I did a lot of digging there a while ago. We found that in his time people were writing all sorts of things."

Yes, governors, court officials and army officers wrote out laws and orders and sent them all over the country. Workmen and foremen wrote out reports for employers. Girls and boys and rich, elegant ladies and gentlemen wrote letters full of family doings just as we do now.

In Moses' time people wrote words made up of letters or syllables and different materials and methods were used to write. One way was to press the shapes of the letters onto the surface of soft clay with a small, three-cornered instrument called a stylus. Some wrote with pen and ink on parchment made from skins of animals and many used paper made from the papyrus plant which grew beside the Nile River.

Of course Moses knew how to write. The Egyptians were writing long before Moses was born, and since he was brought up as the son of a princess in the palace of the Egyptian king, he must have received the highest form of training and education that that rich land could give. Our surest proof that Moses wrote came from the lips of the Lord Jesus who said, "He (Moses) wrote of Me" (John 5:46).

We must not let ourselves be confused by those who neither know the Bible nor the facts about it. As you read it, try to find out what it really teaches and then believe it. Jesus Himself quoted the Old Testament Scriptures.

For Thinking and Doing:

1. Read Psalm 119:89; John 5:39.
2. If your faith is tested by someone who doubts the Bible, what can you do?
3. How can your own reading of the Bible strengthen your faith in it?
4. Are you asking God each day to help you understand and have faith?

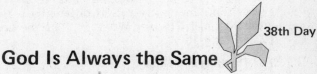

38th Day

God Is Always the Same

"For I the Lord do not change" (Malachi 3:6).

During many centuries before Christ came to earth, the books of the Old Testament were being written. This part of the Bible was finished about four centuries before His birth. The Bible used by Jesus and His disciples contained only the books of the Old Testament, for the New Testament was not written until after the Lord Jesus had returned to heaven.

A testament is a promise by which one agrees either to give or to do something for another. It can also be a covenant whereby one or more people make a promise or agree together to do some special thing.

In the Old Testament we are told of several special promises or agreements which God made with certain people. For instance, after the flood, which wiped out all those dwelling in the earth except Noah and his family, God promised Noah that never again would water cover the earth as a judgment against sin. The rainbow was given as a sign that God would keep His promise. Other things promised under the Old Testament were often blessings connected with men's life on earth.

After Christ's coming to earth, His death, resurrection and return to heaven, God began to deal with people in a better way. The blessings He now promises are the unfolding of those

61

promised by the old agreements. These priceless blessings come to us through the Lord Jesus Christ because of what He did and is doing for us now.

The latter part of the Bible tells of what Christ has done and what God agrees to give us because of Him, so the books from Matthew to Revelation are called the New Testament.

There are many differences between some of the Old and New Testament teachings about God, and because of this some people have thought that either the Bible tells about two Gods or that what the Old Testament writers say of Him is false. Neither is true.

It is true that in old times God did not deal with people as He does now. The human race was younger then and people lived differently. Your parents treat you differently as you grow older. Your parents do not change, but you do. So it is with God. He is always the same, but He deals differently with different men at different times. His own Word is, "I am the Lord, I change not" (Malachi 3:6, KJV).

For Thinking and Doing:

1. Read Hebrews 1:1-3; II Peter 1:20-21.
2. Put Hebrews 1:1-3 into your own words.
3. Does anything in these verses fit in with the main thought in today's reading?
4. Memorize II Peter 1:21.

39th Day

The Original Writings

"The word of our God will stand forever" (Isaiah 40:8).

If we could put ourselves back into Palestine in the time of Christ, we might join a family of godly Jews walking to their church service Saturday morning. The building would be a court or school house and called a synagogue.

Entering, we would see the men and women seated on opposite sides. There would be hymns, prayer and Scripture reading, but the rabbi, or reader, would have a Bible quite unlike ours. The Bible in those days contained no pages, but was on long strips of parchment rolled around a stick at each end to form a scroll. Every word was printed by hand in Hebrew. At this time only the Old Testament books had been written. In all the synagogues the Scripture portions were greatly treasured, and no wonder! Here is their story.

The writers of the books of the Old Testament probably made only the one, original writing of each book. Because God was the real Author, what they wrote was without mistake of any kind. But it was not enough to have just one copy of anything as valuable and wonderful as the Word of God. The original writings would wear out in time, so men made copies. From these copies still others were written. This work was kept up through the centuries and was usually done by men called "scribes." It was tedious work.

The scribes used the utmost care and patience, because to put a wrong letter into a single word might change the meaning of a whole sentence. They dared not, they must not change what God had said. They were not allowed to write several words at a time, but had to say every word aloud and put it down before going on to the next word. Then as the scribe finished a page or column, he had to count each word and each letter to see if he had the same number that was in the part he was copying. We are told that if even one tiny mistake was made, the whole thing was destroyed and had to be done all over again. You can imagine that these men would be most careful to have their copies exactly right.

How thankful we can be that men were willing to do their best so that we could have the precious Scriptures.

Where are the original writings of Scripture now? Crumbled into dust probably. God could have kept them for us, but perhaps He knew that men would have fought to possess such a priceless treasure or would have worshipped the Bible itself more than the God who gave it.

For Thinking and Doing:

1. Read Psalm 12:6; II Timothy 3:16-17.

2. What new thought was there in today's reading for you?

3. Suggest some things for which we should be thankful as we read our Bible.

4. How could you become better "equipped for every good work"? (II Timothy 3:16-17).

Early Manuscripts

"The Lord gave the word: great was the company of those that published it" (Psalm 68:11, KJV).

Since the original writings of Scripture are gone, how can we be sure that our Bible is not full of mistakes? Let's find out. Copies of those original writings are called manuscripts, meaning "something written by the hand of man." To shorten the word we call such writings "MSS." There are over 1,500 MSS copies of the Old Testament.

During many years scholars who understand the Hebrew and Greek languages have examined these ancient MSS in order to take out all mistakes, for in spite of the scribes' careful efforts, a few mistakes did creep in. Corrections were made like this: Suppose that in one MS is was written that a certain king had two sons. However, 1,200 other MSS said he had five. Because the 1,200 all agreed, it would show that there were five sons and that one of the scribes had put down the wrong number in his copy.

We do not have the originals of the New Testament books either. However, there are thousands of copies in Greek, the original language. Some of these copies are of the entire books, and there are also about 4,000 copies of parts of the New Testament. These are written on papyrus or parchment.

Some of these parts of the New Testament are found in letters which Christians wrote to one another. Many of these were written while Christ's apostles were still living, and others were written only a few years later. The poorer Christians of those days wrote on pieces of baked clay called "shards." Eighty-four per cent of the New Testament has been found copied onto such pieces. Taken all together, these different writings give us true and complete copies of the entire New Testament.

So carefully have the scholars worked to correct the MSS of all errors, that we are now told that possible changes still needed can hardly be more than a small fraction of one per cent of the whole.

The Bible which most people read was translated from Hebrew and Greek into English and published in 1611 A.D. Because its printing was made possible by King James of England, it is called the King James, or Authorized, Version. It is a precious, wonderful Book. However, in 1611 Bible students had very few Scripture MSS to work with. Since then hundreds more have been found, and all these have helped to make words and expressions much clearer. From these, other translations have been made into modern English.

For Thinking and Doing:

1. Read I Peter 1:24, 25.

2. What facts about the way the Bible came to us do you think it is important to remember?

3. What is the most important proof to you that the Bible is the Word of God?

4. How can we help others to believe it?

God Knows All Things

"He knows about everyone, everywhere . . . nothing can be hidden from Him to Whom we must explain all that we have done" (Hebrews 4:13, LNT).

The first four words in the Bible are, "In the beginning God." In all our living, thinking and planning we should begin with God. It is the wise thing to do, for sometime each of us will have to answer to Him for all we have said or done. It is the safest, happiest way because only God has the power to keep us from sin and harm and to supply our every need.

God's Book tells of some things we cannot understand, for God and many of His ways are mysterious and strange to us. That should not surprise us, because in heaven and throughout the universe there surely are many kinds of living beings and things unknown to man and for which we have no words. To explain them to us, God would have had to use heaven's language. God's life, ways and thoughts as well as thsoe things which surround Him are infinitely higher and unlike our own. But could you trust and worship a God who was so like yourself that you could understand all about Him?

Although we cannot understand 'how, we know by faith that God sees, hears and knows all things. "God . . . knows everything" (I John 3:20). "The Lord searches all hearts, and understands every plan and thought" (I Chronicles 28:9). This very moment

65

God knows every work, thought and thing taking place throughout the universe. Looking into the past and into the future, He clearly sees all that has been, is now and shall be. "Known unto God are all His works from the beginning" (Acts 15:18, KJV). "Thus saith the Lord . . . who, as I . . . declare . . . the things that are coming" (Isaiah 44:6, 7, KJV). No wonder King David said, "Such knowledge is too wonderful for me; it is high, I cannot attain it" (Psalm 139:6).

It may trouble you that God knows your every thought, word and act, but be thankful instead. How can the Lord comfort us unless He knows our fears and sorrows? He cannot strengthen us unless He understands our weaknesses. Only as He sees our secret sins can He speak to us about them and lead us in the right ways. Because the future which is hidden from our eyes is known to Him, we may go on safely. His love is leading. "Do not fear, only believe" (Mark 5:36).

For Thinking and Doing:

1. Read Job 31:4; Psalm 19:14; Isaiah 46:5, I Chronicles 28:9.
2. As God looks into your heart with what is He pleased and with what is He grieved?
3. What thoughts do you have as you apply Job 31:4 to your own life?
4. Can you honestly pray the prayer of Psalm 19:14?

42nd Day

God Is Almighty

"Power belongs to God" (Psalm 62:11).

There is no life in matter, but there is energy. Scientists make use of the energy and power in the atom, but they cannot explain the sources of its power. "Power belongs to God." How much power has God? "With God all things are possible" (Matthew 19:26). Notice that word "all." There is not a thing, person or law of nature beyond the reach of God's control. Whatever He wills to do He can do, for God is all powerful, "upholding the universe by His word of power" (Hebrews 1:3). "In Him we live and move and have our being" (Acts 17:28).

How can God's power reach throughout the whole universe? It is because His presence is everywhere in a way we cannot understand. "He is not far from each one of us" (Acts 17:27). "Can a man hide himself in secret places so that I cannot see him? says the Lord. Do I not fill heaven and earth?" (Jeremiah 23:24). Someone has said, "He is closer than breathing, nearer than hands or feet."

Here again we must believe what we cannot understand, but this should not be difficult. Out beyond the things we know, there are vast realms where God "lives and moves," and where life, things and ways are quite unlike our own. That is also true of things of earth. Even a short time ago men did not realize that we are surrounded by an ocean of sounds. Now, however, the receiving sets of our radios gather them up and bring them to us. The sounds were always there, but human ears are not made to hear them without the help of special instruments. We live in a world filled with forms of life and creatures which no one had ever seen or known about until the microscope showed them to us.

Light is believed to consist of vibrations or wave motion. Very short waves produce the ultraviolet ray; very long waves produce rays called "infrared." Both red and violet rays are absolutely real, yet they are invisible to us. Radar impulses, X-rays and other electronic rays are unseen and unfelt by man, yet they reach out and go through darkness, distance and substance, revealing that which without their help man could not see or know. Already we have machines that see better than eyes.

As we think of these things we can better understand how God's presence can be very real, and yet be unheard, unseen and unrecognized by man. Also, by faith we can know His presence in our lives.

For Thinking and Doing:

1. Read Isaiah 57:15; Psalm 34:18.

2. What comfort do the statements about God's power and presence bring to you?

3. Say in your own words how a person can have a "contrite and humble spirit."

4. What additional thought about God do you get from Psalm 34:18?

God Is Three in One

"The Lord our God is one Lord" (Deuteronomy 6:4).

Often just one word can have a meaning for us which others do not know about. The telephone may ring and a voice say, "This is Sue" or "This is Jim." That is more than just a name to you; it stands for your very special friend. "In the beginning God . . ." The word "God" in the first verse in the Bible has a meaning many do not understand.

Most of the Old Testament was written in Hebrew, and in that language the word for God was "Elohim," which tells us a very important thing about God. In the English language "God" seems to mean just one person. That is partly true. "The Lord our God is one Lord," but Elohim is like our word "group." That is, just one group but made up of a number of people. The One God is eternally three distinct Persons: God the Father, God the Son (the Lord Jesus Christ), and God the Holy Spirit.

In the Bible God's three-in-oneness is taught in many ways. In Genesis 1:26 God said, "Let us make man in our image, after our likeness." Those words "us" and "our" show that God is more than one. Yet in Genesis 1:27 it also says, "So God created man in His own image." That word "His" stands for just one. God's servant Isaiah once heard the three Persons of God asking, "Whom shall I send, and who will go for us?" (Isaiah 6:8). So here again there is the "I" of oneness and the "us" of more than one.

God's three-in-oneness is clearly shown in the New Testament. One day the Lord Jesus Christ went to John the Baptist to be baptized, and as He was being baptized, suddenly "the heaven was opened and the Holy Spirit descended upon Him in bodily form, as a dove, and a voice came from heaven, 'Thou art My beloved Son'" (Luke 3:21, 22). There was God the Son in His human body, God the Holy Spirit, and God the Father speaking from heaven.

In the New Testament you will constantly read of these three Persons: the Father, the Son and the Holy Spirit. You will also notice that usually the word "God" means God the Father.

How thankful we should be that God tells us about Himself and wants us to know Him. We can count on Him to help us know

Him when we trust Him to do so. Those things about Him which we do not understand we can ask Him to make clear to us.

For Thinking and Doing:

1. Read Genesis 2:24; Luke 11:13; Romans 8:3-4; John 5:18; 10:33.

2. Find references in Roman 8:3-4 to the Father, Son and Holy Spirit.

3. According to John 5:18 and 10:33, Who did Jesus claim to be?

4. Will you ask God to help you trust Him for anything you do not fully understand?

Father, Son and Holy Spirit

". . . Father . . . Son, and . . . Holy Spirit" (Matthew 28:19).

You may ask, "How can God be just one and yet be three?" We do not know; neither do we know how it is that our spirit, soul and body are joined to make one person.

Into my house and into yours there comes a wire along which flows an electric current. That current shows itself in three different ways. In my electric stove it is heat, in the lamp it is light, and in the radio it is sound. Does this prove that there are three different currents or three different kinds of current? No. It is just that one current, undivided and unchanged in everything that makes it what it is, acts in three distinct ways.

God is one in all that makes Him God. All three Persons of God, being one, have the same eternal life; all are all knowing, all powerful and present everywhere. God is one in His character of perfect love, perfect holiness and perfect justice. He is one in what He wills, plans and desires. Yet in many ways these three Persons who are God show forth by the things they do that they are each distinct one from the other.

For instance, it was not God the Father who became man, lived on earth and died to save us. It was God the Son, and it is the Son who is coming back to rule over the earth. "The Father has sent His Son as the Savior of the World" (I John 4:14). Someday Jesus shall come "in His glory, and all the angels with Him . . . before Him will be gathered all the nations" (Matthew 25:31-32). God the Son said of God the Spirit, "When the Spirit of truth comes, He will guide you into all the truth" (John

69

16:13). "And when He comes, He will convince the world of sin and of righteousness and of judgment" (John 16:8).

It is God the Father to Whom we usually pray. Jesus said, "When you pray, go into your room and shut the door and pray to your Father who is in secret; and your Father who sees in secret will reward you" (Matthew 6:6). Jesus also taught His disciples to pray in His name in John 14:13.

Do not think of these three Persons of God as a strange and faraway "something." You are very real to God. No one knows you as well as He does. No one in the world is more interested in you or loves you more dearly, and no one can do so much for you in every way.

Believe God's Word. Speak to Him now, quietly in your heart, and ask Him to make Himself very real to you. Then you do your part and count Him most important in all your plans and for your needs in life.

For Thinking and Doing:

1. Read John 17:5, 20-22; II Corinthians 13:14; I Thessalonians 5:23.

2. What claims of Jesus do you find in John 17:5, 21, 22 that He is equal with God the Father?

3. How would you explain to someone how God is three Persons, yet one?

4. Pray that God will each day make Himself real to you as you read His Word.

45th Day

Angels

"Are they not all ministering spirits?" (Hebrews 1:14).

Is man the only creature in the universe who can know God and understand His wonderful works? Did God create the myriads of planets and stars only to show what He can do? Is this small earth the only place where there are living beings?

For centuries men have wondered about these things and have searched the skies with telescope and spectroscope. However, when scientists are asked if they know of living beings on any planet besides the earth, the answer is, "We do not know."

However, we can know because in His Word God has told us of an "innumerable company" of living ones called angels. Who are they and what are they doing? They are spirit-beings created by God. Some are the "holy angels," who serve and worship the Lord continually. "The Lord of hosts, He is the King of glory" (Psalm 24:10). These myriad hosts are "His angels . . . that do His commandments, hearkening unto the voice of His word . . . His hosts . . . that do His pleasure" (Psalm 103:20-21, KJV). They dwell with Him in the realms of light and glory and are strong, pure, singing, praising and full of gladness because they dwell in the presence of God and are obedient to His perfect will.

There are other angels besides these. They also are living beings created by the Almighty. However, instead of continuing in the presence of the Lord, they are now outcasts, evil and cruel. They do not obey God. Their mighty master is himself a created angel "called the Devil and Satan" (Revelation 12:9).

The Bible seems to teach that angels fill a large part of God's kingdom. "His kingdom rules over all" (Psalm 103:19). We are told of "invisible . . . thrones . . . dominions" and of "authorities" and "principalities" (Colossians 1:16). This indicates angels have different rank and class. Some have greater power and authority than others and a higher form of service. It is evident that in realms unseen by us there are definite dwelling places where these things take place. This is true of all the angels, both good and bad. On earth, too, angels carry on their work. Countless are the contacts that men have had with angels, as we shall see in the next lesson.

You sometimes hear someone say, "You are an angel." But angels are not merely men with kind thoughts and deeds. As you read the Scripture verses which speak of angels, you will soon see that idea doesn't make sense. For example, look at Matthew 25:41 and II Thessalonians 1:7, 8.

For Thinking and Doing:

1. Read Psalm 148:1-5; Psalm 91:11-16; Hebrews 1:5-14.

2. What do you learn about angels from reading the above verses?

3. According to Hebrews 1:14 what do angels have to do with you?

4. Do you understand from Psalm 91:11 why we speak of a "guardian angel"?

Angels Speak for God

"An angel of the Lord descended from heaven" (Matthew 28:2).

The word "angel" means "messenger." Angels bear God's messages from heaven to earth. They have appeared in the form of ordinary men and at other times were surrounded by an unearthly light. In the wicked town of Sodom there lived one righteous man named Lot. One evening there came two angels to him who said, "We are about to destroy this place . . . the Lord has sent us . . . Arise, take your wife and your two daughters . . .Flee for your life" (Genesis 19:13-17). Thus God sent a warning all the way from heaven to that one man so that he might escape the fiery destruction of the city of Sodom.

One night on the cold hard floor of a prison cell, a man named Peter lay chained and asleep. The next day he was scheduled to die because he had dared to preach about the living Christ. Suddenly, unseen by soldier guards, an angel entered the cell. He awoke Peter, loosened his chains and raised him up. "Get up quickly," he commanded. "Wrap your mantle (garment) around you and follow me" (Acts 12:7-8). Past the unseeing soldiers and through an angel-opened door they went out into the street and safety. God and heaven must have seemed most real to Peter and Lot, these two men to whom angels had come.

To Mary, the angel Gabriel brought word that she was to be the mother of the Holy Child Jesus. Later an angel directed shepherds to the place of His birth. Sometimes angels brought a message that was for the whole world—for you and me. It was so in that night when, to a few simple shepherds, God's bright messenger proclaimed these words of hope, "Good tidings of great joy, which shall be to all people . . . And suddenly there was with the angel a multitude of the heavenly host praising God" (Luke 2:10-13, KJV). And no wonder they praised, for they announced the glorious tidings that there was born "a Savior, which is Christ the Lord" (Luke 2:11, KJV).

Angels spoke, too, at the time of Christ's resurrection and ascension. "For an angel of the Lord descended from heaven . . . His appearance was like lightning, and his raiment white as snow . . . But (he) said . . . Jesus, who was crucified . . . is not here; for He has risen" (Matthew 28:2-6).

"As they were looking on, He was lifted up . . . And while they were gazing into heaven as He went, behold two men (angels) stood by them in white robes, and said . . . This Jesus, who was taken up from you . . . will come in the same way as you saw Him go into heaven" (Acts 1:9-11).

For Thinking and Doing:

1. Read Genesis 19:12-26; Acts 12:5-11.

2. What was the most interesting to you about the deliverance of Lot and his family?

3. Does anything in Acts 12:5 tell you why Peter was rescued from jail that night?

4. What kind of prayer was it that God answered?

47th Day

Satan

"Jesus . . . (was) tempted by the devil" (Matthew 4:1).

In addition to the evil angels who we have read about, the Bible also tells us of their leader. His name is Satan and he is also called the devil. He even tempted Christ, but without success.

Although Satan is unseen, his works and influence are all around us. In many ways he tempts us and fights against us all, for the Bible teaches that he is ever working to destroy men's souls and turn them away from God. He uses many means to try to make us disbelieve or neglect God's Word. If he can succeed in this, his battle is almost won because God's Word is the weapon the Lord has given us by which we can overcome the power of the devil.

We must understand that the devil is not just a principle of evil or an evil force. In Matthew 4:1-11 we find Jesus addressing the devil as a person; he is a personal spirit-being. We are warned against him, for he is always the enemy of God and is at war with all who follow and serve Him.

Satan was created as a beautiful, wonderful angel called the "son of the morning" (Isaiah 14:12, KJV). He had a throne of authority under God and was described as "full of wisdom and perfect in beauty." His home was in heaven "till iniquity (sin) was found in (him)" (Ezekiel 28:15). That sin was pride, for Satan "said in (his) heart . . . I will exalt my throne above the stars of God . . . I will be like the Most High." But God said "Thou shalt be brought down to hell. How art thou fallen from heaven, O

Lucifer, son of the morning!" (Isaiah 14:12-15, KJV). You see, the devil thought that he was so wise and great that he was equal with the All-Glorious One who made him, and for that blasphemous thought God cast him down.

What a fearful, solemn time it was when that mighty, powerful angel became filled with hatred toward the Lord and when his great desire and that of his myriad of followers was to destroy and bring to nothing every work and plan of God! Satan is called "the prince of the power of the air" in Ephesians 2:2. He is the governing head over a great kingdom which is made up of evil spirit-beings and men who also refuse to have the Lord rule over them. These are called the "sons of disobedience" (Ephesians 2:2). There are two kingdoms in the universe: Satan's kingdom and God's kingdom (Matthew 12:26, 28). Everyone is in one or the other. When we choose to obey God and Christ is our Savior, we belong to His kingdom.

Of course this wicked one could have no power at all unless the Lord allowed it, but in the end his doom is sure. The apostle John saw into the future and said, "The devil . . . was thrown into the lake of fire (hell)" (Revelation 20:10). All God's enemies will someday be put down.

For Thinking and Doing:

1. Read John 8:44; I Thessalonians 3:5; Revelation 12:9.

2. What do you learn about Satan and his actions from the above verses?

3. How did Satan's sin of pride show in the choices he made?

4. Proverbs 16:5 says that everyone that is proud or arrogant is an "abomination to the Lord." Can you think of reasons why?

48th Day

The King of Glory

"Thus says the Lord: 'Heaven is My throne'" (Isaiah 66:1).

Heaven is the dwelling place of God. All who live there with Him are absolutely satisfied and perfectly happy. No sin can ever enter there, nor sickness and sorrow; there is no pain and no death.

If you could this moment look into heaven, the most glorious sight you would see would be a Man, One who is like, yet unlike, us here on earth. He is called "Wonderful Counsellor, Mighty God" (Isaiah 9:6). Yet this Majestic One has scars of nail wounds in His hands.

This Man is "King of kings and Lord of lords" (Revelation 19:16). Unnumbered angels bow in worship before Him; the mighty seraphim cover their faces in His holy presence. Yet there is the scar of a spear wound in His side.

The brightness of the glory of this Person outshines the noonday sun. All heaven is lighted by His splendor. Not a star moves in its orbit and not a man draws breath that He does not uphold and keep. Yet in this Man's feet are scars of cruel wounds.

His "origin is from of old, from ancient days" (Micah 5:2). His power and authority are "far above all rule and authority and power and dominion, and above every name that is named" (Ephesians 1:21). The Man is "crowned with glory and honor" (Hebrews 2:9). Once, however, He meekly wore a crown of piercing thorns.

Who is this wondrous Person? It is "the man Christ Jesus" (I Timothy 2:5). It is God the Son. He did not always have the form of a man, but there came a time when something tremendous had to be done if sinners were to be saved and brought to God. This work could only be accomplished by one who was both God and man. Because He loved us, the eternal, glorious Son of God left heaven and came to earth to live in human form.

He did not suddenly appear as a man of power and wealth, making a great show of Himself. He began His earthly life as a tiny, helpless baby, and through most of His life Jesus labored as a carpenter in a quiet little town. He whose home was heaven sought no riches and honor for Himself; instead He was always helping others. Then one day He died, nailed upon a huge wooden cross. But that was not the end, thank God!

Because the body of Him who is Life could not be kept in death, Jesus Christ arose from the grave and He lives in heaven now. "I am . . . the living One; I died, and behold I am alive for evermore" (Revelation 1:17, 18). He alone is both truly God and truly man.

For Thinking and Doing:

1. Read Colossians 4:1; I Thessalonians 1:10, 4:16; Philippians 2:5-11.

2. From Philippians 2:5-8, can you trace the steps which Jesus took when He came down from heaven?

3. What do you learn about heaven in Colossians 4:1; I Thessalonians 1:10, 4:16?

4. What do you especially like to think about concerning heaven?

His Coming Foretold

"He will be great, and will be called the Son of the Most High" (Luke 1:32).

Hundreds of years before Christ's birth God had word pictures of a Coming One written into the Old Testament. These so perfectly describe the Lord Jesus that anyone reading the Old Testament should be able at once to see that He is the promised Coming One. These word pictures are part of our Lord's credentials.

In Genesis 22:15-18, 26:1-4, 28:13-14 and in Jeremiah 23:5-6, we are told that this Promised One would be born of the Hebrew race, of the line of Abraham, Isaac and Jacob, and from the family of David. Luke 3:31 and 34 gives these four names among Jesus' ancestors.

The angel Gabriel said to the young virgin Mary, of whom Jesus was born, "You will conceive . . . and bear a son, and you shall call His name Jesus. He will be great, and will be called the Son of the Most High . . . The Holy Spirit will come upon you, and the power of the Most High will overshadow you; therefore the child to be born will be called holy, the Son of God" (Luke 1:31-35). This was predicted 700 years before in Isaiah 7:14.

God told where the Child would be born. "You, Bethlehem . . . who are little among the clans of Judah, from you shall come forth for Me One who is to be ruler in Israel, whose origin is from of old, from ancient days" (Micah 5:2). That was the prophecy and here is the fact. "Jesus was born in Bethlehem of Judea in the days of Herod" (Matthew 2:1).

This Coming One was to be a prophet to the Jews, that is, He would give God's message to these people and would tell them of things to come. "The Lord said to (Moses) . . . I will raise up for them a prophet like you from among their brethren; and I will put My words in His mouth" (Deuteronomy 18:17-18). Jesus was that prophet. He said, "The Father who sent Me has Himself given me commandment what to say" (John 12:49).

Although some envied and hated Him, multitudes followed the Lord to hear His message, and many "wondered at the gracious words which proceeded out of His mouth" (Luke 4:22), and said, "No man ever spoke like this man!" (John 7:46). "Jesus . . . was a prophet mighty in deed and word" (Luke 24:19). The prophecies about Jesus, their fulfillment and His own words were His divine credentials. "These are written that you may believe that Jesus is . . . the Son of God" (John 20:31).

For Thinking and Doing:

1. Read Matthew 1:18-25; 2:1-15.
2. What impresses you most as you read the familiar Christmas story?
3. Matthew 1:2-23 gives two names for the Child who was born of Mary. What are they and what do they mean?
4. What do these names mean to us for our daily lives?

Divine Credentials

"Behold, I stand at the door and knock; if any one hears my voice and opens the door, I will come in to him and eat with him, and he with me" (Revelation 3:20).

We often need to know if a person is who and what he says he is. For example, suppose five scientists in Colorado were working on a secret weapon for the Government. One day a stranger arrives who claims he has been sent by the President to take charge of the work. Would the other scientists be willing to believe him? No, for if this man had come to do such important work, the other men would have been told about his coming. Probably his photograph would have been sent to them also. When the stranger came he would be expected to show letters from the U. S. Government as proof that he was the right person. He would show these letters as his credentials.

When the Lord Jesus came to earth He looked just like other men, but He claimed that He was the "Son of God" (John 10:36), and also claimed, "I have come down from heaven" (John 6:38). He said, "The Father who sent Me has Himself given Me commandment what to say" (John 12:49). "I and the Father are one" (John 10:30), so that "He who has seen Me has seen the

Father" (John 14:9). "No one comes to the Father but by Me" (John 14:6). To those who would turn to God, Christ promised, "I give them eternal life" (John 10:28). He claimed that He had "All authority in heaven and on earth" (Matthew 28:18). The Lord Jesus said He was both God and man.

How could people know if what this Stranger said about Himself was true? How did the Man Christ Jesus dare to make such claims? It was because he knew who He was, and His credentials proved it. You will be reading of them: His words, His works, His character. They prove He is worthy of our love and trust.

However, many do not believe that Jesus Christ was God as well as Man. "He was a very good and wonderful man," they say, "but He was not God." But think. The Lord Jesus said He was one of the Persons of God and equal with the Father. Did He lie? He claimed to have all power in heaven and on earth, to be able to give eternal life to men. Was this also a lie? If it were, then He was not a good man, but a wicked man. We know Christ could not have been that kind of person, so He must have been just what He said—God the Son. We have the record of His wonderful words and deeds to prove it.

For Thinking and Doing:

1. Read Matthew 9:35; Luke 9:1-6; Acts 10:38; Matthew 11:2-6.

2. Which of the credentials of Jesus do you think are the most impressive?

3. According to Matthew 11:2-6, what reasons did Jesus give to John the Baptist that He was the One who was to come according to prophecy?

4. Do you in your heart believe Jesus is the Son of God?

51st Day

The Miracles of Christ

"When the people saw the sign which he had done, they said, 'This is indeed the prophet who is to come into the world!'"
(John 6:14).

There are many proofs that Jesus, the Man who lived in the country of Palestine nearly 2,000 years ago, was really God.

Reports of Him had spread from town to town. Thousands of people had told what they had seen with their own eyes; they, at least, could never doubt that mighty miracles were being done. I can imagine that an excited group of people gathered in the city of Nain one day. All were trying to talk at once. A number had been walking toward the town with the crowd that followed Jesus. As they drew near, there came through the city gates a funeral procession. The coffin held the dead body of a widow's only son. It was a time of great sorrow for the mother, but oh! what a marvelous thing Jesus did! He stopped "and touched the (coffin) . . . and He said, 'Young man, I say to you, arise.' And the dead man sat up, and began to speak" (Luke 7:14-15). The people praised the Lord and said, "God has visited His people!" (Luke 7:16).

On another occasion Jesus taught five thousand people new things about God and healed the sick. How wonderful it all was. So they stayed on and on until it was time for supper. No one had brought any food except a small boy who had five barley loaves and two small fish. But what were they among so many hungry people? Then something happened. There were two small fish and five barley loaves, yet out from the miracle-working hands of Jesus there passed bread and fish enough for all that multitude of thousands. "And all ate and were satisfied. And they took up what was left over, twelve baskets of broken pieces" (Luke 9:17).

These two stories tell only a little part of what the Lord Jesus did while He was here on earth. "He went about all Galilee . . . healing every disease . . . among the people. So His fame spread throughout all Syria: and they brought Him all the sick . . . demoniacs . . . paralytics, and He healed them" (Matthew 4:23-25).

The Lord Jesus did mighty works for the people of His day, and He will do mighty things in your life if you have faith in Him. As we read of Him and His marvelous works we can know that He was truly God.

For Thinking and Doing:

1. Read Matthew 9:18-26; John 20:30-31.
2. What do you learn about faith from Matthew 9:20-22?
3. According to John 20:30-31, why was that book written?
4. What impresses you most about the feeding of the 5,000?

Jesus Knows Us

"But when Jesus perceived their thoughts, He answering said unto them, What reason ye in your hearts?" (Luke 5:22, KJV).

The miracle works of Christ prove Him to be all powerful and all knowing.

Peter found this to be true. In a town beside the Sea of Galilee a tax collector asked Peter if Jesus had paid the tribute money to the treasury in the temple. Peter spoke to the Lord about it. Jesus asked Peter to do a strange thing. "Go to the sea," He said, "and cast a hook, and take the first fish that comes up, and when you open its mouth you will find a shekel; take that and give it to them for Me and for yourself" (Matthew 17:27). Surely only God could have known that 1) there was a fish in the lake with money in its mouth, 2) there would be just the right amount to pay the tax, and 3) the money would be in the mouth of the first fish Peter would catch.

Do you know just how, when and where you will end your life on earth? Can you tell in advance anything that will happen at the time of your death? No. But Jesus could. Again and again His enemies among the Jews tried to kill the Lord by different ways which always failed. But one day Jesus looked into the future and told His disciples, "We are going up to Jerusalem; and the Son of man will be delivered to the chief priests and scribes, and they will condemn Him to death, and deliver Him to the Gentiles to be mocked and scourged and crucified, and He will be raised on the third day" (Matthew 20:18-19).

Notice that there are nine special things the Lord said would take place at the time of His death. Turn now to Matthew 26:1-5, 14-16, 47, 57, 66-68 and 27:1-3, 26-36. It was not the Gentiles, but some of the Jews, who hated Christ and wanted Him killed. Unless He were God, how could the Lord have known that the Gentiles, not the Jews, would kill Him and in the very way described?

We read also that Jesus knew men's thoughts. Peter loved the Lord and boasted that he would never deny Him. But Christ looking forward warned Peter that before a certain time he would three times deny his Lord, and Peter did. (Matthew 26:33-34, 69-75).

Jesus also knows the future. In Luke 21:5-24 He foretold the destruction of Jerusalem, and those very things were done about 40 years later when Titus attacked it. Yes, Jesus, the Son of God, knows all our ways and thoughts.

For Thinking and Doing:

1. Read Matthew 26:33-34, 69-75; Matthew 28:20; I Chronicles 28:9.

2. What specific comfort does it bring you that Jesus knows all about you?

3. What difference should this make in your thoughts and inward emotions?

4. What does Jesus' promise in Matthew 28:20 mean to you?

Our Savior and Friend

"The Father sent the Son to be the Saviour of the world" (I John 4:14, KJV).

The first four books of the New Testament, which give the story of Christ's life on earth, are called the Gospels. They tell of God the Son, the eternal Lord, leaving heaven's riches for earth's poverty. The King of glory willingly exchanged the worship of angel hosts for the scorn and hate of evil men. The Holy, Almighty One came down and wearied Himself in self-denying service for the poor, the sick, the sinning and the despised. He who is Life and the giver of all life gave Himself up to a cruel death.

Now this is most amazing. There had to be a compelling reason why God the Son should become man and do and bear such things. It was all part of God's plan, and that plan is of utmost importance to men and all creation.

The life story of Jesus is marvelous. Neither Satan nor wicked rulers could cause Him fear or turn Him from the right. How noble He was in every way. His quiet patience was that of strength and not of weakness. There was no sign of pride nor of complaining. You never find the Lord Jesus thinking of His own comfort or pleasure. People of every sort felt free to ask for His help, and by the love and kindness of His heart and in the wisdom of God, He met their needs. The Savior warned people of the awful results of sin and turned men's hearts to God.

81

All of us have been disappointed by those we thought were true and loyal friends. But when you see the Lord Jesus as He is shown to us in the Gospels, you realize that He is worthy of your love and trust, for He never fails. "Jesus Christ is the same yesterday and today and for ever" (Hebrews 13:8). He is still the same Lord although He is not now on earth. Count on Him; He wants your trust and He is a Friend who will never let you down.

It is most important for you to realize that the Lord came to earth to be our Savior and Friend. He is always with you to meet all your needs and to keep you from sin and harm.

For Thinking and Doing:

1. Read I John 4:9; John 10:10, 27, 28.
2. What problems are there in your life for which you need wisdom and help?
3. Ask the Savior to help you with these problems and thank Him today that you can always trust in Him.
4. Memorize John 10:10b.

54th Day

Why Our Savior Came

"For the Son of man came to seek and to save the lost" (Luke 19:10).

Why did God the Son become man? It was because some day each of us will stand before Him to be judged for everything we've said and done and for all our way of life. "Each of us shall give account of himself to God" (Romans 14:12). "The Father . . . has given all judgment unto the Son" (John 5:22). Jesus learned by experience how much it sometimes costs to do God's will. As a man, He experienced the temptations that we do, though He did not sin. The Lord suffered from pain, misunderstanding, weariness, cruelty and loneliness. Therefore, He is able to understand our experiences and is the One who can judge all who shall stand before Him in a way that is both merciful and absolutely fair.

The human life of Jesus is a picture of what God wants us all to be. We must realize that Christ is our example and that His holy, noble life is the yardstick or standard by which God measures our lives. That is a solemn thought, isn't it? It would be hopelessly discouraging if the Lord had not come to our help. But He said, "I am come that they might have life, and . . . have it more abundantly" (John 10:10, KJV). This means that Jesus has made possible for us a life that is above our natural life and is beyond anything that we could ever do or be. It is the very life of Christ Himself in us, because He has promised that if we ask Him to come into our hearts, He will dwell there. Therefore, we do not have to live the Christian life all on our own, for He is with us to help us.

In every way the Lord Jesus showed His interest in our welfare by His love and kindness. But what about God the Father? He sometimes seems so far away. Is He stern, harsh and not interested in us? No indeed. God the Father does care, for Jesus said, "I and the Father are one" (John 10:30). The Persons of God are so truly one in their nature and character that Christ told the disciples, "He who has seen Me has seen the Father" (John 14:9). Do you wish to see what God the Father is like? He is exactly like the Lord Jesus Christ who came and lived among men so that He might show us, in words and ways that we can understand, what God is like.

> We can see only a little of the ocean,
> Just a few miles distant from the rocky shore,
> But out there—far beyond our eye's horizon,
> There's more—immeasurably more.
> We can see only a little of God's loving—
> A few rich treasures from His mighty store;
> But out there—far beyond our eye's horizon,
> There's more—immeasurably more.
>
> —Selected

How can you be sure God loves you? "God showed His great love for us by sending Christ to die for us while we were still sinners" (Romans 5:8, LNT).

For Thinking and Doing:

1. Read I John 4:9-10, 19; John 16:27.
2. Explain as you would to a friend what I John 4:9, 10 means to you.
3. What is our part according to John 16:27; I John 4:19?
4. Is this your own experience?

For Our Sins

"He is the forgiveness for our sins, and not only ours but all the world's" (I John 2:2, LNT).

Today you will be reading of a glorious, yet most awful, event in the history of the world in the words of Scripture. As you read it, remember it was for you. It was, of course, for all mankind, but it was for you as though there was no other.

"It was evening . . . Jesus . . . went . . . to the Mount of Olives; and the disciples followed Him. Judas . . . also knew the place . . . And . . . Judas came . . . and with him a great crowd with swords and clubs, from the chief priests and the elders of the people . . . They . . . laid hands on Jesus . . . Then all the disciples . . . fled.

"And they led Jesus to the high priest . . . The chief priests and the whole council sought testimony against Jesus to put Him to death . . . Many bore false witness against Him . . . But He was silent . . . The men who were holding Jesus mocked Him . . . they also blindfolded Him . . . and struck Him . . . and some began to spit on Him.

"They bound Him and led Him away and delivered Him to Pilate the governor . . . Pilate said to them . . . 'What shall I do with Jesus . . . ?' They all said, 'Let Him be crucified!' And he said, 'Why, what evil has He done? I have found in Him no crime deserving death' . . . But they were urgent, demanding with loud cries that He should be crucified . . . So Pilate, wishing to satisfy the crowd . . . and having scourged Jesus, delivered Him to be crucified. Then the soldiers of the governor took Jesus . . . and they gathered the whole battalion before Him . . . And plaiting a crown of thorns they put it on His head . . . and . . . they mocked Him, saying, 'Hail, King of the Jews!' And they . . . struck Him on the head. And when they had mocked Him they . . . led Him away to crucify Him.

"When they came to a place called Golgotha, there they crucified Him. When they had crucified Him . . . they watched Him there. And the people stood by, watching; but the rulers scoffed at Him, saying 'He saved others; let Him save Himself, if He is the Christ of God, His Chosen One!' And Jesus said, 'Father, forgive them; for they know not what they do.' There was darkness over the whole land until the ninth hour. And about the ninth hour Jesus cried with a loud voice . . . 'My God, My God, why hast Thou forsaken Me?' . . . And He said, 'It is finished . . . Father, into Thy hands I commit My spirit.' And having said this He breathed His last . . . And behold, the curtain of the temple was torn in two, from top to bottom; and the earth shook, and the rocks were split . . . The centurion and those who were with him . . . said, 'Truly this was the Son of God.' One of the soldiers pierced His side with a spear." (From Matthew 26-27; Mark 14-15; Luke 22-23; John 18-19).

For Thinking and Doing:

1. Read Romans 5:6-8; I Peter 3:18; Isaiah 53:5-6.
2. What part of today's reading has brought you some new thought about God's love for us?
3. Why did Jesus die for us according to I Peter 3:18?
4. Memorize Isaiah 53:6.

56th Day

He Has Risen

"He is not here; for He has risen, as He said" (Matthew 28:6).

Jesus Christ, the Lord of life, was dead and buried, but He had said that on the third day He would rise again. His enemies did not believe this, but they feared that His disciples might take away His body and pretend He had risen. So a stone was placed at the door of the tomb and sealed. Soldiers were also set to guard it.

As the Lord's body was carried to the grave, "women . . . followed, and saw the tomb, and how His body was laid . . . And . . . Mary Magdalene, and Mary the mother of James, and Salome, bought spices, so that they might . . . anoint Him. And very early on the first day of the week they went to the tomb when the sun had risen . . . And looking up, they saw that the stone was rolled back; for it was very large . . . An angel of the Lord descended from heaven and came and rolled back the stone, and sat upon it. His appearance was like lightning, and his raiment white as snow. And for fear of him the guards trembled and became like dead men. But the angel said to the women, 'Do not be afraid; for I know that you seek Jesus who was crucified. He is not here; for He has risen . . . Come, see the place where He lay.'

85

"They departed . . . and ran to tell His disciples . . . but these words seemed to them an idle tale, and they did not believe them . . . Peter . . . with the other disciple (John) . . . went toward the tomb . . . Peter . . . went into the tomb; he saw the linen cloths lying, and the napkin, which had been on His head . . . rolled up . . . by itself. Then (John) . . . also went in, and he saw and believed.

"That very day two of them (the disciples) were going to . . . Emmaus, about seven miles from Jerusalem . . . and . . . Jesus Himself drew near and went with them. On the evening of that day . . . the doors being shut where the disciples were . . . Jesus came and stood among them and said unto them, 'Peace be with you . . . ' But they were . . . frightened, and supposed that they saw a spirit. And He said, 'Why are you troubled? . . . See My hands and My feet, that it is I Myself; handle Me, and see; for a spirit has not flesh and bones as you see that I have . . . ' And He . . . ate before them . . . Then the disciples were glad when they saw the Lord." (From Matthew 28; Mark 16; Luke 24; John 20).

For Thinking and Doing:

1. Read I Corinthians 15:3-4; Luke 24:36-43.

2. The main message of the apostle Paul is contained in I Corinthians 15:3-4. Name the three parts of that message.

3. How did Jesus prove His resurrection to the disciples?

4. What difference does it make to us that Jesus is risen from the dead?

57th Day

Christ's Resurrection and You

"If you confess with your lips that Jesus is Lord and believe in your heart that God raised him from the dead, you will be saved. For man believes with his heart and so is justified, and he confesses with his lips and so is saved" (Romans 10:9-10).

It would be interesting to stand for an hour on a street where crowds of people hurry by and ask each one these three questions: 1) Do you believe that Jesus Christ really lived on earth and that He was crucified, dead and buried? 2) Do you believe that Jesus' body came out of the grave and that He is living in that resurrected body now? 3) Does it mean anything to you that He is living now?

Many of those questioned might just stare or laugh. One might say, "It is impossible for a dead person to come to life, for there are certain natural laws which cannot be broken." Another might answer, "Even if it were possible, there is no proof that Jesus rose from the dead. Perhaps His soul lives on somewhere, but not His body. As to what a living Christ would mean to me, why, I've never thought about it." So they would go on their way to the office, school or shop.

To deny an important fact because we don't want to face it does not get rid of that fact. To push it away because we aren't interested does not change its importance.

The resurrection of Jesus' body is of vital importance to all, and that includes you. The Bible teaches that just as truly as you are alive today, just so surely will you sometime stand before the risen Christ and see Him in His body, face to face.

If our Lord did not rise from the dead, the Old Testament prophets were false. If His body has gone to dust in the grave, the New Testament is false and the Christian faith crumbles. Then, too, we who rest our hopes on the living Christ perish.

The Lord Jesus claimed, "I have power to lay it (His life) down, and I have power to take it again" (John 10:18). He foretold His return to earth, saying, "The tribes of the earth . . . will see the Son of man coming on the clouds of heaven with power and great glory" (Matthew 24:30).

Therefore, if the Lord Jesus did not rise as He claimed He would, He either did not have the power to do so or His words were not true. If either of these were so, Jesus would stand forever condemned by God, angels and men as a deceiver. This is unthinkable.

For Thinking and Doing:

1. Read I Corinthians 15:3-8, 13-22; Romans 10:9-11.

2. What does I Corinthians 15:3-8 tell you of the proof of Christ's resurrection?

3. Put into a few words of your own Paul's statements in I Corinthians 15:17-19.

4. According to Romans 10:9-10 why is our belief in Jesus' resurrection important?

Christ's Return

"I will see you again" (John 16:22).

On December 1, 1941, no war was being fought in the United States or in the Hawaiian Islands. In the quiet of early morning on December 7, bombs exploded over Pearl Harbor. Hundreds lay dead and wounded. Sorrow and fear gripped millions of hearts, for then war began between the United States and Japan. The battle moved westward to the Philippine Islands. There outnumbered American forces were being defeated and were fighting desperately to push the enemy back. Civilians were imprisoned, persecuted and bombed.

One night a small American boat slipped away from the shore of one of the islands. It carried General MacArthur, who was needed elsewhere, but to those left behind his pomise was, "I will return."

There followed years of bloody war before the tide of battle turned and our defeat changed to victory. Then General MacArthur did come back to the Philippines. His return meant that he was able to keep his promise. It was a sign of the victory which set free the starving prisoners of war and brought an end to battle wounds and death.

Thousands of years ago God created the first man and woman and gave them a beautiful garden called Eden to be their home. Into that quiet, happy place Satan let loose the deadly "bomb" of sin, that awful thing that destroys men's souls and bodies. Right there and then the man and woman were defeated and there began on earth the terrible battle between good and evil which has never ended. Sometimes it seems that sin is more wide-spread than ever and that the power of Satan, the enemy of men's souls, is seen everywhere. Sin and death seem victorious. Even God the Son hung, dead, upon the cross. He seemed defeated. The holy, mighty Lord of life lay in the grave.

But wait. Just before His death Christ promised His disciples, "I will come again" (John 14:3), and "I will see you again and your hearts will rejoice" (John 16:22). Could the Lord really keep that promise? At Easter we often sing:

Death cannot keep His prey—
Jesus, my Savior;

He tore the bars away—
Jesus, my Lord!
Up from the grave He arose,
With a mighty triumph o'er His foes;
He arose a victor from the dark domain;
And He lives forever, with His saints to reign.
Hallelujah! Christ arose!

—Robert Lowry (adapted)

By His resurrection Jesus proved He is conqueror over Satan's hosts and over death. No longer can Satan keep the souls and bodies of men bound in sin and death, for a living Savior delivers us from sin and gives eternal life to all who trust Him. What a wonderful Savior is Jesus our Lord!

For Thinking and Doing:

1. Read Genesis 2:15-17; 3:4-7; Hebrews 2:14-15.
2. Did Eve's actions show she believed God or Satan? (Genesis 2:17; 3:4, 6).
3. Think of some instances where we can make the same mistake.
4. Why does Hebrews 2:14-15 say that Jesus took on Himself our human nature?

59th Day

Certain Proofs

"To them He presented Himself alive . . . . by many proofs, appearing to them during forty days" (Acts 1:3).

In Acts 1:2, 3 we are told that during the forty days between Christ's resurrection and His return to heaven He appeared to His disciples "to whom also He shewed Himself alive . . . by many infallible proofs" (Acts 1:3, KJV). Infallible means sure. If one of your friends died and later you heard from others that he was alive again, what would you accept as sure proof of it? Don't you think the surest proof would be to see and talk with him yourself and to touch his living body? You simply couldn't doubt that your friend lived if you and others saw him walking about, eating

89

and drinking. Then if he reminded you of things you had done and spoken of together, you would be positive he was the same person you had known before.

The apostle Paul tells us that Christ "was buried, and that He rose again the third day . . . And that . . . He was seen of about five hundred (disciples) . . . of whom the greater part remain unto this present" (I Corinthians 15:4-6, KJV). Since most of those five hundred were still alive when Paul wrote those words, he would not have dared to write them if they were not true.

No wonder the disciples were sure their Master had come back to life. Jesus walked and talked with two disciples as they journeyed toward Emmaus and He explained to them the Scriptures. Christ did not show Himself to unbelievers. But to those who loved Him, He seemed most anxious to prove that He was the same Jesus they had known before He was crucified. They could always trust His love and power. Not only did the Lord show Himself to the disciples, but He let them handle Him so that by touch, as well as by sight, they could be sure. He ate with them and reminded them of things He had said before His death.

One disciple, Thomas, was not with the others when Christ appeared to them the first time. He certainly was a doubter. When the disciples said, "We have seen the Lord," he wouldn't believe it. He said, "Unless I see in His hands the print of the nails, and place my finger into the mark of the nails, and place my hand in His side, I will not believe!" How kind Jesus was to that unbelieving heart. For later, when Thomas was with the other disciples, "Jesus came and stood among them, and said . . . to Thomas, 'Put your finger here, and see My hands; and put out your hand, and place it in My side; do not be faithless, but believing.' Thomas answered Him, 'My Lord and my God!' Jesus said to him, 'Have you believed because you have seen Me? Blessed are those who have not seen and yet believe'" (John 20:24-29).

These last words of promise are spoken also to all of us who have never seen the Lord Jesus. We, too, shall receive a wondrous blessing if we believe and accept Him as our Lord and our God.

For Thinking and Doing:

1. Read John 21:1-14; I Peter 1:8.
2. What proof of Jesus' resurrection seems the surest to you?
3. Is I Peter 1:8 true of you?
4. What does I Peter 1:9 say is the result of our faith in His resurrection? See also Romans 10:9-10.

Jesus Is King

"To Him was given dominion and glory and kingdom" (Daniel 7:14).

There are those who think that Jesus was only a man sent from God to teach us how to live and to give us the example of His noble, self-sacrificing life. They suppose He died as a martyr for His high ideals and that, although His influence remains, death ended His existence. Nothing could be farther from the truth. Let's see why.

By the Old Testament prophets God gave promises of a time, yet future, when a mighty king will come and reign over the whole earth. To Him will be given "dominion . . . and (a) kingdom, that all peoples, nations, and languages should serve Him; His dominion is an everlasting dominion" (Daniel 7:14). "This is the name . . . The Lord Our Righteousness" (Jeremiah 23:6). Prophecies in the Bible foretell that Jerusalem will be the capital of the vast kingdom of the world Ruler, the "Lord of lords and King of kings" (Revelation 17:14).

This promised King is living now, for He is none other than the glorious Son of God. Our Christ is coming back to earth as He said He would. He will not reappear as the poor and lowly Jesus, but as the triumphant, supreme Ruler of the universe to destroy God's enemies. He said, "The Father . . . has given all judgment to the Son" (John 5:22), and "When the Son of man comes in His glory, and all the angels with Him, then He will sit on His glorious throne" (Matthew 25:31).

Paul speaks of the time, "when the Lord Jesus is revealed from heaven with His mighty angels . . . inflicting vengeance upon those who do not know God and upon those who do not obey the gospel of our Lord Jesus. They shall suffer the punishment of eternal destruction and exclusion from the presence of the Lord" (II Thessalonians 1:7-9). "Then shall the Lord go forth, and fight against those nations" that have been against Him (Zechariah 14:3, KJV). "And His feet shall stand in that day upon the mount of Olives, which is before Jerusalem" (Zechariah 14:4, KJV). "Behold, He is coming with the clouds, and every eye will see Him, every one who pierced Him" (Revelation 1:7). "And one shall say . . . What are these wounds in Thine hands?" (Zechariah 13:6, KJV).

These words from the Bible tell where the coming King will stand. They speak of wounds in His hands and say that all shall see Him. What can this mean but that it is the risen Christ who shall return in His resurrected body? "He (God) has fixed a day on which He will judge the world in righteousness by a Man whom He has appointed, and of this He has given assurance to all men by raising Him from the dead" (Acts 17:31). You see, we can be absolutely sure that "the man Christ Jesus" will some day judge the earth because He was raised from the dead and is coming again. What a thrilling and awful time that day will be. It may be very soon that every eye shall see the living Lord.

For Thinking and Doing:

1. Read Philippians 2:9-11.
2. What thoughts in today's reading are new to you?
3. What does Philippians 2:9-11 tell us of Christ's return?
4. Why can Christians look forward with joy to Christ's return?

61st Day

Men Who Bore Witness

"This Jesus God raised up, and of that we all are witnesses" (Acts 2:32).

Let us suppose that one day you recognized robbers running from a bank that they had just robbed and where they had killed a man. They were brothers who had once worked for your father. It was a terrible thing. A few weeks later these men were arrested, and after being questioned, were to stand trial for the crime of thieving and murder. Meanwhile, you received a letter warning you not to appear as a witness and threatening to harm you and your parents if you did. What would you do? To deny you knew them would let two dangerous men go free. To tell about them could mean death to you and your family.

The disciples who saw the Lord after His resurrection had just as hard a choice to make. Religious leaders had hated Christ and killed Him. As He was taken away to be tried and later crucified, His followers all "forsook Him and fled" (Matthew 26:56). They feared that they, too, might be killed.

When Jesus was buried His enemies probably thought they would never again be bothered by His frightened disciples, yet a few days later these same disciples dared to teach that Christ was risen from the dead. They went into the temple and accused His enemies of murder, saying, "Jesus of Nazareth . . . you crucified and killed . . . but God raised Him up" (Acts 2:22-24). "God exalted Him . . . as Leader and Savior . . . And we are witnesses to these things" (Acts 5:31, 32). "We cannot but speak of what we have seen and heard" (Acts 4:20).

Did the Jewish council produce the dead body of Jesus to prove that the disciples were wrong? Of course that was impossible. Instead they tried to silence these witnesses by beatings, imprisonment and even death. However, through all the persecutions these men insisted they had seen the risen Lord. How sure they must have been. For although men will tell lies to save their lives or to gain money or power, none would be so foolish as to make up a story and insist upon its truth, knowing it would bring him terrible suffering or death.

There was a sudden change in these disciples from cowardice to courage and from unbelief to faith. There is no way to explain this change except that they knew—beyond any doubt—that there really was and is a resurrected Christ.

For Thinking and Doing:

1. Read Acts 2:22-24; 4:1-4; II Timothy 3:12; II Corinthians 5:20.

2. In what ways can a Christian suffer for his faith today?

3. What example do the early disciples give us of their loyalty to Christ?

4. Put II Corinthians 5:20 into your own words and explain what you think it means to be an "ambassador for Christ."

62nd Day

Saul Is Changed

"Though I formerly blasphemed and persecuted and insulted Him; but I received mercy" (I Timothy 1:13).

One noon soon after Jesus' death most of those who had crowded the broad road leading from Jerusalem to Damascus had taken shelter from the sun's fierce heat. A few still traveled on, such as peddlers, donkeys with loads piled high, and their drivers straggling alongside. A group of Roman soldiers hurried toward the city. Their leader was a young, highly-educated Jew who was also a Pharisee. He was grim and angry, a fiery patriot, all-out for God and the Jewish religion. His name was Saul and he hated the Christians.

But why? It all had to do with Jesus who was to some a mighty Prophet, and to others he was the Jewish Messiah and coming King. Jesus had worked miracles and claimed to be the Son of God, greater than Abraham, Moses and angels. The high priests thought they had put an end to all this. Jesus had been condemned and had died a criminal's death. But He had come to life again; hundreds said they had seen Him. Thousands were believing and were worshipping Jesus Christ as the living God. Saul was infuriated and was trying to stamp out this "blasphemy."

As Saul went on to Damascus a light brighter than the noonday sun shone around him. Falling to the ground he heard a voice saying, "Saul, why do you persecute Me?" Saul said, "Who are you, Lord?" There came the answer, "I am Jesus" (Acts 9:4-5). The despised Jesus was dead. But no, He was not dead, for then and there Saul saw in heaven the risen, living Lord. For a time he was blinded by that glorious sight.

There was no need for swords and soldiers any longer. Saul's one desire now was to know Christ better and to follow Him always.

Do you say this might have been a dream? Impossible. Dreams don't blind one's eyes. Then also, Saul (later called Paul) was changed completely and forever by that sight of Christ. If you read II Corinthians 11:22-33, you will see what he suffered for His dear Master's sake, going to a martyr's death at last. All of Paul's New Testament writings show that he knew, loved, served and would sometime see again his living Lord. This sudden, wonderful change in Saul is one of the proofs of Christ's bodily resurrection.

For Thinking and Doing:

1. Read Acts 9:1-9; I Timothy 1:12-16; Philippians 3:4-8.

2. What impresses you most about Paul's experience on the Damascus road?

3. Why does Paul say he received mercy in I Timothy 1:13?

4. What did Paul consider worth the loss of everything else according to Philippians 3:8?

Heaven

"Now we live in the hope of eternal life because Christ rose from the dead ... it is kept in heaven for you" (I Peter 1:3-4, LNT).

Forty days after Christ came back from death to life, He went away. Where did He go? He went back to His home in heaven, God's dwelling place.

What is heaven like? It is said of our Lord that by Him "all things were created, in heaven and on earth" (Colossians 1:16). Because the Bible says there are "things" in heaven, heaven must be a place. The Bible says, "The Lord's throne is in heaven" (Psalm 11:4). Heaven is not just a dream, nor is it simply a happy feeling or a great empty space where spirits float about. God's home is just as real a place as New York, London or Tokyo.

"The Lord has established His throne in the heavens and His kingdom rules over all" (Psalm 103:19). Far, far away, beyond the vast reaches of the groups of unnumbered stars, Christians believe there is this glorious, unseen world. In that place God rules over all that is in heaven and upon earth, over every living creature and over every great and small thing in the whole universe, seen and unseen.

It would take days to name the many beautiful and interesting things which our God has made for man's use and pleasure here on earth. The Bible tells us that heaven is much more beautiful and glorious then anything we could imagine. "No mere man has ever seen, heard or even imagined what wonderful things God has ready for those who love the Lord" (I Corinthians 2:9, LNT). In the last chapters of the Bible we are told that heaven is a place of matchless glory. There are riches and splendor that cannot be explained and beauty that can only be described as being like clear and shimmering gold, pearls and precious stones. A light unknown to earth floods that heavenly land. "There shall be no night there ... they need no light of ... sun, for the Lord God will be their light ... the glory of God is its light" (Revelation 21:25; 22:5; 21:23).

Jesus spoke of heaven as His Father's house. God's servants, the angels, live there. God's family lives there too. It is made up of all His own dearly-loved sons and daughters—those who belong to Christ. These are called His saints. As a loving human father shares

95

his riches with his children, so God will share the priceless heavenly riches with all who belong to Him.

> O bright Land,
> O fair Land of everlasting day;
> O Land secure and changeless,
> Which shall never pass away!
> Your streets and courts are filling
> With a radiant, raptured throng;
> And voice of saints and angels
> Swells the joyous shout of song!
> Ten thousand times ten thousand,
> The myriad saints above
> Have entered now the presence
> Of the glorious King of love!
> His death has their deliverance
> Wrought from Satan, death, and sin;
> His hand has opened wide the gate
> Of heaven to let them in.

—Anonymous

For Thinking and Doing:

1. Read John 14:2-3; Matthew 6:9-13.
2. What impresses you most about heaven?
3. According to John 14:2-3, where did Jesus go and what did He plan to do?
4. Are you helping to fulfill the prayer of Matthew 6:10?

64th Day

We Shall See God

"We can't even imagine what it is going to be like" (I John 3:2, LNT).

What a wonderful heavenly life is waiting for all of God's children. It will not be spent "just sitting around and playing a harp." That is man's foolish idea. The Scriptures teach that heaven is a busy place and that we who are Christ's shall be living there in resurrected bodies which shall never grow tired or sick. We shall each do that which God's love has planned for us and that which we most enjoy. "In Thy presence there is fullness of joy . . . pleasures for evermore" (Psalm 16:11). Think of the overflowing happiness that we will have, not wishing for anything more or different ever again.

Best of all, we shall see and know our glorious Lord. Speaking of that future time, God has said that He will "dwell with them, and they shall be His people, and God Himself will be with them . . . He will wipe away every tear from their eyes, and death shall be no more, neither shall there be mourning nor crying nor pain any more, for the former things (sorrows of earth) have passed away . . . And His servants shall worship Him . . . and . . . reign for ever and ever" (Revelation 21:3, 4; 22:3-5).

But there is another, awful side to this thrilling picture, for there are millions who will be forever shut out of God's home; they are not of His family. God is holy and heaven must always be kept the "holy place." This is why the Lord has warned that "nothing evil will be permitted in it—no one immoral or dishonest—but only those whose names are written in the Lamb's (Christ's) Book of Life" (Revelation 21:27, LNT). "The fearful, and unbelieving . . . and murderers . . . and idolaters, and all liars, shall have their part (not in heaven, but) in the lake which burneth with fire . . . which is the second death" (Revelation 21:8, KJV).

How solemn. The unbelieving—all who refused to believe God's Word—are counted in with murderers. Also included will be all those "fearful" of the sneers of the unbelieving or of the difficulties of the Christian life and who chose the easy, careless, down-hill way, turning their backs on God.

The privilege of living in heaven is given only to those who believe God's Word and accept Christ as their Savior, becoming God's children.

For Thinking and Doing:

1. Read I John 3:1-3.
2. What do you like best about the description of heaven?
3. Would heaven be heaven if evil or sin could enter it?
4. Have you ever thought how wonderful is the promise, "we shall be like Him"? What does this mean to you?

65th Day

Adam's Sin

"When Adam sinned, sin entered the entire human race" (Romans 5:12, LNT).

Is it possible for a person to be both alive and dead at the same time? The Bible explains that it is: a man can be physically alive, but spiritually dead. Genesis 1:26 and 27 tells us that God created Adam and Eve in His likeness. God who is a Spirit-Being gave them a spirit, a soul and a body. They were given a life and a nature which in many ways was like His own and which joined them to Him. They were given a mind with which to understand God's plans and works. They were companions of the Holy and Almighty One.

The home of Adam and Eve was in the garden of Eden, a beautiful place where they had everything they needed. "Out of the ground the Lord God made to grow every tree that is pleasant to the sight and good for food, the tree of life also . . . and the tree of the knowledge of good and evil" (Genesis 2:9).

There was only one thing they must not do. God said, "You may freely eat of every tree of the garden; but of the tree of the knowledge of good and evil you shall not eat, for in the day that you eat of it you shall die" (Genesis 2:16-17).

For a time all went well. Then something happened. The devil entered the garden and persuaded Eve to disobey the Lord by eating from the forbidden tree. Eve "took of its fruit and ate; and she also gave to her husband, and he ate" (Genesis 3:6).

What a terrible choice they made when they chose to obey the devil instead of God. It was the beginning of man's sin, and sin made a most dreadful change in the spirits, souls and bodies of Adam and Eve. Now their bodies would have to suffer pain, illness and death. "Sin came into the world . . . and death through sin" (Romans 5:12). No longer were they good and innocent of wrong. Evil became part of their very nature so that they were capable of all sorts of sin: pride, cruelty, meanness, lying, envy, hate, unbelief toward God, and the other evils we know so well. Through sin their souls were affected; they were now dead spiritually "through the trespasses and sins" (Ephesians 2:1). All of this was passed on to their children and all succeeding generations.

Think of all the suffering caused by sin and you will realize how awful it is. Think of how it must grieve our Heavenly Father who is all that is pure and holy.

For Thinking and Doing:

1. Read Genesis 3:22-24; Romans 5:12, 17, 19; Psalm 139:23, 24.

2. Why do you think God guarded the tree of life after Adam and Eve had sinned? (Genesis 3:22-24).

3. Think of ways we can lose out through sin like Adam and Eve did.

4. Memorize Psalm 139:23, 24.

Dead Spiritually

"He who has the Son has life, he who has not the Son of God has not life" (I John 5:12, KJV).

Do you remember God's warning to Adam and Eve? He said that in the day they disobeyed Him and ate the forbidden fruit they would surely die. They did eat. Would the Lord do as He had promised? Yes, for as soon as they sinned their bodies began to decay and go slowly but surely on toward death like branches which are cut off of a vine. Although Adam and Eve lived many years after that day they sinned, they did die and physical death became the lot of all men.

When the man and woman ate the fruit, was it their hands and mouths that sinned? Or was it the evil desire in their heart, their soul, which made them choose to disobey? It was not the hands or mouth; it was the soul that sinned. First came the wish and then they decided to eat the fruit. Their hands and mouths had to obey their wills; they took and they ate.

God is the ruler of His universe. His word and law is, "The soul that sins shall die" (Ezekiel 18:4). When a man's body dies his soul and spirit leave his body; they are separated from it.

When Adam and Eve were created God gave them a human nature. He also gave them a kind of life by which they were united with Him: a spiritual nature that could know and have fellowship with Him. God's Spirit was in man's spirit.

In the day that Adam and Eve sinned their souls became separated from God and they were cut off from Him. No longer did their spirits and souls possess that God-like kind of life they received from Him at creation. They still had their human nature and were strong and intelligent. They continued to live physically, but they did not have God's kind of life. They became dead spiritually.

What about your soul? Are you "dead . . . (in) sins" (Ephesians 2:1), separated "from the life of God" (Ephesians 4:18), "having no hope (for the future) and without God" (Ephesians 2:12)? Christ came so that this need never be true of us. God has promised, "He who believes in the Son has eternal life" (John 3:36).

For Thinking and Doing:

1. Read Romans 3:10-12, 23; I Corinthians 15:22; I John 5:12.
2. Put into your own words the main thought in Romans 3:10-12.
3. What are the two divisions describing all men in I Corinthians 15:22 and I John 5:12?
4. In which division do you choose to be?

67th Day

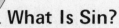

What Is Sin?

"Your iniquities (sin) have made a separation between you and your God" (Isaiah 59:2).

I once read of a mother and her children walking happily down a hilly road. Suddenly she heard a roar from behind. Turning, she saw that a rushing, driverless truck was almost upon them. Quickly she threw to the side of the road the child she was carrying and violently pushed the others beyond reach of the crushing wheels. The children were bruised as they fell, but do you think they got angry and said their mother was cruel to treat them so roughly?

God's Word hits us pretty hard sometimes. When He talks to us about our sins it is because He wants to push us into the way of life and safety. "He is not willing that any should perish (die)" (II Peter 3:9, LNT).

Why is it that all of us sin, even when we do not want to? We sin because Adam and Eve did, for of course their children were born with that same kind of nature. That sinful nature has been passed down from each parent and to each child in all the world. By one man, Adam, "sin came into the world . . . and death through (because of) sin, and so death spread to all men because all men sinned" (Romans 5:12). The fruit which grows on a tree shows what kind of tree it is. Just so, sins are the fruits that show we have sin in our nature.

What is sin? Sin is anything that separates us from God and anything in us that is less than God's standard for us. Do you remember that He says, "The soul that sins shall die" (Ezekiel 18:4)?

You may think your sins don't matter and that you know lots of people who do much worse things than you do. Yet only one bullet, shot into your heart, can kill you as surely as 60 bullets. One sin can cause a soul to die, just as one spot of cancer in your body means you are in danger of dying from cancer. Perhaps you answer, "I do not feel that my soul is dead. I feel very much alive in every way." As a person you are alive physically. However, the Bible teaches that the sinner, the person without Christ, is dead spiritually (Ephesians 2:1).

The important question is, "Will you choose Christ as your Savior from sin? If so, you will have eternal life (I John 5:12).

For Thinking and Doing:

1. Read I John 1:8-10; James 2:10.
2. If a person denies that he sins, what is true of him according to I John 1:8-10?
3. Read James 2:10 and give an example of "one point."
4. What is our part and what will Christ do according to I John 1:9?

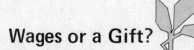

Wages or a Gift?

"The wages of sin is death, but the free gift of God is eternal life" (Romans 6:23).

Do you ever work for wages and to earn money? Suppose your employer should hand you the money you earned and say, "I hope you appreciate this very nice gift." You would be indignant and say, "Gift! I earned this money; it's mine by right!" Wages and gifts are quite different, aren't they?

God says, "The wages of sin is death" (Romans 6:23). The wages (the punishment or penalty) which our sin has earned is death. He also says, "But the free gift of God is eternal life" (Romans 6:23). He is willing to give us something we could never earn.

In a crowded courtroom a condemned man stands before the judge. The man is guilty of a serious crime. The law has decreed that for this crime he must either pay $500,000 or die in the electric chair. The man has no money with which to pay. He is in despair, for he must die. Now he sees the awfulness of his sin. The kind judge pities the man. He says, "You are guilty of this crime for which you should be put to death, but I will take your punishment upon myself. I will pay the money you owe so that you can go free. You need not die, for I will save you." To the judge it would mean giving all the money he had to pay the

101

penalty of another man's sins. To the criminal it would mean the gift of life instead of the death his sin had earned.

This story is a picture of what God has done for us. As judge He must uphold the laws He has made and punish sin by death. What would happen if sin were not dealt with? But in great love He has made a way so that our souls may be set free from death and that we might have the gift of eternal life. God has taken upon Himself the punishment of our sins. That is why Jesus, God the Son, left heaven and became man: so that in a human body He could die in our place, just as though He were the sinner.

"While we were yet sinners Christ died for us" (Romans 5:8). "The Lord has laid on Him the iniquity (sin) of us all" (Isaiah 53:6). While God's holy Son hung upon the cross, the sins of everyone were counted against Him—yours and mine included. "Who His own self bore our sins in His own body on the tree" (I Peter 2:24, KJV). What wonderful love. Heaven's best was given to save earth's worst. How we should thank God that he longs to save us from death and to give us eternal life.

For Thinking and Doing:

1. Read Isaiah 53:3-6; I Peter 2:24.

2. What would our world be like if there were no punishment for wrongdoing?

3. What does I Peter 2:24 tell us was the reason Christ bore our sins at the cross?

4. How does II Corinthians 5:15 tell us we should live?

69th Day

God's Gift of Life

"Thanks be unto God for His unspeakable gift" (II Corinthians 9:15, KJV).

If you could choose only one gift for yourself what would it be? Would it be a car or a TV set, or would you ask for $1,000,000 so that you could buy that TV set, a car and more? It would be nice to have such things while you're on earth. Of course some day all earth's treasures will be left behind; they are not used in the life to come. But God has gifts for you which are more glorious and valuable than man has ever known. They may be yours forever. Just as the one gift of $1,000,000 could buy many costly things, so God's gifts come to us through just one Person—the Lord Jesus Christ.

Let's think of one of these priceless gifts, eternal life. Perhaps you think of eternal life as something in the future and not very interesting or giving you happiness today. But because it is God's kind of life, it must be very wonderful.

"Eternal" in one sense means always, never ending. Eternal life also can mean a quality of life, the kind of life that knowing God can bring (John 17:3). The word "eternal" is used to describe God's character and nature as well as meaning He is always the same. His nature never changes. Forever He is powerful, wise, holy and righteous. He is eternal love and eternal joy. All that God is, He is forever.

God wants to share His life with you in all its beauty and joy. "For God so loved the world that He gave His only Son, that whoever believes in Him should not perish (soul death) but have eternal life" (John 3:16). "The free gift of God is eternal life in Christ Jesus our Lord" (Romans 6:23).

The gift of eternal life is for you. Say this over in your heart, "God, my Heavenly Father, offers to share with me, a sinner, His very own kind of life both now and forever."

Not only this, but He has also made it possible for you to have the thrill of having the Lord Jesus live out through you His nature of love, goodness, courage and joy in your life now on earth. When God gives you His gift of eternal life, it means you then become His own dear child and have His loving care. "Bless the Lord, O my soul" (Psalm 103:1). "The Lord has done great things for us; we are glad" (Psalm 126:3).

For Thinking and Doing:

1. Read Mark 8:34-36; James 1:17; John 3:16.
2. Put Mark 8:36 into your own words.
3. What are the three main statements of John 3:16?
4. What do you think "belief" in Jesus really means? Is it more than just believing in your mind?

70th Day

The New Birth

"Ye must be born again" (John 3:7, KJV).

One night a man named Nicodemus came to Jesus. Perhaps he wished to have a quiet talk away from the crowds that usually

103

followed our Lord during the day. He was a Pharisee, which meant that he was very religious, moral and well educated.

Probably Nicodemus wanted to learn more about the Kingdom of God. He had just begun to explain this when the Lord said a surprising thing, "Except a man be born again (anew), he cannot see the kingdom of God . . . Ye must be born again" (John 3:3, 7, KJV). What? Must a person go back and be born of his mother all over again? Impossible. But it's not that, Nicodemus, for then you would have the same old human nature. No, every man must be born anew; he must be given a nature and life fitted to dwell in God's home and kingdom.

We should be able to understand this, for even on earth there are different sorts of life. The unknowing life of a plant is not at all like the self-conscious life of an animal, and an animal is, in turn, unlike a man, who thinks and acts in a higher way. For example, think of a fish. Its body and way of life are suited to the water, the element in which it lives. The fish could not live as a man or even exist upon the earth unless it were given a new nature and a body prepared for that sort of life. Just as truly, it would be impossible for man in his earthly body and sinful human nature to live in the holy, glorious kingdom of God. No wonder Jesus said that we must be born anew. We must have a different kind of life.

How can we get that wonderful new life? Let's see. When you were born was it through any effort of your own, or were you able to give life to yourself? Most certainly not. The Lord tells us that we can only receive this new life which is eternal as a gift. No amount of good works can give us this new life. God plainly says, "The free gift of God is eternal life" (Romans 6:23). It is "not your own doing, it is the gift of God—not because of works, lest any man should boast" (Ephesians 2:8, 9).

It is because of God's love that we, who are unable to do anything to secure it ourselves, may have this priceless gift. Although in God's love and grace the gift is free to us, it was not cheap to Him. It cost God all the awful suffering and death of His dearly-loved Son.

For Thinking and Doing:

1. Read John 3:1-7, 15, 16; John 17:2, 3.
2. Does John 3:3 mean everyone?
3. Who can give us the nature and life fitted to dwell in God's kingdom? See John 17:2.

4. Will you ask Him to give this gift to you?

Saved

"For God sent the Son into the world . . . that the world might be saved through Him" (John 3:17).

"Saved" is such a happy word. A plane crashes and falls into the ocean. A ship comes near and rescues the drowning people. A child is trapped high up in a burning building. A fireman fights his way through the flames and carries the child out. All saved: brought out of a place of danger and death into one of life and safety.

God has used this happy word to describe being born again, because when a person is born again he is taken out of a place of danger and death and is brought into eternal life and safety. Just as the drowning people and the trapped child could not save themselves, so we cannot save ourselves; God must do it. "God sent the Son into the world . . . that the world (all people in it) might be saved through Him" (John 3:17). "God sent His only Son . . . that we might live through Him" (I John 4:9).

Jesus died for the sins of everyone in the world. Then will everyone be saved? No. Millions of people will perish because there is something we must do. First you must realize your need of what Christ did for you and turn away from what you know is sin. Then you must believe that the Lord Jesus paid the penalty for your sin on the cross. To really believe in Christ as your Savior means you believe He died for your sin. "Believe in the Lord Jesus, and you will be saved" (Acts 16:31). "By (God's) grace (kindness) you have been saved through faith" (Ephesians 2:8). You must trust God to do His part after you have done yours.

A teacher held up a piece of money before a Sunday school class and offered to give it to the first fellow or girl who would come and get it. All seemed interested but no one moved. Finally a girl came up and took the money. Now it was her own. Any of the others could have had it, but only one believed the offer enough to hold out her hand and receive it.

God offers eternal life to all who believe that the Lord Jesus died for their sins and will take Him, that is, receive Him into their hearts. "To all who received Him . . . He gave power to become children of God" (John 1:12). If you ask the wonderful Savior to come into your heart and life, He will do so. He will forgive your

105

sins and give you His own life. There is a well-known picture of Christ standing outside a door. The door has no doorknob. When asked about it, the artist said, "That is the door of the human heart; it must be opened from the inside." Christ has promised, "If any one . . . opens the door, I will come in" (Revelation 3:20). "God gave us eternal life, and this life is in His Son. He who has the Son has life" (I John 5:11-12).

For Thinking and Doing:

1. Read Revelation 3:20; I Timothy 2:3-4.

2. Have you ever asked the Savior to come into your heart and life? If not, kneel down in the quietness of your own room and ask Him to come in today.

3. What does the Savior promise to those who open the door of their hearts?

4. According to I Timothy 2:3-4, what is God's desire?

72nd Day

Another Birthday

"To all who received Him . . . He gave power to become children of God" (John 1:12).

Have you really asked Jesus to come into your heart and given your heart to Him? If you have, you have "passed from death to life" (John 5:24). You are forgiven and are in God's family. You now have two birthdays: the first is when you were born into your own family and the second is the day you were born into the family of God. It will be a glad reminder if you will put both dates in the spaces below and sign your name.

Born the first time _____

Born Again_____

Signed _____

Now that you are in God's family, His enemy the devil will try to discourage or disturb you. The first thing he may ask is, "Do you think you're really saved? Do you feel any different?" Perhaps you will have to admit that you don't feel that you are born again, but God did not promise to give "feelings" when you received Christ. He promised to save you and to give you eternal life.

106

The record of your birth into God's family is in His Word. Look it up in your Bible. "You are all sons of God, through faith (in Christ Jesus)" (Galatians 3:26). "Born . . . of God" (John 1:13). "We are God's children now" (I John 3:2). In heaven your name is "written in the Lamb's (Jesus') book of life" (Revelation 21:27). Think of all Jesus suffered so that you could become His own dear child. Would He fail to keep His promises when He so longs for you to be saved? Of course not.

The devil will do all he can to make you doubt God's Word, for if he can get you to do that, the rest will be easy. If you find yourself doubting, you can be sure Satan is putting lying thoughts into your mind. Our Lord has told us that "the devil . . . is a liar . . . and there is no truth in him" (John 8:44). Our Lord has promised, "resist (stand against) the devil and he will flee from you" (James 4:7).

Read God's precious and true promises again and again. Say them aloud and memorize them. God's promises are the sure way to help you know you are His child. "The Word of our God will stand for ever" (Isaiah 40:8).

For Thinking and Doing:

1. Read Psalm 103:12; Hebrews 8:12; I John 2:12; John 6:37.
2. If a person wants to come to Jesus to be saved, what wonderful promise is true for him in John 6:37?
3. What do you learn from Psalm 103:12, Hebrews 8:12, and I John 2:12 about what happens to your sins when you are saved?
4. Express your gratitude to your Heavenly Father today for His wonderful gift of eternal life.

73rd Day

Growing Up

"So that we may no longer be children" (Ephesians 4:14).

How easy it would be if you could have remained a baby all your life. There would be no dishes to wash or grass to cut and no school work. You wouldn't need to do anything for yourself or for anyone else. You would have no worries, disappointments or discouragements. That would be easy? Yes, but it would also be dull. Think of what you would miss. You would have no friendships, games, fun, or the pleasure that comes through music, reading or travel. Babies are sweet and happy in their baby ways, but who would want to return to babyhood again? You would miss the hard things of life, but you would also have to do without the many pleasures.

God wants His born-again children to grow up. "We are to grow up in every way" (Ephesians 4:15). "Grow in the grace and knowledge of our Lord and Savior Jesus Christ" (II Peter 3:18). It is a strange thing that so many Christians choose to remain babies in God's family. After they are born again, they are content just to live like spiritual infants.

These people are not interested in going to God's school to learn more of Him and the wonders of His kingdom. They have no wish to become strong in soul and spirit and to accomplish great things for God and for others. They are unwilling to do anything that calls for effort, courage or sacrifice. Because they don't want to change and develop, of course these people are weak, flabby Christians. They are not strong enough to stand true to God in difficult places. Their voices are not heard speaking out against evil. Oh no, they might be thought a sissy or odd. They dare nothing for the Lord; therefore, they accomplish nothing.

The Father's will is that each of His much-loved children grow up unto "the measure of the stature of the fullness of Christ" (Ephesians 4:13). He wants us to know the thrill of being linked up with the Almighty in the working out of His glorious plans—the plans which begin on earth and go on through all eternity. God loves His undeveloped, spiritual babies, but He cannot use them to do important work or brave deeds in His vast kingdom. Do you want Him to be able to use you?

For Thinking and Doing:

1. Read Colossians 1:28; II Timothy 3:16-17.
2. Are there any areas in your life where you are still a baby?
3. How many of us are to be mature or grown-up according to Colossians 1:28?
4. In II Timothy 3:16-17 what is it that makes a Christian complete or mature?

Choices

"Walk by the Spirit, and do not gratify the desires of the flesh" (Galatians 5:16).

Before we can learn how to grow and become healthy, happy children of God, we must learn something about our spiritual anatomy. A new girl or boy came into life when you were born again. "If any one is in Christ, he (or she) is a new creation. All this is from God" (II Corinthians 5:17, 18). Now you have two natures: the good nature which is the eternal life that God has put within your soul and your human nature which God describes as the "flesh" (Romans 7:18). As long as you are on earth this human nature will be a part of you, and oh, what a lot of trouble it can make.

The holy, God-given nature will never go along with the desires and plans of the flesh, for they are exact opposites. The one wants you to live for God and to walk guided by His Spirit; the other wants you to live for yourself. It is as though two people are always walking at your side. The one is good, wise, brave and strong, and is constantly longing for you to have the best. The other, though pretending to be a friend, will often get you to lie or to be mean, cowardly and bad-tempered. This one, your "self," insists on having his own way, will lie to you, and lead you into sin and trouble. You must choose to follow your new nature.

For another example think of it this way. Here are two plants growing side by side. The one is a rare, beautiful, fruitful plant; the second is an ugly, poisonous shrub that gives off a bad odor.

The dangerous, selfish companion is a picture of our human nature, ready to lead us into wrong. So also the poisonous, hateful plant is a picture of our sinful life that has its roots in our souls. The illustrations of the true friend and the beautiful plant are like the life which our Lord has given to us, which is His life kept within us by the Holy Spirit.

You need to turn away from your old self, which can make you so much trouble, and choose as your friend and leader the One whose love and wisdom you can always trust: Jesus Christ the Lord. As for the poisonous shrub, do not water it or care for

109

it in any way; cut back every shoot that shows itself. Then do everything you can to cultivate the choice plant so that it can grow. For that beautiful life is "Christ in you, the hope of glory" (Colossians 1:27) and "Christ who is our life" (Colossians 3:4).

Either Christ or the flesh, which is self, will control us. Which life do you choose to feed and follow?

For Thinking and Doing:

1. Read Ephesians 4:22-24; Galatians 5:17; Romans 13:14.

2. In the Living New Testament, Ephesians 4:22, 24 reads, "Throw off your old evil nature . . . Clothe yourself with this new nature." Give examples from everyday life of how you could do this.

3. Can you explain Galatians 5:17 in your own words?

4. Paul urges us to "put on the Lord Jesus Christ" in Romans 13:14. What else does he urge us to do?

75th Day

Solid Food

"Eat God's Word—read it, think about it—and grow strong in the Lord" (I Peter 2:2, LNT).

Centuries ago a young man, doing great things for the Lord, said to Him, "Thy words were found, and I ate them" (Jeremiah 15:16). But how could he eat them? In eating ordinary food, we take into our bodies that which becomes blood, muscles and cells, keeping us alive and healthy. Likewise, as we take God's Word into our hearts and let it do its work there, the life of the Lord Jesus is developed within us. God's Word is the food for our souls. "Man shall not live by bread alone, but by every word . . . of God" (Matthew 4:4). One reason why there are many weak, unhealthy and unhappy children of God is because of their bad eating habits. The Lord says, "Let the Word . . . dwell in you richly" (Colossians 3:16).

Some people are like a person who might take very nourishing food every day, but would not swallow any of it. These people are the ones who read the Bible every day, yet the truth doesn't get down into their hearts to do its work there. So "the message . . . did not benefit them" (Hebrews 4:2). "Blessed rather are those who hear the word of God and keep it!" (Luke 11:28).

Others will swallow only soft foods and refuse anything they have to chew. That is, they read only those parts of the Bible which are simple and easy to understand, those requiring no effort. Then there are those who eat only sweet things. These are the people who love the precious promises of Scripture, but a reproof for sin or a command to be obeyed is not for them. They forget that, "All scripture is inspired by God and profitable for teaching, for reproof, for correction, for training in righteousness, that the man of God may be complete" (II Timothy 3:16-17).

It is possible to only nibble a bit at the Word of God and then, through eyes and ears, fill our hearts and minds with things which are worthless or even coarse and impure.

What do you feed upon? Is your soul healthy and growing in the life of God? Why not decide now to not only read, but also to think about, digest, and feed upon the Word of God. "How sweet are Thy words to my taste" (Psalm 119:103). "I have laid up Thy word in my heart that I might not sin against Thee" (Psalm 119:11).

For Thinking and Doing:

1. Read Job 23:12; I Peter 2:1, 2; Colossians 3:16.

2. Explain, as you would to a friend, what you think Colossians 3:16 means when it says, "Let the Word . . . dwell in you richly."

3. How much time per day do you spend reading and thinking about the words you are reading in the Bible?

4. Memorize Psalm 119:11.

76th Day

Spiritual Exercise

"Bodily exercise is all right, but spiritual exercise is much more important" (I Timothy 4:8, LNT).

"Be doers of the Word, and not hearers only" (James 1:22). Exercise is doing something—action. Neither body nor soul can be strong or healthy unless it is active. There are different bodily exercises; some are necessary and some are for the good of others.

Some kinds are mostly for our own pleasure. Yet even these—swimming, tennis, football or basketball—are not always fun. For if we wish to do better than others in anything, we often have to give up certain pleasures in order to reach our goal and win the reward.

What is the exercise God speaks about? It, too, is action—doing something. It is your mind, heart, lips, hands and feet, all acting in obedience to whatever God tells you to do or be. Jesus' life on earth is our example. His soul and body were always acting in constant, quick obedience to the will and Word of God. While the way was often difficult, yet He was keen, strong and full of joy.

Our souls are to be exercised in different ways, for we are God's athletes. We are, as it were, running a race, going quickly forward along a track of God's choosing. Or we are like wrestlers, though our wrestling is "not against flesh and blood, but against . . . spiritual wickedness" (Ephesians 6:12, KJV). For sometimes the devil and his followers will come strongly against us, and God expects His children to resist and to overcome. Keep "looking to Jesus" (Hebrews 12:2). He is the spiritual athlete's Coach. He will help you and strengthen you to win.

Sometimes we are the Lord's soldiers, fighting in the battle against sin in ourselves or in some of the world's evils. But Christ is the Captain of our salvation, and we can be "more than conquerors through Him who loved us" (Romans 8:37). Jesus calls as volunteers into His army all who will serve Him faithfully and bravely. He needs anyone who is ready to take his "share of suffering as a good soldier of Christ Jesus" (II Timothy 2:3).

What a glorious privilege is ours: to be able to exercise ourselves for God, to run the race and to fight the good fight honorably, courageously and well.

Rewards will go to those who have run straight toward the goal which He has set. Those who have dared to wrestle and fight for Him will receive rich rewards, as only God can give.

For Thinking and Doing:

1. Read I Timothy 4:7, 8; II Timothy 2:5; I Corinthians 9:24, 25.

2. Why does I Timothy 4:8 say spiritual exercise or godliness is of value?

3. Can you think of ways it is of value in your daily life?

4. What does Paul advise us to do in I Corinthians 9:24, 25?

Spiritual Race

"Let us run . . . the race that is set before us" (Hebrews 12:1).

How exciting the athletic contests of ancient Greece must have been. Their athletes were heroes just as ours are today. The apostle Paul, in writing to the new Christians in his churches, often used some illustration from these athletic contests to explain something he wanted them to understand about spiritual exercise. In that day the Greek athlete who practiced for the races had heavy slabs of lead strapped to his legs and waist. On the day of the race these were thrown aside and he ran with ease. Paul used this to illustrate the spiritual race of every Christian.

Sins are like lead weights that drag us down. They make running very difficult. He said, "Let us also lay aside every weight, and sin which clings so closely, and let us run with perseverance the race that is set before us, looking to Jesus" (Hebrews 12:1, 2). The Living New Testament expresses these same verses this way, "Let us strip off anything that slows us down or holds us back . . . those sins that wrap themselves so tightly around our feet and trip us up." Our track athletes are stripped to the lightest clothing; nothing must hold them back. Just so, we must strip ourselves of entangling sins which would trip us up or hold us back in our spiritual race.

> Run the straight race through God's good grace,
> Lift up thine eyes and seek His face;
> Life with its way before us lies,
> Christ is the path and Christ the prize.
> —J. S. B. Monsell

Paul also said, "Fight the good fight of faith" (I Timothy 6:12). The Christian is often referred to as a soldier. We are encouraged by God's promises, such as, "Be strong and of good courage. Do not be afraid or dismayed . . . with us is the Lord our God, to help us and to fight our battles" (II Chronicles 32:7-8). "The Lord of hosts is with us" (Psalm 46:7). "I will not be afraid; what can man do to me? (Hebrews 13:6).

Are you willing, but does it look too hard? Dare to step forward and take your place in the ranks of the runner or the soldier for Jesus Christ. As you obey His call you will find that you do not run or fight alone. Another is there beside you.

113

"Fight the good fight of faith" (I Timothy 6:12). "Everyone who conquers will inherit . . . blessings" (Revelation 21:7, LNT).

Fight the good fight with all they might;
Christ is thy strength, and Christ thy right;
Lay hold on life, and it shall be
Thy joy and crown eternally.

— J. S. B. Monsell

For thinking and Doing:

1. Read I Corinthians 9:26; Galatians 5:7; Philippians 2:16.
2. What are the weights in your life?
3. Look at them and evaluate them. What are they really worth?
4. Who can help you lay them aside? Will you let Him?

78th Day

Our Pilot

"He led them in safety" (Psalm 78:53).

One day a traveler began a journey, enjoying beautiful views under sunny skies. However, during the journey the way often led over high, jagged mountains, across scorching desert, and through furious storms. Finally the traveler arrived at journey's end, safe, comfortable and only a little tired. I was that traveler going many miles in comfort and safety because I journeyed in a jet plane. There was no need for me to work, for the plane's powerful engines bore me up and carried me onward. Yet I had a part to do. No plane could have taken me to my journey's end until I had boarded the plane and trusted myself to the pilot.

When you follow the Lord, it means that you must trust Him too; you will travel with Him day after day. Whether the journey will be long or short depends upon the number of years you live. Who can tell what lies ahead through the days of your life? Only God knows, and all His power and wisdom are ready to carry you safely through whatever comes. "He knows the way that I take" (Job 23:10). He is strong in power "travelling in the greatness of His strength" (Isaiah 63:1, KJV). He is "able to keep you from falling" (Jude 24) into sin or danger.

Yes, the Lord is able to take care of you, but He cannot do it unless you hand over to Him your whole life. God "is able to keep that which I have committed (given over) unto Him," said Paul (II Timothy 1:12, KJV).

That is the secret of safety. God urges His children, "Commit thy way unto the Lord; trust also in Him; and He shall bring it to pass" (Psalm 37:5, KJV).

> He knows; He loves; He cares;
> Nothing this truth can dim.
> He does the very best for those
> Who leave the choice with Him.
> —Author Unknown

Our Lord guides and upholds millions of stars as they move in their courses. He is "upholding the universe by His word of power" (Hebrews 1:3). "By the greatness of His might . . . not one faileth" (Isaiah 40:26, KJV). Surely you can expect Him to keep you, His own, loved child, and to do the very best for you. Commit your life to Him and trust Him. Then through sunny or stormy days you can say, "God is my strength . . . He maketh my way perfect" (II Samuel 22:33, KJV).

For Thinking and Doing:

1. Read Psalm 23:1; Proverbs 29:25; Psalm 40:4; II Samuel 22:31-33.

2. What help does Psalm 23:1 give us for our daily life?

3. If we believe He can make our way perfect, what difference can this make when we have trouble?

4. What promise do you find in II Samuel 22:31?

79th Day

Our Shelter

"Though I walk through the valley . . . Thou art with me" (Psalm 23:4).

You may have heard of the Death March of Bataan of World War II. It was there that hundreds of United States troops were forced to march to prison camps. During the march and in the prisons, our men were so cruelly and horribly tortured that few came through alive. Jesse Miller of the Army Air Corps went through that frightful experience while he was still very young. He has written the following letter to young people:

"Fellows and girls, you may be wondering if it really pays to be a Christian. I truthfully can say that Christ is good, and He is

115

the most wonderful shelter a fellow can ever have. One day, December 8, 1941, He proved Himself to be that 'shelter in the time of storm.' Japanese 'war birds' were laying destruction to our base, Clark Field, in the Philippines. We didn't know what to do. Bombs were falling all around us. The earth was being riddled with machine gun shells; gas tanks were blowing up by the dozen. I had fortunately found a little cove in the earth and I hugged it tight.

"We didn't have a chance, for they came in and caught us with our planes on the ground, destroying almost every one of them. All we could do was to take it. A calm came over me because, you know, I had a 'fox hole' which no man could take away; I was in the hollow of His hand. A Bible verse came to me, which I suppose is my life verse. It has meant a great deal to me since I was saved. 'I am crucified with Christ: nevertheless I live; yet not I, but Christ liveth in me: and the life which I now live in the flesh I live by the faith of the Son of God, who loved me, and gave Himself for me' (Galatians 2:20, KJV). What a shelter! 'No one is able to snatch them (me) out of the Father's hand' (John 10:29), for I am in Christ Jesus.

"It was a strange thing. There in an earthly shelter in the midst of an earthly war, a heavenly voice seemed to say, 'Follow Me.' Many times heavenly things seem a bit strange, but God was calling me to get out of that cove where I was lying, and I did. When the battle was over I walked back. As my eyes fell upon the spot where I had been lying only a few moments before, there welled up a great 'Thank You, Lord.' He had directed the path of this one child of His from a bomb which had struck that very place.

"Fellows and girls, walk with Him. I can truthfully say that even through the battle of Bataan and that horrible Death March of Bataan, through three and one-half years as a prisoner of war, and through disease, pain and hunger, the Lord has proved Himself to be that 'Shelter in the time of storm.'"

—Signed, Jesse L. Miller

For Thinking and Doing:

1. Read Psalm 23; John 10:27-30.

2. Can you think of a time in your own life when you have been in danger, but were protected by God?

3. What was the source of Jesse Miller's calmness?

116   4. What does that promise in John 10:28 mean to you?

Our Call

"He . . . guided them by the skilfulness of His hands" (Psalm 78:72, KJV).

"As He (Jesus) walked by the Sea of Galilee, He saw . . . Peter and Andrew . . . casting a (fish) net into the sea . . . and He said to them, 'Follow Me, and I will make you fishers of men. Immediately they left their nets and followed Him . . . He saw . . . James . . . and John . . . mending their nets, and He called them. Immediately they left the boat . . . and followed Him" (Matthew 4:18-22).

What did it cost these men to follow Jesus? It meant giving up their own affairs for something they knew not. It meant doing the will of Another instead of their own and taking their place beside One who seemed to others to be only a poor and humble carpenter. But they touched the hands of the Son of God; they looked upon His face. They watched the Creator of all things show forth His tremendous power in the miracles He did.

They were part of the small company which He chose to be His nearest, dearest friends and to whom He will give a high place in His kingdom, yet they were called to serve.

When Christ was in the world He was only one Man among a multitude. In other lands there were millions of precious souls He could not reach. So the Lord chose disciples who, when He went back to heaven, would act as His hands to do, His feet to go, and His lips to speak. They must take His place to bring others to God.

How well did Peter fish for souls? By just one sermon on a single day the Holy Spirit used him to bring about 3,000 to Christ. Other thousands have been caught by his written words. And what about young John? I am sure that through the words of John 3:16 alone, myriads have been brought to God. Yes, it costs, but it also pays to follow the Lord Christ.

"Follow Me." This is His call to you. You must count the cost of following. But don't forget to count the overwhelming gain. Kneel down in the quiet of your own room, think these things through within your heart, and talk to God about them. A team captain wants loyal, all-out players. Jesus wants that kind too. Those who love themselves the best or those who are weaklings are not "fit for the kingdom of God" (Luke 9:62). But if your will is to truly follow Him, He is by your side to help you.

You may feel, "Yes, I truly want to, for the Lord has done so much for me. But I fear I can't hold out." That is right; you can't. Jesus does not expect you to. He said, "I will make you . . . " You do the following, and He will do the holding and keeping. "Kept by the power of God" (I Peter 1:5, KJV).

For Thinking and Doing:

1. Read John 10:3, 4; Jude 24, 25; Philippians 1:6.
2. Have you heard His voice calling you?
3. What does Jude 24 tell you Christ is able to do?
4. Memorize Philippians 1:6 and believe it.

81st Day

Our Privilege

"If any one serves Me, he must follow Me" (John 12:26).

> Where's the trumpet and the drum
> For my racing, surging song?
> Where's the leader who can show me
> Where my talents best belong?
> Here in Christ I see the answer—
> Hear the echo singing loud;
> Here in Him, the perfect Leader;
> Here I find the mighty God!
> —Jeanne Farwell Michaelson

Who is it that asks us to follow Him? Are you doing Him a favor when we answer His call? Oh no. He is the One "in Whom are hid all the treasures of wisdom and knowledge" (Colossians 2:3). He is the One by Whom all things "were created, in heaven and on earth, visible and invisible, whether thrones or dominions . . . or authorities—all things were created through Him and for Him . . . and in Him all things hold together" (Colossians 1:16, 17). "God has . . . bestowed on Him the name that is above every name, that at the name of Jesus every knee should bow, in heaven and on earth and under the earth" (Philippians 2:9, 10). The risen Jesus is the Lord of heaven and the Lord of hosts. Some day every living being will bow before Him. Today we have the privilege of following Him.

Let us not think of Christ's call as something impossible or too hard. Let us rather be glad because our glorious Lord has chosen us to live for Him here on earth. As you think of Who it is that calls you, can you not say in gratitude to Him, "Most perfect and loving Savior, I do choose to follow you always as the Master of my life." Then will come the answer, "If any one (girl or boy) serves Me . . . the Father will honor him" (John 12:26).

Christ cannot be the Master of your life until you truly give yourself to Him. We read of those who "first . . . gave themselves to the Lord" (II Corinthians 8:5). You cannot know the Lord Jesus or fully follow Him, and He cannot use and bless you as He wants to, until you, too, have given your whole self to Him. Christ has given Himself for you and given Himself to you forever.

Will you not, if you have never truly done so, give your whole heart and life to Christ, your loving, wonderful Savior?

For Thinking and Doing:

1. Read Psalm 23:2; 25:4, 5, 10; John 12:26.
2. Find some good reasons which are given for following the Lord in Psalm 23:3 and 25:5, 10.
3. What condition is there about serving the Lord and what promises in John 12:26?
4. Memorize Psalm 25:4.

82nd Day

His Way Up

"Truly, truly, I say to you, unless a grain of wheat falls into the earth and dies, it remains alone; but if it dies, it bears much fruit" (John 12:24).

In God's vast kingdom there are high places of honor, service and reward for those who truly follow Jesus. There is such a place waiting for you if you will let God prepare you for it. We can only enter the high place of honor by going God's way, and His way is down! Those who go the highest have first to go the lowest.

The Son of God has gone that way. He came down from heaven to earth to live as a poor man: from a throne and the worship of angels to a shameful death of the worst of sinners. "Jesus . . . for a little while was made lower than the angels . . . because of the suffering of death . . . for every one" (Hebrews 2:9). Now, having gone back to heaven, He is "crowned with glory and honor," and is "able for all time to save those who draw near to God through Him" (Hebrews 7:25). Only by dying could He become the crowned and mighty Savior. Only by dying could He bring men to God.

The call to follow Christ and to win others for Him is a call to follow Him all the way. "A disciple is not above his teacher, nor a servant above his master" (Matthew 10:24). The Son of God could only save the lost and enter highest honor and glory by going down. So as His disciples or followers, there can be no other way for us.

The Lord said, "Unless a grain of wheat falls into the earth and dies, it remains alone; but if it dies, it bears much fruit" (John 12:24). Plant a grain of wheat in the ground. What happens? It loses itself; it decays and dies. But as it dies, out from that one, small, decaying thing a stalk pushes up into the sunlight. The slender stem grows tall and strong. The dying grain lives more fully now. Soon it is bearing, not one, but many grains of ripening wheat.

For our Lord's sake and for the sake of those He wants to save through you, will you follow the Savior all the way—down? As His follower you must be willing to be one of His grains. Let the Lord lead you down if you want a joyful life and a rich reward from Him.

For Thinking and Doing:

1. Read John 12:24-26; Matthew 10:39; Luke 9:24.
2. What does the illustration of the grain of wheat teach you?
3. How do you think the person who loves his life can lose it?
4. What do you think it means to "hate" your life? See the thought given in Matthew 10:39 and Luke 9:24.

83rd Day

Not Worth Keeping

"One has died for all; therefore all have died" (II Corinthians 5:14).

Are you willing to go down with the Lord Jesus so that God can trust you in a high place and make you a blessing? Look back some 1,900 years to a hill outside Jerusalem. There, dying on a cross, hangs God's dearly beloved Son. In God's sight He is not alone. You and I are there also. "Our old self was crucified with

Him" (Romans 6:6). What we are by nature—sinful and sinning—God counts as having been put with Christ upon the cross. There He paid the penalty for our sins; that penalty of death fell upon Jesus instead of on you and me. "For our sake He made Him to be sin" (II Corinthians 5:21). "He . . . bore our sins in His body on the tree (cross)" (I Peter 2:24). Since your sins are part of you, God counted you as being on the cross with Christ.

You may say, "But I was not yet born when Christ died for my sins." That's true. However, God knew you would be born. If He had left you out and had not counted you and your sins as being there with Christ, you would have to bear the penalty for your sin yourself.

God put all that we are in our natural lives into that place of death with Jesus. Our old nature is not worth keeping; it had to go to make room for something better. It was the only way to free us from the power of Satan and sin. "The death He (Christ) died He died to sin, once for all . . . So you also must consider yourselves dead to sin" (Romans 6:10,11). He bore our sins that "we might no longer be enslaved to sin" (Romans 6:6).

We who are God's children are told to think of ourselves as united to Jesus in His death to sin. We might think of the following as an illustration. Suppose you had a strong enemy called "Sin" who made you do his evil will. One day you were killed in an auto accident. Then no longer could your enemy force you to obey him. "Sin" was not dead, but you were dead to him.

God does not say that your sin has died; it is very much alive. But He sees you as having died to it. He only asks that you agree with Him about this even though you cannot understand.

It may seem unreal and a strange teaching of the Bible that you are crucified with Christ. But if you will believe it and let the Lord work it out in your life, you will find it most real indeed. Don't be afraid to accept this death of your old nature. Remember, it is not worth keeping. As you do this, you make room for Christ to live His life in you.

For Thinking and Doing:

1. Read Romans 6:4, 16-18; Colossians 3:2, 3, 5-10.

2. Is it a good thing to become dead to sin or wrongdoing? Name some examples.

3. Why does Romans 6:4 tell us we are to be "buried with Him by baptism into death"?

4. Does repeated sin make us slaves? Can the laws of habit work the other way according to Romans 6:16?

A New Creature

"If any man be in Christ, he is a new creature: old things are passed away; behold, all things are become new" (II Corinthians 5:17, KJV).

There are two great truths in the following verse. See if you can find them. "I am crucified with Christ: nevertheless I live; yet not I, but Christ liveth in me: and the life which I now live . . . I live by the faith of the Son of God" (Galatians 2:20, KJV). Let's take the first part which is death and then life.

You are just one person. When you were born into God's family you received a new life by which you became "a new creature" in Christ (II Corinthians 5:17, KJV). But you also still have what is called "the old man" or "the flesh." This is your sinful, human nature, and it is that which should be kept as dead.

Look at a dead man. He is not determined to have his own way. He doesn't get angry. He is not conceited or untruthful. A dead man is not mean or lazy. He is not interested in wrong or unclean things. It isn't that he could do these things, but won't. He doesn't even want to do them. God can make you just like that, so that your old nature is dead. You won't do these things—you won't even want to. Yet the Lord cannot do this unless you let Him.

First you must believe that in each one of us, that is, in our flesh or sinful, human nature, "nothing good dwells" (Romans 7:18). You must be willing to accept what God says: that your sin-filled nature is worthless, worthy only of death. This is one of the most difficult things the Lord will ever ask you to do, for we all think we're pretty good.

Not only do we need to think of ourselves as "dead with Christ," but we have also to put this truth to work in our daily lives. For example, suppose that before I was saved, I always wanted my own way, for my will is very strong. But now, as a born-again person, I realize that I have died to that sin of always wanting my own way. No longer do I let sin rule me through my will. Instead, my strong will is set to please God. It is the same with all other things and thoughts that are not like Christ. To refuse the desires and ways of my old nature is to count it as being dead.

As the temptations and desires come, look up to your living Lord and say, "Lord, I died to this sin with You. With your help, I refuse to do it." He will give you victory and the joy of overcoming and living a new life of adventure in the special nearness and power of Christ.

For Thinking and Doing:

1. Read II Corinthians 5:14-17; Ephesians 4:22-24.

2. Can you think of some old things in your old nature that you would like to be rid of?

3. How can you put the teaching of today's lesson to work in your life?

4. Think of the characteristics you would like to have Christ help you develop in your new nature. Will you ask Him to help you?

Christ in Me

"It is no longer I who live, but Christ who lives in me" (Galatians 2:20).

Paul, as a Christian, could say that in his old nature he had died with Christ. But he didn't stop there. He also said, "Nevertheless I live." It is the same with all God's children. We are to think of our born-again selves as living by faith in the Son of God.

Think of a small boy standing on the edge of a deep, swift-flowing river. He must cross over, but he cannot swim and there is no bridge. What can he do? Nothing. Then a man comes to the boy's help. This man is an experienced swimmer, so the child is strapped to the strong man's back and together they go down into the water. Soon the swimmer steps out of the river onto the far shore; the boy comes up also for he is joined to the man.

Jesus, fastening us to Himself with cords of love, went down into death for us. Just as the man came up out of the river onto the far bank, so the Lord Jesus came up out of death and the grave, returning to heaven. Just as the child came up from the river because he was joined to the man, so God sees you as being risen with Christ and sharing in the very life of the Lord Jesus. "For if we have been united with Him in a death like His, we shall certainly be united with Him in a resurrection like His" (Romans 6:5). "But if we have died with Christ, we believe that we shall

123

also live with Him" (Romans 6:8). "The life He lives He lives to God" (Romans 6:10). "So you also must consider yourselves . . . alive to God in Christ Jesus" (Romans 6:11).

We know that sometime even the bodies of God's children will be in heaven, but He wants us to think of ourselves as being with the Lord Jesus now. We are told to "walk in newness of life"(Romans 6:4). We are to be like a certain coal miner who inherited a large sum of money. Do you suppose he went right on working in the mine? No, not he! He cast aside his pick, his dirty old clothes, and all his ways of poverty. He began to live and behave according to the newness of life which was now his by the possession of riches.

We, too, should gladly strip ourselves of things of the old life and realize that because we are joined to Christ, we are lifted high above the low level of a sin-filled life. We are always to live according to our place with Christ, that is, in newness of life in Him.

For Thinking and Doing:

1. Read Hebrews 13:20, 21; Ephesians 4:24; I John 4:12; Ephesians 6:10, 11.

2. How is the new you described in Ephesians 4:24?

3. Who is it that dwells in the Christian according to I John 4:12 and Galatians 2:20?

4. Who is the Source of our strength for newness of life? See Ephesians 6:10.

86th Day

A Clean Vessel

"If anyone purifies himself . . . then he will be a vessel for noble use" (II Timothy 2:21).

Have you counted your old nature as dead and given yourself to Christ to manage your life? If you have, you should expect things to happen because He loves you so.

In a dark and dirty shop a man worked at repairing clocks and watches. One day I noticed that the shop was entirely changed. All the old stuff was gone and the place was freshly painted. The windows were washed and everything was clean. Attractive pictures hung upon the walls and fine rugs were on the floor. Handsome showcases displayed valuable jewelry and beautiful silverware. The little man was there, still at work, but well-dressed now, smiling and happy. A small sign on the wall explained the change. It said, "Under New Management." Someone who knew what to do and had the money to carry out his plans had taken over.

By nature our hearts and minds are like that shop. The windows of our souls may be so darkened by pride that we cannot see all the sins within. Yet we do see some of them plainly, don't we? These sins may not bother us or we might not want to do anything about them. At times we may try to hide the meanness, lies, and other sins that make our hearts like that dirty shop.

But "God . . . knows the secrets of the heart" (Psalm 44:21). The Bible says our heart is "desperately corrupt" (Jeremiah 17:9), and says, "out of the heart come evil thoughts. These are what defile a man" (Matthew 15:19, 20). "We have all become like one who is unclean" (Isaiah 64:6). How glad we can be that none of us need to remain unclean if we let the new Manager take over everything in our life.

The new owner of the shop did not make it clean and then leave it empty, nor did he try to fix up the old stuff that was in it. He filled it with useful and beautiful new things. That is what the Lord Jesus does with lives given to Him. He will make us pure, attractive, and pleasant to live with by filling our hearts and minds with good things, which are His riches. "The hungry He fills with good things" (Psalm 107:9) and with "the beauty of holiness" (Psalm 29:2). "He . . . giveth strength and power" (Psalm 68:35).

> I am satisfied with Jesus,
> Satisfied as I can be;
> But the question keeps recurring,
> Is He satisfied with me?
> —Author unknown

"Search me, O God, and know my heart! Try me and know my thoughts! And see if there be any wicked way in me, and lead me in the way everlasting!" (Psalm 139:23, 24). "And let the beauty of the Lord . . . be upon (me)" (Psalm 90:17, KJV).

For Thinking and Doing:

1. Read I Samuel 16:7; Proverbs 4:23; I John 1:7-10; Psalm 139:23, 24.

2. Why do you think God looks on man's heart rather than on his outward appearance?

3. According to I John 1:7-10, what do we need to do to have our hearts made clean?

4. Will you pray the prayer of Psalm 139:23, 24?

125

My Choice

"Choose this day Whom you will serve" (Joshua 24:15).
"Know that when He appears we shall be like Him" (I John 3:2).

When we take the Lord Jesus to be the Manager of our lives, we must expect Him to do what the new owner did in his shop. Suppose that He would say to you, "Dear child, this wrong thing must go." Would you reply, "Lord, I'm willing for my worst sins to go; I don't want them either. But my temper must go? I can't give that up. I must have my own way because . . . well, because I like it." Or would you say, "I must forgive that one who hurt me? Never! And, Lord, I couldn't get along without those small lies over in that dark corner."

We are all alike. We see and despise the sins of others, yet we hang on to our own. But God says, "Keep yourself pure" (I Timothy 5:22). "Hate what is evil" (Romans 12:9). We need to hate sin of every kind and our own sin especially. God hates it. Your sin brought Jesus to the agonies of the cross. Your sin harms and weakens you. It hurts others. Above all, it grieves the loving heart of the Lord. He wants you to be close to Him, but sin makes a difference in your relationship just as when a friend hurts you.

What is sin? Sin is wrongdoing of every kind, and it is also the failure to do what is right. "Whoever knows what is right to do and fails to do it, for him it is sin" (James 4:17).

If you are careless about sin and think that it doesn't matter much and if you do not hate it and long to be free from it, perhaps you are not really born again. This is a most serious thing, so do take the matter to the Lord and ask Him to show you what is wrong.

Sin hinders answers to prayer. "If I regard iniquity (sin) in my heart, the Lord will not hear me" (Psalm 66:18, KJV). To regard sin is to know it is there and to do nothing about it. God is absolutely fair in blaming us for being willing to go on sinning and for failing to turn from it and take His way of deliverance.

Your choices make your life. What you choose you finally become. "Wherewithal shall a young man (or girl) cleanse his way? by taking heed . . . to Thy Word" (Psalm 119:9, KJV).

Have you chosen Christ as the Manager and Lord of your

life? If not, will you say to Him today, "Lord, I choose to follow You"?

For Thinking and Doing:

1. Read John 8:31-34; I John 3:1-6.
2. Is John 8:34 true in some area of your life?
3. How can you be free according to John 8:31 and I John 3:6?
4. I John 3:2 contains a promise for us. Think about how wonderful it will be. Does it represent your choice?

My Trust

"For Thou, O Lord, art . . . my trust . . . from my youth" (Psalm 71:5).

> I Gave My life for thee.
> What hast thou given for Me?
> And I have brought for thee
> Down from My home above,
> Salvation full and free;
> My pardon and My love.
> Great gifts I brought to thee.
> What hast thou brought to Me?
> —F. R. Havergal (adapted)

When you start to obey the call of Jesus to trust Him, yield to Him, and follow Him, you may begin to doubt and think, "Of course the mighty Lord can take care of me, but will He? Suppose He leads me in a way I do not wish to go. What if He takes away some of the things I love? No, I cannot give myself and all my ways into Jesus' keeping!"

Satan puts his word in also; he always does when God asks us to step up higher. "Don't choose Christ to rule within your heart," he says. "If you do, you won't have any more fun. It is your life; live it as you please. How can you trust Someone you have never seen?" Satan is the enemy of your highest good. He knows, but does not mention, the countless joys and blessings which the living Christ pours into yielded hearts and lives. Nor does Satan mention the tragedy he brings into lives he governs.

Jesus speaks to your heart, challenging you to trust and follow Him. "I beseech you . . . by the mercies of God, that ye present (give) your bodies . . . unto God, which is your reasonable

127

service" (Romans 12:1, KJV). Our Lord says it is a wise and right thing to give ourselves to God because of His mercies. "God is love" (I John 4:8).

"We need have no fear of Someone who loves us perfectly; His perfect love for us eliminates all dread of what He might do to us. If we are afraid, it . . . shows that we are not fully convinced that He really loves us" (I John 4:18, LNT).

The great love of our heavenly Father led Him to send His beloved Son to die for you. The love of Christ for you led Him to the suffering of the cross. Surely you can trust such love to only do you good and never harm you. His promise is, "I will never leave thee, nor forsake thee" (Hebrews 13:5).

Jesus never fails; He will not fail you. Trust Him. Will you say today, "Lord, You are my Trust; I give myself to You"?

For Thinking and Doing:

1. Read Romans 12:1, 2; Deuteronomy 31:6, 8; Psalm 37:3-5.
2. How does Paul describe God's will for us in Romans 12:2?
3. What is the reason given in Deuteronomy 31:6, 8 that we should not fear?
4. Memorize Psalm 37:5.

89th Day

Yielded

"Yield yourselves to God" (Romans 6:13).

God does wonderful things for His children. He also does wonderful things in and through them if they will let Him. God cannot do wondrous things through us until our members—heart, lips, hands and feet—are given over to Him. That is why we are told, "Yield yourselves . . . and your members to God as instruments of righteousness" (Romans 6:13).

An instrument is that which a person uses to do a certain thing; it is a tool or a weapon. It may be a pen used to express one's thoughts, a hammer to build a house, or a sword to defeat an enemy. Pens, hammers and swords can do nothing by themselves. They are useless until they are taken into the hand of the writer, the builder, or the soldier.

Our Lord wants to use us as pens to express His thoughts, for in Him "are hid all the treasures of wisdom and knowledge" (Colossians 2:3). As hammers, we are not able in our own strength to build up poor, sinful lives into things of beauty for God to live in. No, "I, the Lord, have rebuilt the ruined places" (Ezekiel 36:36). Only as swords in His hands can we win victories over the devil. "You are not able . . . to fight with him" (I Samuel 17:33). "The battle is the Lord's" (I Samuel 17:47).

Jesus said, "Without Me ye can do nothing" (John 15:5, KJV). We can be on the go, like a person on a merry-go-round, but we won't get anywhere or do anything that counts for God and for eternity until we let the Lord work first in us and with us, and then through us.

All around you there are those who do not know God's truth and whose lives are run by sin and fear. These are held like slaves by Satan. Will you give yourself and your members wholly to the Lord so that He can use you? The pen, hammer and sword have no power of choice, but you, a person, can choose or refuse to yield yourself to Christ.

> Christ has no hands but our hands
> To do His work today;
> He has no feet but our feet
> To lead men in His way.
> He has no tongue but our tongue
> To tell men how He died;
> He has no help but our help
> To bring them to His side.
> —Author unknown

Do your hands, feet and tongue serve Christ? "Yield yourselves unto God, as those that are alive from the dead" (Romans 6:13, KJV).

For Thinking and Doing:

1. Read Romans 6:13-17; John 15:1-11; Romans 12:1, 2.
2. How are we made clean according to John 15:3?
3. Why does Christ say, "Abide in Me"?
4. What are we to yield to God according to Romans 12:1 and Romans 6:13?

Victory in Christ

"Thanks to be God, who gives us the victory through our Lord Jesus Christ" (I Corinthians 15:57).

One of God's great heroes was the apostle Paul. God chose him to make Christ known to the nations both by his teachings and by his life. Paul became one of those men of whom it was said, "These . . . have turned the world upside down" (Acts 17:6). What exciting stories he could tell of adventures on land and sea and of the great things which the Lord did for him and through him.

But best of all, Paul learned how to live in newness of life. How did Paul, who sometimes failed, become so triumphant? He learned that the secret of victory over sin is, "Not I, but Christ" (Galatians 2:20, KJV). He could say for all the world to hear, "I can do all things through Christ which strengtheneth me" (Philippians 4:13, KJV). "When I am weak, then am I strong" (II Corinthians 12:10). "Strong in the Lord, and in the power of His might" (Ephesians 6:10, KJV) because "Christ . . . lives in me; and the life I now live . . . I live by faith in the Son of God, who loved me and gave Himself for me" (Galatians 2:20).

Is this miraculous life of victory only for a few like Paul? No. The mighty Lord Jesus, who lived in the apostle, lives in you if you are His child. The power for glorious and holy living is the power of the glorious and holy Christ. Christ in you is not just Jesus on the outside helping you. It is far better than that. It is Jesus inside, living His life out through you.

Within you is the real life of the Son of God: His strength, courage, holiness, faith, thoughts, feelings and loving kindness. Our Lord said that this was so. Ask God to help you realize this marvelous fact and your heart will thrill with joy in believing. Everything we need is provided for us in Christ our Lord.

Never give up,
Nor doubt that you shall win.
You must not falter!
Is not Christ within?
Which is the stronger then:
Our Lord? Of sin?

Thanks be to God, who gives us the victory through our Lord Jesus Christ" (I Corinthians 15:57).

Lord Jesus, make Thyself to me
A living, bright reality;
More present to faith's vision keen
Then any outward object seen;
More dear, more intimately nigh
Than the sweetest earthly tie.
                —Author unknown (adapted)

For Thinking and Doing:

1. Read Romans 12:21; Philippians 4:13, 19; I Thessalonians 5:21-24.

2. Do you believe Philippians 4:13?

3. Will you claim today the promise of Philippians 4:19?

4. The Living New Testament expresses I Thessalonians 5:24 this way: "God, who called you to become His child, will do all this for you, just as He promised." Memorize this verse in your Bible.

91st Day

Union with Christ

"Take care to live in Me, and let Me live in you" (John 15:4, LNT).

A man and his wife bought a large lot on which to build a house. Just where the house was to stand, a huge rock lay sunken in the ground. They blasted the rock with dynamite and it was carried off in a truck in broken pieces. The two owners didn't try to dig out the rock or push it away by their own strength. They brought in a stronger force to do the work for them. The rock which was a hindrance to their building could only be removed by a stronger force than theirs.

When we want to build a Christian life, our big hindrance is sin. The force that rids us of the hindrance of sin is Christ Himself, not our own poor efforts. We do not have to live the Christian life ourselves; we have Someone to help us. To each of His own Jesus says a breathtaking thing. "(You are) in Me, and I in you" (John 15:4).

If we were to go to an orchard where the keeper was doing some grafting, we would see him cut a couple of small branches off a certain tree. In the branches of a second tree he would make two openings and in them he does the work of grafting. The two small pieces are bound tightly to the larger branches. Soon the sap of the tree flows through the grafted branches, and they become part of one another. The life of the tree flows into the new part.

131

The Bible tells us, "It is from God alone that you have your life through Christ Jesus" (I Corinthians 1:30, LNT). Another translation says, "You—and it is all God's doing—are in Christ Jesus." This is like the grafting of the tree. We are now attached to Him and His life is in us.

There is something even more wonderful. "Do you not realize that Jesus Christ is in you?" (II Corinthians 13:5). What a marvelous thought. The Lord of heaven is willing to live out His personal life in me. When you believe this and act upon it, your life becomes an entirely new thing and a glorious adventure with our Lord. Christ is our life. His life flows through us like the life-giving sap flows through the tree. Of course you cannot understand the mystery of this union, but you do not need to. You can count it to be real because God says it is.

When were you grafted into the Lord Jesus? It was when you asked Him to come into your heart and took Him to be your Savior. Then God the Father and the Holy Spirit placed you in Christ, and you were given His life. You now live in union with the One who is able to keep you growing as His life flows through you.

For Thinking and Doing:

1. Read Psalm 92:12; Ephesians 4:15; I Peter 2:2; II Peter 3:18; Revelation 3:20.

2. By what does I Peter 2:2 tell us we grow?

3. In what ways are we to grow according to II Peter 3:18?

4. If you are not sure you are grafted into union with the Lord Jesus, make sure today. See His promise in Revelation 3:20.

92nd Day

Bearing Fruit

"A branch can't produce fruit when severed from the vine. Nor can you be fruitful apart from Me" (John 15:4, LNT).

If you live where grapes grow and you walk through a vineyard at harvest time, you can see fine bunches of juicy grapes hanging on the vine. You know that the grapes are the outgrowth of the sap which flows to them from the root and the large main stem which makes the vine. The Lord Jesus likens Himself to this main stem and root, and He likens all true believers to the branches. "I am the vine, you are the branches" (John 15:5). Just as the purpose of the branches is to bear fruit, so Christ says, "I chose you . . . that you should . . . bear fruit, and that your fruit should abide (remain)" (John 15:16).

Christ promises that if we let Him live in us—in our hearts— our lives will be fruitful. "He who abides in Me, and I in him, he it is that bears much fruit, for apart from Me you can do nothing" (John 15:5). The kind of fruit our Lord wants to see in our lives is the fruit of the inner life, which is spiritual fruit. First, new traits of character will be developing in you; the kind of personality which is His purpose for you will be formed.

Paul tells us that, as Christ's branches, we are to be filled "with the fruits of righteousness" (Philippians 1:11) and that such fruits are, "love, joy, peace, patience, kindness, goodness, faithfulness, gentleness and self-control" (Galatians 5:22, 23). He tells us that when Christ controls our lives He will produce this kind of fruit in us.

Imitation fruit won't do. In certain shops one can find lovely-looking grapes, but they are made of wax. Some people are like these. Outwardly their personalities may seem attractive, but their pleasant words and ways are not for real. Their thoughts are critical and mean; in their inner lives they are neither kind nor good. Sooner or later their real character shows.

Even some who claim to be Christians may be trying to imitate Christ by pretending to have fruit. They do not let Christ really govern their inner lives. To all these He says, "Apart from Me you can't do a thing. Take care to live in Me, and let Me live in you" (John 15:5, 4, LNT). When He lives in our hearts and is Manager of our lives, then He promises we will bear much fruit.

> Have Thine own way, Lord!
> Have Thine own way!
> Hold o'er my being
> Absolute sway.
> Fill with Thy Spirit,
> Till all shall see
> Christ only, always,
> Living in me.
> —A. A. Pollard

For Thinking and Doing:

1. Read John 15:1-17.
2. What does Christ promise in John 15:7?
3. Would you like to have the spiritual fruit mentioned in

paragraph three above? (Galatians 5:22, 23).

4. Will you ask Him to fulfill His purpose and develop these fruits in your inner life?

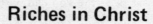

Riches in Christ

"My God will supply every need of yours according to His riches in glory in Christ Jesus" (Philippians 4:19).

This is a true story. A very old man had lived alone for years in a tiny, rickety, one-room shack. He was shabby and thin and always seemed half starved. In winter his poor old body shivered in the biting cold. Finally the old man died, and police went into the little house to gather up his few belongings. Imagine their surprise in finding a bank book which showed that the man was not poor at all. He possessed hundreds of thousands of dollars which had been placed in the bank to his account. He had great wealth, but the riches did him no good for he did not use them.

When you took the Lord as your Savior you not only received salvation, but you also received the fullness of His pure, strong, beautiful life. "Christ in you" (Colossians 1:27). "From His fullness have we all received" (John 1:16). Realize that spiritual riches are more valuable than material wealth. Just as truly as the old man should have drawn money from the bank to supply his needs, so should you make good use of everything that belongs to you in the Lord Jesus.

How can you do this? First believe God that "all things (of Christ) are yours . . . and you are Christ's" (I Corinthians 3:21, 23). Remember that Christ's life is in you, and that He is living every moment of every day. That fact is just as real as the money in any bank in your home town. Because this is true, act in faith. His promises are like blank checks. Fill in your name and receive whatever you need of His resources for your daily life.

What are your needs now and for the day stretching before you? Is it confidence or happiness? Perhaps you need patience or truthfulness. Whatever it is, speak to your ever-present Savior about it. Tell Him of your need, that in faith you look to Him to supply it, and that you take from Him His security, His joy, His patience and His truthfulness. You may not feel any different at once, but very simply count on the understanding Lord to do as you ask. Expect it, and as you trust, His life will be working within you.

134

A quick turning to Jesus at any time—and taking—will change defeat into victory. "They who trust Him wholly, find Him wholly true."

For Thinking and Doing:

1. Read Romans 11:33; I Timothy 6:17, 18; Ephesians 2:7.
2. Give some examples of uncertain riches and of those God gives us to enjoy (I Timothy 6:17).
3. What are your special needs? Will you claim the promise of Philippians 4:19 for them?
4. Memorize Philippians 4:19.

94th Day

The Promise of the Holy Spirit

"It is best for you that I go away, for if I don't, the Comforter won't come. If I do, He will—for I will send Him to you" (John 16:7, LNT).

Black night descended upon Jerusalem, and a group of men prepared to commit murder. The Man they hated and envied must die. In another part of the city Jesus and 11 of His disciples were together. Christ knew He was about to be taken and crucified. He knew that beyond death and the grave there would be His resurrection and return to heaven. But in this dreadful hour the Lord was thinking of His faithful disciples who had given up all for Him. They had followed Him along the roads of Palestine, daily sharing in His sorrows and labors. Jesus was their Master, Teacher, Lord and Friend. He realized that soon these few followers would be left without Him and would be surrounded by the many evil men who were His enemies and theirs.

The Lord had much to tell His disciples on this last night about His betrayal and the shedding of His blood. They must know that very soon He would "leave the world and go to the Father" (John 16:28). The Lord warned, "The world would love you if you belonged to it; but you don't—for I chose you to come out of the world, and so it hates you. The people of the world will persecute you because you belong to Me, for they don't know God who sent Me" (John 15:19, 21, LNT).

As the disciples began to understand that their beloved Lord was going into suffering and death and that they were to lose Him, their hearts were filled with sorrow. They greatly feared those things which they would have to face alone. Who would be their help?

Then Jesus told them that they need not grieve or fear. He said, "The world will greatly rejoice over what is going to happen to Me, and you will weep. But your weeping shall suddenly be turned to wonderful joy" (John 16:20, LNT). For although His earthly work was finished and He could no longer remain, yet a Companion would come to them from heaven to take His place. "I will ask the Father and He will give you another Comforter, and He will never leave you. He is the Holy Spirit" (John 14:15-17, LNT).

In New Testament language "Comforter" means "one who is called alongside to help." Christ thus gave His disciples the promise that the Holy Spirit would come and would be with them always. This promise is the same today for all who follow Christ and receive Him into their hearts. The Holy Spirit is our Helper and the One who is with you to meet every need.

For Thinking and Doing:

1. Read John 14:16-20, 26-29.

2. The RSV uses the word "Counselor" for the word "Comforter." Try to express what each word means to you.

3. What name does Christ give to the Holy Spirit in John 14:17?

4. What does Christ promise the Holy Spirit will do for the disciples according to John 14:26? Do we need this too?

95th Day

The Holy Spirit of God

"But I will send you the Comforter—the Holy Spirit, the source of all truth. He will come to you from the Father and will tell you all about Me" (John 15:26, LNT).

The first thing to know about the Holy Spirit (also called the Holy Ghost) is that He is God. Those words "Spirit" and "Ghost" do not mean "specter," but that He is a Spirit Being. The Holy Spirit is a person. In speaking of this Coming One, Jesus used the words "He" and "Him." We should never use "it" in speaking of the Holy Spirit.

"The Counselor . . . He will teach you" (John 14:26). "The world . . . neither sees Him nor knows Him" (John 14:17). That He is one of the Persons of the Godhead is shown by the way His name is given an equal place with that of the Father and the Son. "The grace of the Lord Jesus Christ and the love of God (the Father) and the fellowship of the Holy Spirit be with you all" (II Corinthians 13:14).

So truly does God the Holy Spirit share the very life of God the Father and God the Son that sometimes He is called "the Eternal Spirit," "the Spirit of God," " the Spirit of Holiness," or "the Spirit of Christ." There is no disagreement between the three Persons of God: no separate plans, wisdom, will or power. All work together in bringing Their purposes to pass. Before the universe or man was ever made, the three-in-one God counseled together about the work of God the Son, His earthly birth, atoning death, ascension, and future kingdom.

God acted in this same way in creation. Not only did the Father and the Son create the universe and man, but the Holy Spirit also shared this work and did what only God can do. We read, "When Thou sendest forth Thy Spirit, they are created" (Psalm 104:30). "The Spirit of God has made me . . . gives me life" (Job 33:4). "By His Spirit He hath garnished (called forth and made beautiful) the heavens" (Job 26:13, KJV).

The three-in-one God acted when Christ came to earth in human form. The Father prepared a body for Jesus (Hebrews 10:5), the Son Himself took the form of man (Hebrews 2:14, Philippians 2:7), and the Holy Spirit brought about that forming of the Lord Jesus in the womb of Mary before our Lord was born (Luke 1:35).

All through Christ's talk with His disciples recorded in John 14, He speaks of God the Father, the Holy Spirit and Himself as being one. What a joy it must have been to them when they finally realized that He was promising to come to live within them and to be with them always.

You can have that same joy today if you have received Christ into your heart as your Savior and Lord.

For Thinking and Doing:

1. Read Isaiah 40:10; John 14:18-24.

2. In the light of today's lesson and according to John 14:23, can you explain how Jesus and the Father make their home with a believer?

3. What does Christ say is the proof that we love Him? See John 14:21, 23, 24.

4. Can we keep His Word if we do not read it and think about it? Memorize Isaiah 40:10.

The Coming of the Holy Spirit

"When the Spirit of truth comes, He will guide you into all truth" (John 16:13).

In Old Testament times God was known as Creator and Almighty Lord. People who worshiped Him knew something of the Holy Spirit, yet the full truth of the three Persons of God was not made plain.

Before Christ came to earth the Spirit came upon chosen ones as in I Samuel 10:10. By His power these men worked miracles and by His wisdom they taught and prophesied, giving forth the very words of God. However, it seems that the Holy Spirit was not an ever-present Companion to all believers in those days. It was even possible for them to sin so greatly that the Spirit would draw away from them. This was true of David. We hear his sad cry, "O God . . . cleanse me from my sin . . . and take not Thy Holy Spirit from me" (Psalm 51:2, 4, 11). But there was to be a change.

On the last night before Christ's crucifixion He told the disciples that the Holy Spirit would come in a new way. "The Father . . . shall give you another Comforter (to be to them all that Jesus had been), that He may abide with you forever . . . He dwelleth with you, and shall be in you" (John 14:16, 17, KJV). Notice that the Holy Spirit, who had been with the disciples, would from now on be in them forever. Can you imagine how wonderful this promise was to the disciples? One of the Persons of God would be always there within, just as real as their own human spirit and soul. That wise, loving, Holy One would be knowing their every thought of joy or sorrow. He would be going with them every place they went and ready to guide, teach, correct and comfort.

About 53 days after Christ had promised the coming of the Holy Spirit, His disciples were together in Jerusalem praying, praising and waiting. On the day of Pentecost, without warning, "Suddenly a sound came from heaven like the rush of a mighty wind, and it filled all the house where they were sitting. And there appeared to them tongues as of fire, distributed and resting on each one of them. And they were all filled with the Holy Spirit" (Acts 2:2-4). They did not see the Holy Spirit, but they did hear and see something which showed He had come.

The book of Acts has many proofs that the Spirit dwelt within the disciples, such as the miracles they performed, the hardships they endured, and the wonderful changes in their lives. The fearful Peter, who denied his Lord on the night Jesus was arrested, became a bold and courageous leader of the early church by the power of the Holy Spirit.

The Holy Spirit is just the same today as He dwells in a believer's heart. He can make wonderful changes in your life and He is within you to help you.

For Thinking and Doing:

1. Read John 16:12-15; Acts 5:12-16.

2. Could you explain from today's reading the difference Pentecost made to Jesus' disciples?

3. Whose power made Acts 5:12, 15, 16 possible?

4. As a follower of Christ, what difference would you like the Holy Spirit to make in your life?

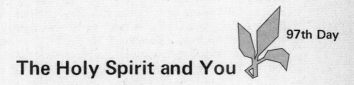

The Holy Spirit and You

"All who are led by the Spirit of God are the sons of God" (Romans 8:14).

We need to know about the Holy Spirit and what He does. Although God is one in His nature and plans, each of the Persons of God has special work to do in carrying out those plans. Let us think of an example. In a miserable little shanty lives a poor, sick widow with her seven children. One day a stranger knocks at the door. He has heard of the family's troubles and has brought a huge load of food and clothes. He explains that he and his two brothers have a warehouse filled with supplies of every kind, and these they freely give to any who are in need. The gifts are really from all three brothers, for they all carry on the work. One of them decides who will be helped and how. The second gets in the supplies, and the third brother delivers that which is sent by the other two. He is the agent by whom the will of the other brothers is done.

139

This story is a simple picture of the work of the three-in-one God toward man. The Holy Spirit is God's agent on earth. It is He who now brings to pass, in the world and in and through man, those things which God the Father wants done and which the Son has made possible. For example: "The gift of God (the Father) is eternal life" (Romans 6:23). "Also the Son gives life to whom He will" (John 5:21). Eternal life is the gift of the Father and the Son and has been made possible by the death of our Lord. It becomes real within us now through the work of the Holy Spirit.

Eternal life is not just life beyond the grave, but it is a quality of life—the kind of life which God gives you when you are born again. "This is eternal life, that they know Thee the only true God, and Jesus Christ whom Thou hast sent" (John 17:3). It is that inner, spiritual life the Holy Spirit develops within us. So it is said, "Anyone who does not have the Spirit of Christ does not belong to Him" (Romans 8:9).

Jesus said, "When He (the Spirit) has come He will convince the world of its sin" (John 16:8, LNT). All over the world the Holy Spirit continually works in men's hearts and shows them through the Word of God and by their own conscience that they are guilty of sin and that they must turn away from it to God. It is the Holy Spirit who speaks this way to your heart. "His Holy Spirit speaks to us deep in our hearts, and tells us that we really are God's children" (Romans 8:16, LNT). "So now we can obey God's laws if we follow after the Holy Spirit and no longer obey the evil nature within us" (Romans 8:4, LNT).

Thy Holy Spirit, Lord, alone
Can turn our heart from sin.
His power alone can sanctify
And keep us pure within.
Thy Holy Spirit, Lord, can bring
The gifts we seek in prayer.
His voice can words of comfort speak,
And still each wave of care.
—H. E. Blair

For Thinking and Doing:

1. Read Romans 8:26 and reread all the verses quoted in today's reading.

2. Name the things these verses say the Holy Spirit does for us.

3. What reason is given in Romans 8:26 for our need of the Holy Spirit?

4. Memorize Romans 8:26.

Controlled by the Holy Spirit

"You are controlled by your new nature if you have the Spirit of God living in you" (Romans 8:9, LNT).

What would you think of a girl who was just married to a splendid, loving husband but would turn to him and say, "Now I expect you to provide everything I want or need, but I do not care to know you better or have anything to do with you"? Or suppose a young man was taken into partnership in a successful business. Do you think he would succeed if he said to the head of the firm, "I am not really interested in you or in your business. All I want is my paycheck"?

If you truly belong to Christ, the Holy Spirit is in you. It is a closer union than that of husband and wife or that of partners in business. Yet so many Christians pay no attention to the Holy Spirit. They are not interested in knowing Him, although they want the blessings He gives. If we take time to learn about the Spirit, we can come to really know this Holy One Himself.

Our Lord described Him as "the Spirit of truth (Who) . . . will guide you into all truth" (John 16:13, KJV). "He shall teach you all things" (John 14:26, KJV). "He shall testify (witness) of Me" (John 15:26, KJV). He is the Spirit of truth, for He is the Author of God's Book which is truth. He teaches us the truth through the Scriptures. He reveals Christ, Who is "the Truth" (John 14:6). The Holy Ghost is called the Spirit of Christ because He was sent by Christ and He enables us to become acquainted with our Lord and Savior. Because He is the Holy God, He is also called the Spirit of Holiness and is ever seeking to make men whole, or holy. This True and Holy One is the Spirit of "wisdom and understanding . . . of counsel and might . . . of knowledge" (Isaiah 11:2).

Because God's work on earth is put in charge of the Spirit, He guides and leads God's children in the right way. "As many as are led by the Spirit of God, they are the sons of God" (Romans 8:14, KJV). In the Living New Testament, Romans 8:5 reads, "Those who let themselves be controlled by their lower natures live only to please themselves, but those who follow after the Holy Spirit find themselves doing those things that please God."

Do you follow His leading in your heart; are you controlled by Him, seeking to please God?

141

For Thinking and Doing:

1. Read Galatians 5:16, 17, 19-21, 25, 26.

2. Reread the verses quoted in today's reading. What additional things did you learn that the Holy Spirit does for us?

3. If we are led by the Holy Spirit in our daily walk or life, what command does Galatians 5:16, 17 give us and why?

4. According to Galatians 5:26, what else should be left out of our lives?

99th Day

The Holy Spirit's Work

" I ask God . . . to give you power through His Spirit to be strong in your inner selves" (Ephesians 3:16, TEV).

The story is told of a poor orphan girl who lived in a bare, unheated, attic room. One evening, returning to the attic after a day of hard work, she could hardly believe what she saw. The room, once so cold and empty, was now full of lovely things: good food, warm clothes, pretty furniture and books. A cheery fire burned in the fireplace. Every few days new things appeared. She did not see or know who brought them, but the gifts proved that someone had been there. Someone knew about her and really cared!

It may be difficult for you to realize that Someone you have never seen dwells within you. He has entered so quietly you may not even feel that He is there. But the changes in your life prove the presence of the Holy Spirit. Because you were born again, you are interested in the things of Christ and you long to know Him better and truly please Him. The Lord Jesus explains this work of the Spirit, saying, "He will take what is Mine and declare it (make it known) to you" (John 16:14). You now have the comfort of knowing you are in the heavenly Father's loving care. "We know how dearly God loves us, and we feel this warm love everywhere within us because God has given us the Holy Spirit to fill our hearts with His love" (Romans 5:5, LNT).

Are you finding courage to stand true to the Lord? If so, it is because you are being made strong in your inner life by the Holy Spirit. Are you now understanding the Scriptures better? If so, that is proof that the truth is being "revealed . . . by His Spirit," so "that we might know the things that are freely given to us (by) God" (I Corinthians 2:10, 12, KJV).

Every time you realize you have sinned against the Lord, it is the Holy Spirit showing you that sinful thing. "When He comes He will convince the world of sin" (John 16:8). Although you may not know the Holy Spirit very well and all the teaching about Him may be new to you, if you are a child of God, you can believe that He is within you. God says that He is, and that is enough. But you have added proof by the change which is being made in your thoughts and life. Act as if the Holy Spirit is within you and you will find it to be true. In your daily life you act as though you can get music through the radio. You believe it, turn the knob, and get results. In the same way the Holy Spirit will prove that He is in you when you act in faith.

"Those who do what God says—they are living with God and He with them. We know this is true because the Holy Spirit He has given us tells us so" (I John 3:24, LNT).

For Thinking and Doing:

1. Read Psalm 107:1, 2, 8; Psalm 143:10; Job 32:8.

2. For what should we give thanks to God according to Psalm 107:1, 2, 8?

3. Make a list of the things which the Holy Spirit does for us that are mentioned in today's reading.

4. Will you pray that He will do these things in your inner life?

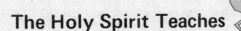 **100th Day**

The Holy Spirit Teaches

"The One who is coming to stand by you, the Holy Spirit . . . will be your Teacher" (John 14:26, Phillips).

The invention of the telephone was probably the finest work ever done by Alexander Graham Bell, for the telephone has been a help to millions of people. In the beginning no one could explain the telephone as well as Mr. Bell himself because, of course, the man who made it knew the most about it.

The writing of the Bible was one of the great works of the Spirit of God, for the men who wrote it spoke as they were "moved by the Holy Spirit" (II Peter 1:21). Because the Holy Spirit is the real Author of this Book, He knows everything about it. The Lord Jesus said the Holy Spirit would "teach you all things" about God and eternal life (John 14:26). He does this through the Bible.

How thankful we can be that this all-wise Teacher is always living within the heart of the Christian to help us to understand God's Word. Whenever you read any part of the Scriptures, pray and ask the Holy Spirit to help you to understand what you read. Also ask Him to do the following things for you:

1. To so use what it says that the things of God the Father and of the Lord Jesus Christ will seem more and more real to your heart.

2. To show you what God wants His children to be and to do, and then to help you to do it and to be it.

3. Perhaps the Holy Spirit will use the Bible to remind you of some sin that must be forgiven and then given up.

4. As you read or memorize some very precious promise, ask the Holy Spirit to give you faith to believe it, that it will become a part of your very life, and that you will learn how to use God's promises for every time of need.

5. That the Holy Spirit will give you a love for God's Word and that it will stay in your heart.

"I have laid up Thy Word in my heart, that I might not sin against Thee." "Open mine eyes, that I may behold wondrous things out of Thy law" (Psalm 119:11, 18). The Living New Testament expresses I Corinthians 2:14 in this way: "The man who isn't a Christian can't understand and can't accept these thoughts from God, which the Holy Spirit teaches us. They sound foolish to him, because only those who have the Holy Spirit within them can understand what the Holy Spirit means."

For Thinking and Doing:

1. Read John 14:23-26; I Corinthians 2:9-14.

2. What promises did Christ give to those who love Him and keep His Word according to John 14:23, 26?

3. Why is it that the person who has not accepted Christ cannot understand His teaching? See I Corinthians 2:14 quoted above.

4. Will you continue to ask the Holy Spirit to be your Teacher in the five ways suggested in today's reading?

You Belong to Him

"The Lord knows those who are really His" (II Timothy 2:19, LNT).

On great open spaces of grassland, cattlemen have herds of animals feeding. There may be thousands of head of cattle, many of them belonging to different owners, but they wander and graze together until a certain time. Then men on horseback ride in among the herds, divide the cattle into groups, and drive them toward the ranches where they belong. There is no trouble over getting the right animals, for each one bears the special mark of its owner, branded or burned upon it with a red-hot iron. That mark is the stamp, or seal, of ownership.

As we look about us we cannot always tell who are truly God's children, but He knows because each one bears His mark of ownership. When you took the Lord to be your Savior, "you were sealed with the promised Holy Spirit" (Ephesians 1:13). The Living New Testament expresses the same verse this way: "All you . . . who heard the Good News about how to be saved, and trusted Christ, were marked as belonging to Christ by the Holy Spirit, Who long ago had been promised to all of us Christians." The mark of God's ownership upon us is the Holy Spirit living in us.

A brand is put on cattle so that the owner will not lose any of his valuable animals. Because of the seal of the Spirit, we know that we are safe in our Lord's keeping. He will constantly care for those He bought at such a very great price. In John 10:28 there is a wonderful promise Christ has given to us: "No one shall snatch them out of My hand." We are forever safe in His keeping.

In Ephesians 1:13, 14, we are told that not only are we sealed with the Holy Spirit, but He is also "the guarantee of our inheritance." A guarantee is a pledge. To illustrate this, one Christmas morning I found an envelope among my gifts. Inside it was a picture of an auto, and tied to the picture car was a small metal key. A note said that the key would fit a new car which I would receive in a few days. Sure enough, the car arrived. The key was the pledge, or promise, that I would surely get something which was already mine, but which I had not yet received.

In the same way the Holy Spirit is given to God's children as a pledge. His indwelling is the promise and assurance that the

Lord has already given us many wonderful and delightful things which are now awaiting us in heaven. "No eye has seen, nor ear heard, nor the heart of man conceived, what God has prepared for those who love Him" (I Corinthians 2:9).

For Thinking and Doing:

1. Read John 10:27-29; I John 3:24; 4:13; Ephesians 4:30.
2. What does Christ say in John 10:27-29 about His sheep?
3. How do we know we belong to Christ according to I John 3:24 and 4:13?
4. In what ways can we grieve the Holy Spirit (Ephesians 4:30)?

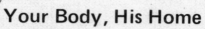

102nd Day

Your Body, His Home

"Dear young friends, you belong to God" (I John 4:4, LNT).

What is your body, and to whom does it belong? You may reply, "My body is that part of me which can be seen and felt; it is made up of flesh, bones, blood, etc. It is that in which my soul and spirit live. It is mine." God answers that if you are a Christian, your body is much more than that and that it does not belong to you. "Your body is the home of the Holy Spirit God gave you, and . . . He lives within you. Your body does not belong to you. For God has bought you with a great price. So use every part of your body to give glory back to God, because He owns it" (I Corinthians 6:19, 20, LNT). If there is one thing we feel belongs to us, it is our body. But God says that it is His.

The Lord Jesus Christ bought us; His death was the price He paid so we might enjoy the safety and privilege of belonging to God. Not only did He buy our souls and spirits back to God, but He also bought our bodies. Some day the bodies of His own are to be changed and fitted to live with Him in heaven. How good it is to know that nothing is left out; every part of us belongs to a loving and almighty Father.

Because the Holy Spirit dwells within you, wherever you are He is hearing what you hear and seeing what you see. Into what sort of places do you take this sinless, glorious Person who is God? What does He look at through your eyes and hear through your ears? Is He sometimes ashamed of what you see and hear and of the way you use that body in which He lives? The Bible tells us to be careful not to sadden this most holy Guest. "Do not grieve the Holy Spirit of God" (Ephesians 4:30). He has come to do God's wonderful work within your heart and bring you joy and blessing. He is there to teach, comfort and guide. He is there to strengthen you to stand against the attacks of Satan, who brings you many temptations.

It is easy to tell if we have grieved the Holy Spirit, for we are conscious of having sinned and we lose our joy. Then we need to ask forgiveness of the Savior, and He restores us to fellowship with Himself again. In our prayers and in the study of His Word, we learn in what ways we may be grieving the Holy Spirit as He speaks to our hearts. "Do not smother the Holy Spirit. Keep away from every kind of evil . . . May your spirit and soul and body be kept blameless" (I Thessalonians 5:19, 22, 23, LNT).

For Thinking and Doing:

1. Read Psalm 51:1, 2, 10, 11; Romans 12:1, 2.
2. For what does David pray in these verses of Psalm 51?
3. The Living New Testament translates Romans 12:1: "I plead with you to give your bodies to God. Let them be a living sacrifice, holy—the kind He can accept. When you think of what He has done for you, is this too much to ask?" What is your answer?
4. Ask God to show you ways you may be grieving His Holy Spirit and ask His forgiveness and help.

103rd Day

His Good Work

"I am sure that God who began the good work within you will keep right on helping you grow in His grace" (Philippians 1:6, LNT).

When you asked Jesus to come into your heart, you may have expected never again to do or say those wrong things you have since learned to hate. Instead you may be more conscious of failure than ever before, and it may seem that you are more often tempted to sin. Most earnest Christians have this experience. It may not mean that you are really sinning more often, but rather that the Holy Spirit is showing up sins you did not realize were there. You might easily miss seeing the dust in a poorly lighted room, but if you raise the shades and let the sunlight in, you see it all. The Holy Spirit is the Light that reveals to us sins we did not see before He came into our lives.

When God reveals failures, confess them to Him at once and ask His forgiveness, but do not become discouraged. It is said that at one time in their history, the Chinese soldiers lost almost every battle. This was because defeated generals got their heads promptly cut off. Because of this the armies never had experienced leaders. Experience in every field of life is essential. We learn by experience and that takes time. This is especially true of the Christian life.

Expect nothing good of yourself and then you won't be disappointed. However, you can expect God to keep His word that "sin will have no dominion (power) over you" (Romans 6:14). Don't be troubled if you do not have complete victory right away. How does fruit grow? A fully ripened peach doesn't burst out from a bare branch overnight. First there is the flower, and then the tiny green knob which holds all the beginnings of the peach—seed, pulp, juice and skin. Yet more sun, rain and sap are needed to fully ripen the fruit. When things are just right, fruit ripens quickly.

Certain new Christians seem to grow more quickly than others. Usually, however, God teaches us little by little. The Lord is not discouraged about you, so don't give up. Remember it is the "sap" of the life of the Lord, the Holy Spirit within you, that will cause you to grow. "He who began a good work in you will bring it to completion at the day of Jesus Christ" (Philippians 1:6).

For Thinking and Doing:

1. Read I Peter 2:2, II Peter 3:18. Reread Philippians 1:6.

2. The King James Version translated I Peter 2:2: "As newborn babes, desire the sincere milk of the Word, that ye may grow thereby." What are we to do so that we may grow?

3. What has God done and what will He do according to Philippians 1:6?

4. Memorize Philippians 1:6.

Broken Contact

"Your iniquities have made a separation between you and your God" (Isaiah 59:2).

A printing firm bought some fine new electric equipment which was to take the place of a machine which was run by hand. It was supposed to do much better work and in less time. The new machine arrived and was set in place. The switch was turned on, but nothing happened. All the power of the electricity was there, ready for use, but somewhere something was wrong. Finally a break was found in one small wire. It was only a little thing, but it stopped the flow of the current into and through the machine. When the two separated ends of the wire were brought together again, the new equipment worked perfectly.

Our Lord wants us to be in good working order like that machine and to be something in which and through which the mighty current of His Holy Spirit can move and work. Sin of any kind will hinder this. It puts us out of touch with the Lord Jesus; it breaks contact and stops the flowing of His life through us.

The Bible contains hundreds of promises telling what God will do in and through His children, but so often these promises have a condition. "You are My friends, if you obey Me" (John 15:14, LNT). "If you abide in Me," the Savior said, "and My words abide in you (are held in your heart), ask whatever you will, and it shall be done for you" (John 15:7). Prayers will be answered if . . .

Are you perhaps missing God's best and His blessing because of broken contact, that is, because you did not obey and abide? There is a way of repair and a Person to do it. First find out where the trouble lies. God's Word and His Spirit's quiet voice speaking within your heart will show you.

Then the moment you know what is wrong, confess it as sin. Be definite and call the sin by its name. It is that special spot which needs to be repaired. It may be more than one place, but tell God what they are and that you are sorry to have failed Him. Do it at once and then believe His gracious promise, "If we confess our sins to Him, He can be depended upon to forgive us and to cleanse us from every wrong" (I John 1:9, LNT). "If anyone does sin, we have an advocate . . . Jesus Christ" (I John 2:1). An

149

advocate is one who comes to our help in time of need. When we turn from sin and confess it, our Lord repairs the broken place and restores happy contact with Himself.

"Call upon Me in the day of trouble; I will deliver you" (Psalm 50:15). Deliverance is available if you call on Him. "If you want to know what God wants you to do, ask Him and He will gladly tell you" (James 1:5, LNT). You will know if you ask.

For Thinking and Doing:

1. Read Isaiah 43:25; 44:22; Psalm 103:10-12.

2. What are the reasons given in these references that God forgives our sins?

3. Think of things in your life that may be breaking contact. If there is something you must give up, ask Him to help you and then give it up.

4. Memorize I John 1:9.

105th Day

I Can, in Him

"For I can do everything God asks me to with the help of Christ who gives me the strength and power" (Philippians 4:13, LNT).

"Do whatever He tells you" (John 2:5). This is not as easy as it sounds. Just ask Paul. In spite of all his efforts to keep from sinning, he once had to admit, "I don't understand myself at all, for I really want to do what is right, but I can't. I do what I don't want to—what I hate" (Romans 7:15, LNT). Haven't you often felt just like that? Thousands of God's children have.

God's Word tells us not to sin. We may start to work on our tempers and unkind tongues. We may do pretty well for a time; then without warning anger may leap out of our hearts and mouths like a tiger from its cage.

We are told to "Love one another" (I John 4:7). Paul tells us, "Love is patient and kind; love is not jealous or conceited or proud, love is not ill-mannered or selfish or irritable, love does not keep a record of wrongs ... its faith, hope and patience never fail" (I Corinthians 13:4-7, TEV). Yet, struggle as we may, we sometimes do grow irritable, jealous and selfish. Impure thoughts enter our minds. Our Lord also says, "Love your enemies, bless them that curse you, do good to them that hate you" (Matthew

5:44, KJV). How can we do this when sometimes it is all we can do to love our friends?

Scripture tells us what our Lord wants us to do and to be. We truly long to please Him, and yet somehow all our trying often ends in failure. How discouraging it is. When we look into our hearts we see so much wrong there that we are tempted to say, "It's just no use for me to try to meet God's standards for a Christian. I might as well give the whole thing up."

All these discouragements are from Satan. He probably defeats more Christians in this way than in any other way. Of course it would be quite unfair of God to expect you to do what is impossible, but He does not expect that. The Lord knew all about our weak, human natures when He took us to be His own loved sons and daughters. He had provided a way by which we can keep His every command. "I can do all things in Him who strengthens me" (Philippians 4:13).

> Distrust yourself, but trust alone
> In Him, for all—for ever;
> And joyously your heart shall own
> That Jesus faileth never!
> —F. R. Havergal

For Thinking and Doing:

1. Reread I Corinthians 13:1-4 and Philippians 4:13. Read I John 4:7-11.

2. What new thought about what love really is like have you received from I Corinthinas 13:1-4?

3. What reason is given in I John 4:11 that we should love one another?

4. Memorize and believe Philippians 4:13.

106th Day

Living by Faith

"The man who finds life will find it through trusting God" (Romans 1:17, LNT).

What is faith? It is to believe or to trust. We use faith every day. You drop a letter in the mailbox, believing it will be delivered to a friend in a distant city. We put our money in the bank, believing they will pay it out to those who cash our checks. We do not think it is foolish to have faith in other people and in what

151

they say and do. Why should we think it is strange or difficult to trust God?

Two children were playing on a hillside as the sun was setting. One said, "See how far the sun has gone down. Awhile ago it was right over that tree and now it is low down in the sky." The other answered, "It is the earth that moves, and not the sun. You know; Father told us." The first child shook his head. He had seen the sun and he knew the earth did not move, for he had been standing on it all the time. "I know what I see," he said. "But I believe Father," replied the other. The other believed in spite of what he saw because he knew his Father could always be trusted.

Our Lord said, "Have faith in God" (Mark 11:22): in God, the glorious One with Whom "all things are possible" (Mark 10:27) and in God "that cannot lie" (Titus 1:2, KJV). Why does the Bible say so much about faith in God? Because "without faith it is impossible to please Him" (Hebrews 11:6). Also because, "He who does not believe God has made Him a liar" (I John 5:10), and to do that is sin.

To have faith in God is, first of all, to believe what He says in His Word and to count His promises as true. Then we are to have faith in God Himself and trust that the mighty Lord is both willing and able to do all that He has promised. "Fully convinced that God (is) able to do what He . . . promised" (Romans 4:21). He is able, no matter how difficult or even impossible the thing may seem.

It is having faith in God Himself when we believe that He is always loving us and working for our highest good; it is when we trust that what He does is best even when we go through hard ways and things seem to be all wrong. Faith has nothing to do with how things seem or how we feel. We are not to wait until we see what God does before we trust Him. No, the promise is for just the opposite, "Did I not tell you that if you would believe you would see the glory of God" (John 11:40). It is first believing and then seeing because we have believed.

For Thinking and Doing:

1. Read Psalm 37:3, 5; Psalm 56:3; Psalm 62:8; Proverbs 29:25; Proverbs 3:5.

2. What are the conditions and the results given in Psalm 37:3, 5?

3. When is the time to trust? See Psalm 56:3 and Psalm 62:8.

4. How fully are we to trust and what are we not to do according to Proverbs 3:5?

Much or Little?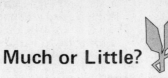

"According to your faith be it done to you" (Matthew 9:29).

Jesus met people in Palestine who were like people today. Many had no faith in Him. For others He performed mighty miracles because they believed in Him with all their hearts. There was a mother who begged Christ to heal her suffering child and who kept on asking and trusting Him to do all she desired. He answered her, "'O woman, great is your faith! Be it done for you as you desire.' And her daughter was healed instantly" (Matthew 15:28).

Peter, in answer to his Master's call, walked toward Him on the water. But Peter grew afraid and as his faith weakened he began to sink. To him the Lord said, "O man of little faith, why did you doubt?" (Matthew 14:21).

Again, there was a time when Christ and His disciples were in a little boat, tossed by great waves upon a very stormy sea. In terror they cried out for fear that they would drown although the Almighty Son of God was with them. They did not trust Him and the Lord spoke sadly, "Why are you afraid? Have you no faith?" (Mark 4:40).

How is it with us as Christians? Do we have great faith, little faith, or sometimes no faith at all? Perhaps you believe that God is able to keep His promises, but you are not sure that He will really do as He says. Then cry to Him, "(Lord) I believe; help my unbelief!" (Mark 9:24). Of course we can always trust Him.

Faith is like a hand which reaches out and takes what God promises and never lets go. Your hand may be a bit weak and may tremble a little, but use it anyway and lay hold of what God has for you. It has been said that "Faith is a living power from heaven that grasps the promise God hath given."

May it never be said of us, "He did not do many mighty works there, because of their unbelief" (Matthew 13:58). Yet it is not your faith that does the actual work, but the God in Whom you put your trust.

> O how sweet to trust in Jesus
> Just to take Him at His Word
> Just to rest upon His promise
> Just to know, Thus saith the Lord.

Jesus, Jesus, how I trust Him
How I've proved Him o'er and o'er
Jesus, Jesus, precious Jesus!
O for grace to trust Him more.

—L. M. R. Stead

For Thinking and Doing:

1. Read Luke 17:11-19.
2. What did the lepers have to do which involved faith?
3. When were they healed (verse 14b)?
4. Can you think of an example from daily life where faith and obedience are both necessary?

A Growing Faith

"These trials are only to test your faith, to see whether or not it is strong" (I Peter 1:7, LNT).

Faith will grow. When a tiny seed is put into the ground the first sprout is a weak, frail thing. But wait. Under the sun and rain that little stalk becomes a tall, strong cottonwood tree. Seeds will grow if given proper care. A wise gardener knows what best suits each plant and tree. Some trees need plenty of sunshine; others need shade. Unhealthy branches must be cut away and pests destroyed. At times the tree may have to be transplanted to a different place.

You may feel that your faith is as small and weak as a tiny seed. Yet Jesus said, "If you have faith as a grain of mustard seed . . . nothing will be impossible to you" (Matthew 17:20). If given the right care you will find that "your faith is growing abundantly" (II Thessalonians 1:3).

You may ask how. First, "Faith cometh by hearing, and hearing by the Word of God" (Romans 10:17, KJV). This does not mean it is enough to simply read the words of Scripture or hear them through our ears. Rather, just as tree roots draw up into themselves the water and minerals which are in the earth, so must we take God's Word into our hearts to believe and truly obey it. "Be doers of the Word, and not hearers only" (James 1:22). Then as you read the Bible record of what God did for those who trusted Him, you will realize how you can trust Him too.

Our loving heavenly Father is a wise gardener. He knows how to cause the small seed of faith to grow. Some Christians develop

154

best in the sunshine of a smooth, easy life; they would wilt and go down under trouble. Others can only learn to trust through the clouds and rains of difficulty and trial. God's desire that we should grow in faith is one reason why He allows so many changes to come to us—sometimes the sunshine of gladness and sometimes the shade of disappointments and troubles.

If you are brave enough to ask God to give you strong faith, then you must expect things to happen. They will be the Lord's answers to your prayers. He will commence working with His growing plant. You may have to be freed from the pests of harmful friendships. He my transplant you from a life of ease into one of difficulties. It won't be pleasant, but it will be right. Faith trusts, even though we cannot understand.

Don't be like the person who plants a seed, digs it up to see if it is growing, and pokes it into the ground again. Set your thoughts on the God who is willing and able to keep His promises. "Those who trust Him wholly, find Him wholly true."

For Thinking and Doing:

1. Read I Corinthians 16:13; Colossians 1:23; 2:5; James 1:3.
2. What quality of faith is described in the verses above?
3. According to James 1:3, how do we develop that quality of faith?
4. Memorize James 1:3.

Trust and Obey

"*Abraham trusted God and when God told him to leave home and go far away to another land which He promised to give him, Abraham obeyed. Away he went, not even knowing where he was going*" (Hebrews 11:8, LNT).

Long years ago a small group of men and women started on a journey. Neighbors and relatives questioned their leader. "Why do you leave home, Abram, when you are well and happy here in Ur?"

"I go because the God of glory appeared to me and said, 'Go from your country, and your kindred, and your father's house.'"

155

"Where are you going then?"

"I do not know. He only said, 'Go to the land that I will show you and I will make of you a great nation, and I will bless you, and make your name great, so that you will be a blessing' (Genesis 12:1, 2). I must obey, and these others are journeying with me."

And so, "By faith Abraham obeyed when he was called to go out to a place which he was to receive as an inheritance" (Hebrews 11:8). With his little band of fellow travelers Abraham started forth, "not knowing where he was to go," but "fully convinced that God was able to do what He had promised" (Romans 4:21). Behind lay the many friends and the busy, prosperous city. What lay ahead? Would it be hardship and loss? Perhaps the cruel kings of the lands they would travel through would seek to destroy them. But with them every moment would be that mighty Lord who would not fail to keep His Word.

Did he have troubles? Yes, Abraham had them, for his faith had to be exercised to grow. But as he continued believing and obeying, God kept adding blessings until "Abraham was very rich in cattle, in silver, and in gold" (Genesis 13:2). At the close of his life we read "the Lord had blessed Abraham in all things" (Genesis 24:1). It was far beyond what Abraham had ever dreamed or hoped.

The same God who led Abraham has plans for you. He "will bless you . . . so that you will be a blessing" (Genesis 12:2) if you have faith to obey Him and follow as He leads. You may not understand why God tells you to do a certain thing, but God never makes a mistake. To trust only what we understand is to have no faith at all. We need not fear as we go forward with God.

> Trust and obey,
> For there's no other way
> To be happy in Jesus,
> But to trust and obey.
> —V. H. Sammis

For Thinking and Doing:

1. Read Genesis 15:2-6; Romans 4:13, 18-22.

2. What promise of God did Abraham believe according to Genesis 15:2-6?

3. What does Romans 4:20, 21 say about Abraham's faith?

4. Why do you think Abraham's faith was counted for him as righteousness? (Romans 4:22).

Faith Brings Victory

"By faith the walls of Jericho fell down" (Hebrews 11:30).

To Abraham and his families, the Israelites, God promised to give the beautiful, fertile land of Canaan. At last the time came when the people, led by Joshua, were going in to take what God had promised. The unarmed Israelites had been quiet slaves in Egypt, but the Canaanites were fierce and warlike. At the very entrance to their land stood the high-walled city of Jericho. Would the Israelites trust God and go forward?

"When Joshua was by Jericho . . . the Lord said to Joshua, 'See, I have given into your hand Jericho, with its king . . . and mighty men of valor. You shall march around the city, all the men of war, going around the city once. Thus shall you do for six days. And seven priests shall bear seven trumpets and on the seventh day you shall march around the city seven times, the priests blowing the trumpets . . . and all the people shall shout with a great shout, and the wall of the city shall fall down flat.'"

Joshua and all the people did exactly as God told them. The priests blew loud on the trumpets, the Israelites gave a great shout and "the wall fell down flat, so that the people went up into the city . . . and they took the city." (from Joshua 5 & 6).

Can't you just imagine how it was? How those in Jericho must have laughed at the silly Israelites who were just marching around the walls and blowing trumpets. They probably were still laughing on that seventh day when suddenly there came a horrible sound of crumbling, falling bricks and stones. God had honored the faith of the Israelites and given them the land He had promised them because they obeyed Him.

Archaeologists, digging in the place where Jericho once stood, have since uncovered the remains of the fallen walls. The scattered pieces showed that God keeps His Word.

Does some "Jericho" stand in your path? Is there something or somebody that makes it seem as if God's promises and plans for you can never come true? If so, have faith in God. "Commit your way to the Lord; trust in Him, and He will act" (Psalm 37:5). Turn the whole thing over to God and go forward as He leads; then watch the Lord fulfill His Word to you and work things out.

157

For Thinking and Doing:

1. Reread the story of Jericho in your Bible in Joshua 6:1-5, 8, 11, 14, 16, 20.

2. What promise did God give to Joshua according to verse 2?

3. How much faith was involved in what the people were asked to do?

4. In what position were they when God's power brought down the walls? What does this teach you?

Faith Stands Firm

"The fire had not had any power over the bodies of those men" (Daniel 3:27).

An amazing story of the faith of three young Israelites is told in the book of Daniel. It was a festival day in Babylon in the year 600 B.C. In the broad plain of Dura there stood an enormous statue of Nebuchadnezzar, the mighty king of the empire. The sun glinted from the golden image with a dazzling light. It shone upon the multitudes who had come from temples, palaces and huts and were streaming in from all over the land to bow in worship before this great image of their king. "Whoever does not fall down and worship shall immediately be cast into a burning fiery furnace" (Daniel 3:6).

The royal orchestra began to play. As stalks of wheat bend low before a strong wind, the people bowed before the shining image of the proud Nebuchadnezzar. From his high and jewelled throne he watched them; everyone was worshiping him as a god.

No, not everyone. There were three young men in that crowd who had been brought to Babylon as captive slaves. These three, Shadrach, Meshach and Abednego, loved the one true God and His command was, "You shall not make for yourself a graven image. You shall not bow down to them... I am the Lord your God" (Exodus 20:4, 5). Which would they have: life and riches or a horrible death and God? They chose. They stood erect and would not bow down.

Then Nebuchadnezzar in furious rage commanded that these men be brought to him. They came. They saw the cruel, red-hot furnace and held firm to their faith in God, saying, "Our God whom we serve is able to deliver us from the burning fiery furnace; and He will deliver us... O king. But if not... we will not serve

158

your gods or worship the golden image" (Daniel 3:17, 18). Then the king was "full of fury . . . and he ordered the furnace heated seven times more than it was wont to be (usually) heated" (Daniel 3:19). Then these three men were cast into the fiery furnace.

But King Nebuchadnezzar became very astonished and said to his counselors, "Did we not cast three men bound into the fire? . . . But I see four men loose, walking in the midst of the fire, and they are not hurt. The fourth is like the Son of God" (Daniel 3:24, 25, KJV). It was true! The Lord had joined the three faithful men to work a glorious deliverance. The astounded king called the young men to come out from the furnace and gave them high places of honor in his great empire. What a story of faith!

Just as the fiery experience was for them a place of safety when the living King of glory came down to be their Companion in the flames, so Christ Himself will be your Companion in every trouble and test when you stand faithful to Him.

For Thinking and Doing:

1. Read this story in your Bible in Daniel 3:1, 4-6, 8, 13-28, 30. Read also Nahum 1:7.

2. What great truth taught in the Bible does this story illustrate for us?

3. Think of some examples when we have to stand firm in our loyalty to Christ today.

4. Can we know He is with us to help us in time of trouble?

112th Day

Faith Gives Peace

"Be still, and know that I am God" (Psalm 46:10).

The Lord Jesus had returned to heaven. Those who had crucified Him were determined to wipe out His faithful followers. King Herod killed James and arrested and imprisoned Peter. "The night before he was to be executed, he was asleep, double chained between two guards with others standing guard before the prison gate" (Acts 12:6, LNT).

Peter, facing a horrible death, was sleeping; he was not scheming how to escape and he was not lying awake trembling with fear or feeling sorry for himself. He was at peace: his mind and heart were undisturbed and free from fear and worry. He was at rest because he trusted Jesus. Peter knew the Lord could deliver him from death if it was His will, but if it were not, by dying he would all the sooner see the One he dearly loved. Jesus had said, "Let not your heart be troubled" (John 14:1). "I am with you always" (Matthew 28:20). That meant in life or death, so Peter slept.

Peter had a wonderful deliverance, as an angel led him out of prison. He also had remarkable faith as he slept peacefully that night when his life was in danger. His friends were all praying for him. "Earnest prayer was going up to God from the Church for his safety all the time he was in prison" (Acts 12:5, LNT).

Have you ever gone to bed at night, but no rest came? Your body was quiet, but your thoughts went here and there. Perhaps you were remembering that thing you should have done, but didn't, the unkind or untruthful words that day, or some sin which no one saw but God. The safe way to get rid of such thoughts is to tell God at once how sorry you are and to ask Him to show you how to make things right; only then can your heart be at rest.

Perhaps things had gone wrong through no fault of your own, and you were worried, frightened or upset. You can take one of God's promises and expect in faith that He will fulfill it for you. Set your thoughts on God, on the One who knows and cares, the kind and mighty One who is your Father in heaven. Why get upset when you can turn everything over to Him? Take His promise: "Thou wilt keep him in perfect peace, whose mind is stayed (is resting) on Thee: because he trusteth in Thee" (Isaiah 26:3, KJV).

As you trust, the Lord will change things or give you strength to bear them. Trust and be at rest, for God gives us peace of heart. "Peace from Him Who is and Who was, and Who is to come" (Revelation 1:4). Peace from Him "Who is," to care for all the problems of today; "Who was," and so is able to straighten out yesterday's tangles; "Who is to come," to be with you in every tomorrow.

For Thinking and Doing:

1. Read the story of Peter's escape in Acts 12:1-17.

2. Were Peter's friends praying in complete faith? Compare verse 5 and verse 15.

3. Do we sometimes pray with no real faith?

4. Take one of God's promises that fits some difficulty you are having and really count on it.

In Training

"No distrust made him waver concerning the promise of God, but he grew strong in his faith" (Romans 4:20).

Dick, a young neighbor, was a football fan. He seemed to think and speak of nothing else. He read the rules of the game and watched other players. He was determined to get on the school team. Yet how could he? Dick was a skinny youth with no muscles, but he had plenty of grit. He didn't sit down and moan, "I'll never make it." instead he pitched right in. Alone or with friends he had workouts in the back yard. He was thrown, knocked about and bruised, but he stayed with it. Now Dick is strong, with muscles as hard as bricks, and captain of his school team.

Most of us start out with weak faith, but using it will make it strong. Reading stories of God's heroes and how they became strong in faith, such as the stories of Abraham and Peter, encourages our own faith. Yet it is not enough to know of others' faith. The Lord knows that faith cannot become strong without exercise, so He lets things come into our lives which will force us to use our faith and trust Him.

For instance, you may turn a matter over to God for Him to work out, and it might grow worse. You may ask Him to do a certain thing, but the answer might not come at once or in the way you had hoped. You may beg the Lord to remove some trouble which seems too hard to bear another day, but there might be no change. These things are not to weaken you, but to cause you to keep on trusting in the love and wisdom of God. Your faith is being exercised.

It is faith in action when you let the Lord manage your affairs. It is faith acting when you refuse to be worried, but keep on believing God's promises even in the hard places. All these difficult things are workouts, and although our heavenly Coach sometimes allows us to be bruised, He is training us to become members of His team and to be strong in faith and able to do great things for Him.

"Strange and difficult indeed you may find it; but the blessing that you need is behind it," it has been said. "Blessed are those who have not seen and yet believe" (John 20:29).

Trust Him when dark doubts attack you.
Trust Him when your faith is small.
Trust Him, when to simply trust Him
Seems the hardest thing of all.
—Author unknown

For Thinking and Doing:

1. Read I Timothy 4:7, 8; I Corinthians 9:24-27.

2. What kind of training is more important than bodily exercise according to I Timothy 4:7, 8?

3. What does Paul say all athletes must develop?

4. Where are you exercising your faith in your daily life?

114th Day

What Is Prayer?

"Men ought always to pray" (Luke 18:1, KJV).

In a far-off land two travelers walked a road together; one was a Christian and the other was a Buddhist priest. As they walked and talked the hands of the priest whirled a small wheel-shaped box which held a few prayer papers.

"To whom do you offer the prayers within your wheel?" the Christian asked.

"To no one in particular."

"Well, what special things do you pray for?"

"I do not pray for any special things," the priest answered.

Is this what Jesus meant when He said men ought always to pray—a constantly whirling wheel or words continually spoken, but to no one in particular nor for any special thing? No indeed. "Thus says the Lord . . . call upon Me . . . pray to Me, and I will hear (pay attention to) you" (Jeremiah 29:10-12). "When ye pray say, 'Our Father, which art in heaven" (Luke 11:2, KJV). True prayer is someone on earth getting in touch with Someone in heaven.

Prayer is not simply having good, religious thoughts. True prayer asks for particular things. "Whatever you ask in prayer, you will receive, if you have faith" (Matthew 21:22). "In everything by prayer . . . let your requests be made known unto God" (Philippians 4:6).

Prayer is asking, looking, trusting
To receive good things from God.

Prayer is seeking for His wisdom
By the Spirit, through the Word.
Prayer is fighting 'gainst the devil
Who would throw the Christian down.
Prayer is working, keeping at it,
Till the victory is won.

            —Anonymous

Prayer is really talking with God and listening to what He would say to us by the Holy Spirit within our hearts. We come to Him in worship and reverence for all that He is: glorious, holy, all wise, our loving Father. Christ has taught us to bring our requests to Him and ask for the things we need, both spiritual and material. Prayer is fellowship with Him and knowing He is with us and loves us.

Being thankful and praising God for His goodness to you is a good way to begin your prayer. Include others in your requests and do not forget to ask God to guide you and keep you in His ways.

If you say, "There is no time to pray," time must be taken from something else. Prayer is a great part of God's plan of blessing for your own life and for the lives of others. Are you faithfully making the time each day to read your Bible and pray? We always make time for the things we really want to do.

For Thinking and Doing:

  1. Read Matthew 6:5-15.

  2. Why do you think it is important to get alone for prayer?

  3. List the things for which Jesus taught us to pray.

  4. Will there be anything new in your prayers because of today's reading?

115th Day

Why Pray?

"You do not have, because you do not ask" (James 4:2).

Some people are like the men Job tells about, who said of God, "What profit do we get if we pray to Him? We have everything we want. Why should we pray?" They turn their backs on the One who said, "Call to Me and I will answer you" (Jeremiah 33:3).

Do you ever ask yourself, "Why pray?" You, too, may feel it is a waste of time or that God doesn't seem to answer prayer. Didn't the Lord Jesus say, "Your Father knows what you need before you ask Him" (Matthew 6:8)? Since the all-powerful God knows each person's need, why doesn't He give His help without being asked? Why is it that God does not save souls or do His work in the world unless His people pray?

If our heavenly Father gave and did all that we need without our asking, we would lose more than we gained, for true prayer is not just a way of getting what we want. The most important thing about prayer is that it puts us in touch with the living God. Prayer is a time when we can talk over matters with Him. Then God by the Holy Spirit speaks to our hearts about our personal affairs, guiding, comforting, strengthening, showing us where we fail or sin and what to do about it.

From near and distant places the radio gathers its messages of sound, yet only those can hear who tune in. So God is also ready and longing to speak to hearts, but only those who tune in by prayer receive the heavenly message.

What is prayer as seen from God's side? He knows that if there were no need for prayer, most Christians would grow careless and leave God out of their lives. He loves us too well to let that disastrous thing happen. Prayer keeps us depending on the Lord. He has asked Christians to pray, and to do so proves that we love Him and want to obey Him. It means we care for His interests as well as our own.

Why pray? Here are a few reasons:

1. Because there are things we will never receive unless we do.

2. Because God is willing to answer prayer and promises to do so.

3. Because prayer brings God's best blessings into our lives.

4. Because Christ prayed much and He is our example.

5. Because the Lord Jesus tells us to; that proves its importance.

6. Because our inner life grows stronger when we keep in close touch with God.

7. Because we are given the great privilege of praying for others and bringing blessing to them.

"We will give ourselves continually to prayer" (Acts 6:4, KJV).

For Thinking and Doing:

1. Reread today's opening verse and Matthew 6:9; 21:22; James 5:13-16.

2. Fit each one of the above verses with one of the seven reasons we should pray.

3. Which reasons seem the most important to you?

4. Which verse in today's reading meant the most to you?

Prayer Is Asking

"Ask whatever you will, and it shall be done for you" (John 15:7).

The storekeeper of a little shop around the corner has a busy time. Some girls come in for a quart of ice cream, a boy wants tennis balls, and a woman buys fresh peaches. So it goes all day. Those who come ask for particular things; they pay the proper price and get what they want.

The Bible tells of people who prayed to God for certain things and received what they asked for. Some of the things seemed rather small and some were great impossibilities, but God granted their requests. Elijah "prayed fervently that it might not rain, and for three years and six months it did not rain on the earth" (James 5:17). Hezekiah, about to die, prayed for healing. Hannah asked God for a son. King Solomon asked for wisdom and understanding. A man born blind asked that he might see. Christ's disciples asked that they might have more faith. You, too, may talk to God about every desire and need, for the Lord does not say, "In some things," but, "in everything" we are to make our wants known to Him.

You can pray anytime and anywhere. Peter prayed from a housetop; David prayed within a cave; Daniel prayed from a lion's den; Jonah prayed while in the belly of a huge fish; and Paul prayed in a prison. Most of us pray in our own room on our knees, but we can lift our hearts in prayer wherever we are and at any time.

God hears and answers a few words or many. A king prayed long and earnestly as he dedicated the beautiful temple to God. Peter, in a time of sudden fear and need, simply said, "Lord, save me" (Matthew 14:30). We may speak aloud to God or quietly within our hearts. It is often good to speak aloud to God, just as we would to a friend, as we kneel to pray.

When should we pray? "Pray at all times" (Ephesians 6:18). "Evening and morning and at noon He will hear my voice" (Psalm 55:17). You should have at least one definite time for prayer each day. You may also want to just speak to God within your heart about special things throughout the day.

The person who is speaking to God and the prayer itself are far more important than the time, place, or kind of prayer. "The Lord looks on the heart" (I Samuel 16:7) of the one who prays. We must be in earnest and be obedient to His Word. "The earnest prayer of a righteous man has great power and wonderful results" (James 5:16, LNT). "The eyes of the Lord are toward the righteous and His ears toward their cry" (Psalm 34:15).

"Give ear to my words, O Lord . . . for to Thee do I pray" (Psalm 5:1, 2).

For Thinking and Doing:

1. Read Psalm 27:7, 8; Psalm 48:1, 9; Psalm 62:1, 2, 5, 8.

2. What do you learn about prayer from these verses from the Psalms?

3. Is there a thought about prayer in today's reading that is helpful to you?

4. What promise are you claiming from today's verses?

117th Day

Prayer Is Listening

"Let me hear what God the Lord will speak" (Psalm 85:8).

In the small booth of a radio station a man was broadcasting. He heard no voice except his own and saw nothing except what was in that small room. This broadcaster was sending out a call for help for hundreds of people made homeless by a flood. But was anyone listening to him? He soon got the answer, for gifts came pouring in of money, food and clothes. These all proved that his call for help was heard.

Men are sending satellites and space ships far, far into outer space. As they fly in their courses at terrific speed, the tiny instruments they carry send messages back to earth so that we can know more about the universe which is all around us.

We are like the man in the radio booth. We do not see the One to Whom we pray. Is God really there and listening? Then these things we asked for begin to come, and we realize our prayers were heard by a living Person. We are like the scientists who listen for the messages sent back to earth by the space ships and satellites. We need comfort, help, guidance, wisdom or courage to do what is right. We send up our ship of prayer. We listen carefully and soon word comes down to us from God. He may speak to us through some verse in His Book or somehow He will speak to our hearts. And always it will be exactly what we need.

Our prayers go farther and faster than any space ship. They go right into heaven and into the heart of our loving, heavenly Father. No satellite can enter heaven and send back messages to us. But there is a God in heaven who has said, "Call to Me, and I will answer you" (Jeremiah 33:3). "Ask, and it will be given you" (Matthew 7:7). "The Lord hears the prayer" of His own dear children (Proverbs 15:29). "He will surely be gracious to you at the sound of your cry; when He hears it, He will answer you" (Isaiah 30:19).

It is to the praying Christian that God gives a noble part in the working out of all His plans. The wisest and greatest of all people, old or young, are those who pray and whose prayers are being chosen by God to carry out His will down here on earth. Will you be one of those chosen ones?

The Psalms are filled with prayers; you can use them as your own whenever they express your own thoughts and needs. They can become a guidebook to teach you to pray.

For Thinking and Doing:

1. Read Psalm 145:18, 19, 21; Psalm 146:1-8; Psalm 85:8.
2. What assurance about prayer is given in Psalm 145:18, 19?
3. For what reasons does the psalmist praise the Lord in Psalm 146:1-8?
4. To whom will God speak according to Psalm 85:8?

118th Day

Confident Prayer

"We receive from Him whatever we ask" (I John 3:22).

The Lord Jesus promises His children, "If you ask anything in My name, I will do it" (John 14:14). "How wonderful!" we exclaim and start praying for all sorts of things. But wait. What else does the Word say? "This is the confidence which we have in Him, that if we ask anything according to His will He hears us. And . . . whatever we ask, we know that we have obtained the requests made of Him" (I John 5:14, 15). Isn't it wonderful? Yet there is that big "if."

God promises to do as we ask if we pray for that which is His will; therefore, we need to discover what His will is. We are told, "Do not be foolish, but understand what the will of the Lord is" (Ephesians 5:17).

How can we find out God's will? Read the promises in God's Word. He will never erase what He has written; He will not change His mind. "I am the Lord, I change not" (Malachi 3:6, KJV).

These are some of the promises given for things in His will:

1. He promises wisdom as to what you say or do, where you go and when, to help you with your studies at school, in your choice of friends, and for every other thing. "If any of you lacks wisdom, let him ask God . . . and it will be given him" (James 1:5).

2. God is more interested in you than you are. He is ready to give you all that is necessary to make you like Christ—a true Christian. "This is God's will—your growing holy" (I Thessalonians 4:3, Berkeley).

3. He is willing to supply every need of yours, such as food, clothes, money for college, or a job. "My God will supply every need of yours according to His riches in glory in Christ Jesus" (Philippians 4:19).

4. He will give us "richly all things (all right things) to enjoy" (I Timothy 6:17, KJV).

As you read the Bible you can find many other wonderful things God is willing to do for His asking children. Go to God in prayer about them and say, "This is what I ask, dear Lord; this is what You have promised." "God said, 'Ask what I shall give you'" (I Kings 3:5). "My covenant (promise) will I not break" (Psalm 89:34, KJV).

For Thinking and Doing:

1. Reread all the verses in today's reading. Read Colossians 1:9.

2. How can we be confident of answered prayer according to I John 5:14, 15?

3. How important is it to ask God for wisdom? See Colossians 1:9.

4. Memorize the promise that means most to you and claim it.

Prayer for His Will

"If any man's will is to do His will, he shall know" (John 7:17).

> Lord, I have shut the door.
> Speak now the Word
> Which, in the din and crowd
> Could not be heard.
> Hushed now my inner heart;
> Whisper Thy will;
> While I have come apart,
> While all is still.
> —William Runyan (adapted)

There is always much to pray about which the Bible does not speak of specifically. How can we know God's will about such things? For instance, if I am to attend a Christian conference, I'll need to pray for extra money, but does God want me to go? I would like to ask the Lord to make me a good football player so as to be a witness for Him on the school team, but would He rather have me doing something else? My best friend and my sister are trying to win the same scholarship for college. Both are Christians; both are praying for it and want me to pray for them. How shall I pray, for both cannot win?

It's all right to ask for money for the conference and for help to make the team, but be sure to turn everything over to the Lord to do as He knows is best. Tell your heavenly Father that these things are what you want if He is willing to give them and that if He is willing, you fully trust Him to do it. If the answer does not come, you will know that He has some better plan for you. When praying about the scholarship, pray that God will enable the girl of His choice to win.

No, we may not always know our heavenly Father's will, but there is One who does. You remember that the Lord Jesus spoke of the Holy Spirit as One called alongside to help us and to help us pray. Often we do not know what prayers to offer nor in what way to offer them, but "the Holy Spirit helps us with our daily problems and in our praying. For we don't even know what we should pray for, nor how to pray as we should, but the Holy Spirit prays for us with such feeling that it cannot be expressed in words . . . He pleads for us in harmony with God's own will" (Romans 8:26, 27, LNT).

Because the Spirit is one of the Persons of God, He knows exactly how God the Father wants us to pray. Many times the Lord is only waiting for His children to ask so that He may begin to give. Deep down in our hearts there are joys and sorrows, hopes and discouragements, longings and fears which confuse and worry us. The Holy Spirit, who lives within each Christian, knows all these things; He knows just how we should pray about them. So we are to be "praying always . . . in the Spirit" (Ephesians 6:18, KJV), putting ourselves under His control and guidance when we pray.

For Thinking and Doing:

1. Read Romans 8:26, 27; Mark 3:35; Hebrews 13:20, 21; Acts 13:22; Luke 22:41, 42.

2. According to Romans 8:26, 27, Whose help do we have in knowing God's will?

3. How is David described in Acts 13:22?

4. How did Jesus conclude His prayer in Luke 22:4l, 42.

120th Day

Prayer in His Will

"Thy will be done on earth" (Matthew 6:10).

There was trouble in the land of Israel. For three and one-half years there was no rain. Crops withered and died under the blazing sun. Would all the people and animals perish also?

God had a plan and told it to His servant Elijah. "I will send rain upon the earth" (I Kings 18:1). That was a wonderful message for starving people. Yet Elijah did not hurry away to spread the good news. Instead he climbed to a lonely hilltop and there he bowed himself down on the ground and earnestly prayed for the rain which the Lord had already promised to send. Was that strange? No, for God uses His children's prayers as a means of getting His will done on earth. Our Lord said, "Pray then like this,

Our Father . . . Thy will be done on earth, as it is in heaven" (Matthew 6:9, 10).

The Bible teaches that this world is moving toward tremendous events—wonderful things which will cause His people much joy and terrible things, causing those without God to cry out in terror. Nations will be changed, governments will fall, and there will be amazing happenings. God has plans concerning all these things, but so has the devil. In His Word God shows us a picture, or pattern, of His plan for the future of this earth and Satan's way of hindering it. Part of these two patterns seems to be quickly taking shape around us now. Perhaps the last pieces of the puzzle are being put into place.

God's plans are fully carried out as His people pray according to His plan. If by prayer you and I are not helping to bring about God's will on earth, we are making it easy for Satan to work in his evil ways. Communism and all other godlessness are part of Satan's plan; God's plan is that both people and nations should believe in and follow Christ. We should pray for our nation and its leaders. We should pray for missionary work so that those who have never heard the Gospel may hear its good news of God's plan of salvation through Christ.

The Lord calls you into partnership. Your family, friends, church, school, nation and the world are all to be reached by God through prayer—your prayers. Our part is to pray; His part is to work as we pray.

In the Army there are certain groups of trusted men trained for all kinds of service. They have no regular place of duty and are sent only where the commanding officer sees there is a special need. Our prayers for others should be like that, with our Commanding Officer, the Holy Spirit, directing our prayers to the very place, person or thing where God sees they are needed. He will guide you by some Scripture verses, or He may just use your mind and guide your thoughts. "In everything by prayer" (Philippians 4:6). "By the Spirit which He has given us" (I John 3:24).

For Thinking and Doing:

1. Read I Kings 18:1, 41-46; Matthew 18:12-14.

2. How many times did Elijah have to continue his prayer for rain? See I Kings 18:43.

3. What does this teach us about prayer, even prayer in God's will?

4. What statement in Matthew 18:14 can be the basis of prayer for those who do not know God?

Powerful Prayer

"The earnest prayer of a righteous man has great power"
(James 5:16, LNT).

Men have learned to make their minds work for them in wonderful ways. They realize that iron and steel are not only much stronger than man's body, but that they never get tired and want to quit. So men have invented all sorts of machines: engines to move huge locomotives, to generate electricity, to cut through mountains, and to lift tremendous weights. Although there is great power in these engines, it lies idle until man pushes a button or pulls a lever; then the power is released and goes to work.

God is "glorious in power" (Exodus 15:6). "With God nothing will be impossible" (Luke 1:37). Nothing is impossible. But most of the time we do not have God's power working for us because we do not pray. For although prayer can do nothing of itself, it is one of the levers which sets free the mighty power of the Lord. And He never grows tired or decides to quit.

> There is an Eye that never sleeps
> Beneath the wings of night!
> There is an Ear that never shuts,
> When sink the beams of light.
> There is an Arm that never tires
> When human strength gives way.
> There is a love that never fails,
> When human loves decay.
>
> There is a power which man can wield,
> When human help is vain
> That Eye, that Heart, that Arm to reach,
> That listening Ear to gain.
> That power is prayer, that reaches high
> Through Jesus to God's throne;
> It moves the Hand which moves the world,
> And brings the answer down.
> —James A. Wallace (adapted)

Through God prayer becomes one of the mightiest forces in the universe, affecting minds, hearts, bodies, people and things. It can go wherever God can go. It can travel any distance and into any place. Walls cannot keep prayer out nor shut it in. As we pray He changes things and people. As we pray God will give the results. "As for me, far be it from me that I should sin . . . by ceasing to pray for you" (I Samuel 12:23).

For Thinking and Doing:

1. Read Matthew 28:18; II Corinthians 4:7 Ephesians 1:19; II Peter 1:3.

2. According to Matthew 28:18, how complete is Christ's power?

3. What reason does II Peter 1:3 give us that we may have power in prayer?

4. Ask God to teach you how to pray effectively.

122nd Day

Persistent Prayer

"Keep on asking and you will keep on getting; keep on looking and you will keep on finding" (Luke 11:9, LNT).

> Did you come to Him believing,
> Trusting on, yet not receiving,
> Tho' His promise
> You have claimed and made your own?
> And you know He walks beside you,
> Yet His love has long denied you
> Just the blessing
> You most covet from His throne?
> —Marjorie Lewis Lloyd

Have you been asking God to make real that which He has promised? Although you pray and pray there may be no sign of an answer. You might think, "It seems as if God has forgotten. I might as well give up asking or expecting." Jesus says Christians "ought always to pray and not to faint" (Luke 18:1, KJV). What does a person do who faints? He gives up and flops. We need to keep on praying, for it often takes time for God to answer prayer.

Perhaps you are wanting to do or be some special thing for Him. Remember the Lord can't accomplish His best work using half-made instruments; He has to make us worthy of the trust. The greater the thing asked for, the greater the time it takes to prepare a life to receive it. So He keeps us waiting. It strengthens our faith; it teaches patience and humility of heart, and we learn how to live in the control of the Holy Spirit. Sometimes when no answer comes and we ask God to show us why, He lets us see the hindering sins we did not know were there. Then we realize our help can come from God alone.

173

It may be that you feel led to pray earnestly for some particular blessing and nothing happens. That need not mean your prayer is wrong, but rather that Jesus is answering, "Yes, I know your love and how you want to please Me, but you are not yet ready for the answer. First there are lessons to learn of trust and obedience so that I can be your life. Your prayer is the very thing I want for you. Believe in Me. In the right time the answer will come."

"I am the Lord . . . they shall not be ashamed that wait for Me" (Isaiah 49:23, KJV). "For I know the plans I have for you, says the Lord: plans for welfare . . . to give you a future and a hope" (Jeremiah 29:11). "The Lord is good to those who wait for Him" (Lamentations 3:25). In the waiting time, keep close to the Lord. "Be still, and know that I am God" (Psalm 46:10). It is the Almighty One who is working for you. "Rest in the Lord, and wait patiently for Him" (Psalm 37:7, KJV). All He asks of you is a loving faith and obedience. He is both kind and just and wants to answer your prayer.

For Thinking and Doing:

1. Read Luke 11:5-13.
2. What reason did He give that the friend was given what he asked?
3. What do you think this story of Jesus is meant to teach us?
4. What gift does He say we should ask for?

123rd Day

Expectant Prayer

"If you ask anything in My name, I will do it" (John 14:14).

Few people in civilized countries hide away money in an old sock beneath a mattress. Instead it is placed in a bank for safekeeping. The money can be drawn out at any time by using a check, either for one's self or as a way of paying money to another.

Someone has said that most Bible promises are like checks which we receive as gifts, for in them we read what is given to us by God. Let's think about your check promises in this way:

1. You must take it to the right bank—to God.

2. You must sign your name on the back of the check, showing you are the person to receive the money. Are you sure you truly bear the name of "Christian" and have the right to use God's check promises?

3. One would not expect to be given more money than the check promised; nor should you be satisfied with less. Read carefully to see exactly what the Lord promises and expect to receive it. Is God less to be trusted than a bank?

4. The money will be actually given only when you hand the check to the bank. The check is the reason that you can claim and get the money. Are you expecting to receive from God? "Produce your cause, saith the Lord; bring forth your strong reasons" (Isaiah 41:21, KJV). You can hand God's promise to Him, saying, "This, Lord, is the reason why I expect to receive."

5. The signature on your check is the most important part. Without that you have nothing. The Lord Jesus said, "If you ask anything in My name, I will do it" (John 14:14). Everything God promises and gives to a Christian comes to him only through the Lord Jesus and because he is Christ's. It is only because we are His—we are in Him and He is in us—that we may expect answers to prayer. "In Him (Christ) all the promises of God are "Yes" (II Corinthians 1:20, Berkeley). Thus we must always ask in the name of Jesus, and anything to which He says "Yes" will be done.

> His love has no limit,
> His grace has no measure,
> His power has no boundary
> Known unto men,
> For out of His infinite
> Riches in Jesus
> He giveth, and giveth,
> And giveth again.
> —J. E. Myhill

For Thinking and Doing:

1. Read John 16:23, 24; Psalm 25:11; Psalm 31:3.

2. What specific promise does Christ give in John 16:23, 24?

3. Do you think you could pray in His name for anything which was not in His will?

4. Memorize Psalm 31:3 and use it as your prayer today.

United Prayer

"If two of you agree on earth about anything they ask, it will be done for them by My Father in heaven" (Matthew 18:19).

Some years ago I met with a group of Christians much older than myself. At the close of the meeting each of the others prayed. Then it was my turn. No one moved except me. I shook as though I were about to be shot! Finally I managed to gulp out a few words which sounded like I was being strangled. It was my first time of praying aloud before others, and it put me in a panic. Since then, many times I have thanked the Lord for shoving me into that experience.

Most of our praying is done alone, and through God each prayer made according to His will and from a clean heart has power to bring about what He wants done. Yet it is very important to join with others who pray for the same things, for then the power is multiplied and increased.

When the Lord Jesus taught His disciples that if two agree about anything they ask, it would be done for them, He did not mean that two or more people can get together and lightly say, "Let's agree to pray about this or that." No, it is only when the Holy Spirit puts the same desires for special things into their hearts and then leads them to pray in deep earnestness, that God hears and acts. It is a picture of two or more men standing back to back, striking out against an enemy or of a number joining together to carry a very heavy load.

Jesus also promised His own, "Where two or three are gathered in My name, there am I in the midst of (with) them" (Matthew 18:20). Yes, when two, five or 100 believing, Spirit-led Christians pray together, things begin to happen. It is then that Jesus, Whose power is almighty, joins the group, praying with them and standing with them.

Pray with others whenever possible. Pray aloud, talking to God. Ask Him to open the eyes of your heart so that you will see the needs of others for whom He would have you pray.

> For the days are dark, the work is great,
> And time is slipping away.
> So whatever we think of doing for God,
> We had better do it today.
> —Author unknown

For Thinking and Doing:

1. Read Acts 16:16-34.
2. What were Paul and Silas doing when the earthquake came?
3. What was the wonderful result of their imprisonment?
4. Do you have a Christian friend with whom you can pray? If not, why not find one?

Praise in Prayer

"Always be thankful no matter what happens, for that is God's will for you who belong to Christ Jesus" (I Thessalonians 5:18, LNT).

A Christian business man and an unbeliever were seated together at a table. Before beginning the meal the business man bowed his head and thanked God for the food. The unbeliever sneered. It was not the fashion, he said, for well-educated people to pray at the table. The Christian replied that he always gave thanks for his food. Which are we like: the business man or the unbeliever? Are we so grateful to God for His countless gifts that we tell Him so, or do we accept everything as if we had it coming? We don't like to be treated in that way; neither does God.

Perhaps you think you have very little for which to be thankful. But if you are God's child, you should realize that you are rich indeed. The mighty, all-wise Ruler of this vast universe, Who is your Father in heaven, loves you, cares for you, and guides you now and forever. You have the privilege of prayer and the promise of answers. You know Jesus is your dearest friend and the source of joy and great blessing in your life.

You may have to do without many things that others have, but someday you'll discover that it doesn't matter much. When you are unhappy because of what you don't have, just start thanking the Lord for what you do have and see what happens. "I will praise the name of God . . . with thanksgiving. This also shall please the Lord" (Psalm 69:30, 31, KJV).

"The Lord . . . hath showed me His marvelous kindness" (Psalm 31:21, KJV). "It is good to give thanks to the Lord, to sing praises to Thy name, O Most High, to declare Thy steadfast love in the morning, and Thy faithfulness by night" (Psalm 92:1, 2). Begin your morning prayer by praising God for what He is. Will you thank Him for His kindness, for past answers to prayer, and for the answers which are on their way?

177

Always remember to thank the Lord Jesus for all the blessings you have because you are His.

> Praise the Savior you who know Him
> Who can tell how much we owe Him?
> Gladly let us render to Him
> All we are and have.
>
> —Thomas Kelly

For Thinking and Doing:

1. Read Psalm 103:1-5, 8-14, 17, 18.
2. Name things for which David praises the Lord in verses 1-5.
3. For what does he praise the Lord in verses 8-14?
4. Give thanks to Him today, naming some of His benefits to you.

126th Day

Faith and Prayer

"When you ask Him, be sure that you really expect Him to tell you" (James 1:6, LNT).

Huge locomotives have power to pull thousands of tons of steel and other weights over high mountains and for many hundreds of miles. Yet they cannot do this without rails to run on, and there must be two rails; only one would be useless.

There is no limit to what God can do in answer to prayer, but He works only as His people use the track along which His power moves. This track must also have two rails: one is prayer and the other is faith. It is no use to put down the rail of prayer unless you lay the rail of faith along beside it and for all the way.

The Lord has promised to hear and answer all prayer made according to His will and from a clean heart. If we do not believe God keeps His promises, we should not ask. "Ask in faith, with no doubting, for he who doubts is . . . a double-minded man" (James 1:6, 8). A person of that sort must not expect to receive anything from the Lord.

There is no need to wonder if our Almighty Father in heaven is able to keep His Word, for God the Son tells us that "all things are possible with God" (Mark 10:27). He tells us, "If you have faith as a grain of mustard seed . . . nothing shall be impossible to you" (Matthew 17:20), that is, nothing which is God's will. "Have faith in God . . . whoever . . . does not doubt in his heart, but believes that what he says will come to pass, it will be done for him. Therefore I tell you, whatever you ask in prayer, believe that you receive it, and you will" (Mark 11:22-24).

What are you praying for now? Is it in the will of God? Have you claimed a promise from Him? The Lord asks you about that very thing, even though it seems impossible, "Do you believe that I am able to do this? According to your faith be it done to you" (Matthew 9:28, 29).

> When once His Word is passed;
> When He has said, "I will,"
> The thing shall come at last.
> God keeps His promise still.
> —Author unknown

You may say, "But I have so little faith, and I'm asking for such big things." Don't think about how weak your faith is, but of what God is able to do. "The Lord is able to give you much more than this" (II Chronicles 25:9).

Again you might say, "But I don't feel as if my prayers are being answered." Faith is one thing and feeling is another. Don't trust your feelings, trust God and count on His faithfulness to you.

> For feelings come and feelings go,
> And feelings are deceiving.
> My safety is the Word of God;
> Naught else is worth believing.
> —Martin Luther

For Thinking and Doing:

1. Read Acts 27:1, 2, 13, 14, 18-29; 39-44.
2. Pick out instances, in this exciting story of shipwreck, of how Paul showed his faith.
3. Find a verse that indicates he also was praying.
4. Memorize Matthew 9:29.

127th Day

God Hears

"He is before all things, and in Him all things hold together" *(Colossians 1:17).*

Two people are talking: a non-Christian and a Christian.

"It is no use to pray. Praying is just saying words. God won't change people, things and happenings simply because someone

179

asks Him to!''

"But the words people say to us often make great changes in what we do, both for ourselves and for others."

"Well, perhaps God can sometimes change people, but everyone knows He can't change the physical laws of the universe."

"What are those laws? Physical laws are those things and actions by which the different parts of the universe are kept in order, are kept going on in a regular way, and because of which, when a certain thing happens, the results will always be the same. For instance, under the law of evaporation, damp objects lose their dampness when exposed to the air. Gravity is the force that draws all objects toward the center of the earth."

"Yes, and if God interfered with those laws everything would be upset!"

"Does it upset the law of gravity when a plane flies miles up into the sky? Of course not. It only shows that another force has been brought in—that of a propeller or a jet—which is stronger than the law of gravity. For centuries man thought it was impossible for men to fly, but increased knowledge has made it possible. No man knows enough to say what God can or cannot do. Nor can he tell by how many still-unknown laws the Almighty is governing and working in His universe. Man did not make the laws controlling the universe, nor can he put an end to them. For these laws are the will of God in action."

The Bible tells us God hears prayer, He asks for it, and He answers it. This being so, He must have created all things in such a way as to leave room for answers to prayer, and to keep for Himself the right to change things by making use of other laws, of which man knows absolutely nothing. "Known unto God are all His works from the beginning of the world" (Acts 15:18, KJV). "Who has known the mind of the Lord or who has been His counselor" (to give Him advice)? (Romans 11:34). "His ways (are) past finding out" (Romans 11:33, KJV). "None can . . . say to Him, 'What doest Thou?'" (Daniel 4:35).

To doubt that prayer is answered is to doubt the Father who promises, "Call to Me, and I will answer you" (Jeremiah 33:3). God the Son says, "If ye shall ask anything in My name, I will do it" (John 14:14). "What if some were without faith? Shall their want (lack) of faith make of none effect the faithfulness of God? No indeed; let us hold God to be true, though every man should prove to be false" (Romans 3:3, 4, Williams).

For Thinking and Doing:

1. Read Psalm 4:3; Psalm 145:19; Job 22:25-27; Luke 1:45.
2. What is the basis for the assurance the Psalmist has that God will hear his prayer? See Psalm 4:3; Psalm 145:19.
3. What similar thought do you find in Job 22:25-27?
4. Put your own name in the place of "she" in Luke 1:45.

God Answers

"Since He did not spare even His own Son for us but gave Him up for us all, won't He also surely give us everything else? (Romans 8:32, LNT).

During the world war a submarine lay on the ocean floor. For two days the crew tried in every way to raise it to the surface of the water, but is was no use. Finally the men realized that they were doomed. No ship would come to help them because none knew where they were. Facing a sure and agonizing death, these helpless men sang a hymn of prayer to God. It was a prayer of desperate need and longing from each heart.

> Abide with me: fast falls the eventide;
> The darkness deepens, Lord with me abide;
> When other helpers fail, and comforts flee,
> Help of the helpless, O abide with me.
> —H. F. Lyte

Then to make death a little less awful, the commanding officer gave each man some medicine to quiet his nerves. Suddenly one of the sailors fell, unconscious. As he dropped his body struck a small piece of machinery. There was a sound of something moving. The jammed machinery had been set in motion by that jolt and the submarine rose to the surface and made port safely. This is truly an unusual story, but it illustrates in what unexpected ways prayer can be answered.

The Lord wanted to save those men. "He already knew what He was going to do" (John 6:6, TEV). He was waiting until they called upon Him. Suppose they hadn't called? We miss many blessings through failing to pray. "You do not have, because you do not ask" (James 4:2). We should make the disciples' prayer our own: "Lord, teach us to pray" (Luke 11:1). We should learn, not simply how to pray, but to pray—to do it.

181

We must not grow discouraged when God does not work in just the way and when we think He will. Often the Lord does the utterly unexpected thing, and He may keep us waiting until the very last moment. Although an answer may be delayed, He is never too late. "For My thoughts are not your thoughts, neither are your ways My ways, says the Lord. For as the heavens are higher than the earth, so are My ways higher than your ways and My thoughts than your thoughts" (Isaiah 55:8, 9).

> In His own way they come,
> The answers to our prayers;
> Not always as we thought they would,
> Nor even as we felt they should,
> But in the wisdom of a God
> Who understands and cares.
> In His own time we see
> The things His love has planned.
> And when we find that they are best,
> We wonder that we did not rest,
> But fretted, since we could not see
> The workings of His hand.
> —Author unknown

For Thinking and Doing:

1. Read Matthew 6:25-33; Isaiah 64:4.

2. What everyday needs does the Lord say will be given to us? See Matthew 6:25-33.

3. What are we to do according to Matthew 6:33?

4. What does Isaiah 64:4 say is our part?

129th Day

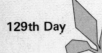

How He Answers

"No good thing does the Lord withhold from those who walk uprightly" (Psalm 84:11).

"Aw, Mom, let me . . . "

"Please, Dad, give me . . . "

Has any boy or girl you know ever said that? We all have and we all know the answers. Sometimes it was "Yes;" that was fine.

It might have been "No;" then we felt mistreated. There were other answers too, such as "Perhaps, I'll see," or "Yes, but not until you are older." So all we could do was wait or try to do everything to convince Mother and Dad that they could trust us and give us what we wanted.

Now that we are older we can understand why parents often have to say "No," "Wait," or "Perhaps." No matter how a child cried for it, no mother would give a child a large, sharp knife to play with. A father would not put a 6-year-old boy at the wheel of a high-powered car and turn him loose to drive alone down a busy street. We have to wait for such things until we are wise and strong enough to use them properly.

God is our Father. When we ask something of Him in prayer, He often has to answer like our earthly parents do. Sometimes the Lord quickly gives what we ask, but at other times it may be hard to understand exactly what He is answering. How can we know? In some cases God always says "No." He will not do what we ask if it would lead us away from Him. Our Lord never gives that which would harm us or another. He also says "No" about everything which is forbidden in his Word. "You ask and do not receive, because you ask wrongly" (James 4:3).

Perhaps you do not fulfill the conditions for the answer He is longing to give you. Are you wilfully going on in some sin, disobedient to His voice within? "If I regard iniquity in my heart, the Lord will not hear" (Psalm 66:18). Don't hang on to anything that is wrong. Confess it as sin and let go of it. Then you have cleared the track and made way for the prayer answers to come through. Are you neglecting God's Word and prayer? "If you abide in Me, and My words abide in you, ask whatever you will, and it shall be done for you" (John 15:7).

There are times when God is trying to teach you something that will help you, or He wants to give you something better than what you asked for. You may be asking for something as valueless as a piece of costume jewelry when He plans to give you some priceless jewel.

Sometimes young people pray to be given the boy friend or girl friend of their choice when God knows that friend would not be best for them and that His choice would be the perfect one. "You do not have because you do not ask" (James 4:2). "You ask and do not receive, because you ask wrongly" (James 4:3). Sometimes God's answer is "Wait." That for which you pray will come in His time.

For Thinking and Doing:

1. Reread all the Scripture verses in today's reading.

2. If you are not having prayer answered, try to find whether the reason may be in those given above.

3. Can you know if you are asking for something forbidden in His Word unless you read it?

4. Claim for yourself the promise of Psalm 84:11.

130th Day

How to Pray

"It is good to give thanks to the Lord" (Psalm 92:1).

Here is Anne, who has just been chosen student body president at school. Of course she wants to succeed in her new task, not only for her own sake, but that she may also be an honor to the school and a help to the students. To be successful Anne must think about four things: members of the school faculty, her own words and actions, what others may do to help or hinder, and the added work and effort expected of her.

God has chosen every Christian for the most important tasks in all the world. One of these is prayer. If we would succeed, we too must take four things into account:

1. God, to Whom we pray.

2. The person or thing prayed for.

3. Our enemy Satan, who is against us.

4. We who pray, and if we really want God's will.

In later readings we shall think about the last three things of which we must take into account as we pray. Today let us think about God, to Whom we pray.

He is able to do and willing to answer. Although we may pray at any time, in order to do real business with God we need a quiet place alone with Him. "When you pray," Jesus counseled, "go into your room and shut the door and pray to your Father who is in secret (or unseen), and your Father . . . will reward you" (Matthew 6:6). It takes faith to speak to someone unseen, but our Lord Jesus would never tell us to do a useless thing. Our Father promises, "While they are yet speaking I will hear" (Isaiah 65:24).

To get alone with God is well worth the time it takes. Shut in with Him and all disturbing things shut out, we can speak to our loving Father as freely as to our dearest friend. Indeed, we may speak more easily to Him, for He knows all about us anyway. "Come now, let us reason together, says the Lord" (Isaiah 1:18). It is as if He says, "Let us talk matters over together. Tell Me all that troubles you, and what you want and need for yourself and others, and I shall speak to you and show you what to do."

It is in the quiet place that we see God and ourselves most clearly. Here we get a glimpse of God. He makes Himself known to us through His Word and the inner voice of the Holy Spirit. We should always kneel in prayer to God, "Who is . . . majestic in holiness" (Exodus 15:11). Jesus Himself kneeled down to pray when He was on earth. So let us go sincerely into His presence because "If My people . . . humble themselves, and pray and seek My face . . . then will I hear from heaven" (II Chronicles 7:14). "O come, let us worship and bow down, let us kneel before the Lord our Maker! For He is our God" (Psalm 95:6, 7).

For Thinking and Doing:

1. Read Matthew 6:5-15.

2. What do you think is the reward mentioned in Matthew 6:6?

3. For what things does Christ teach us to ask in the Lord's Prayer?

4. Which are we more likely to ask for, and what important things do we sometimes fail to ask for?

Hindrances to Answers

"It is good that one should wait quietly for the salvation of the Lord" (Lamentations 3:26).

It is easy for a strong man to move an object weighing even more than himself. It is easy for God to hold up the universe with its billions of speeding, whirling stars. The reason why God and man can handle things so easily is that things have no thoughts of their own; they have no will which refuses to do this or that. But God does not, and man cannot, force another person to think different thoughts. Each of us can keep control of our own thinking and own will if we choose to do so.

Thus today, as we are thinking of the person or thing prayed for we see why things asked for are often received so quickly and prayers for people can remain unanswered for years. It may be prayer for some dear friend or someone in the family whose heart is far from God, uncaring and unsaved. The strong will is set to go its own way—the way that "leads to destruction" (Matthew 7:13). By man's standard, that life may be very good or very bad, but it is perishing because it is without Christ. "Those who are far from Thee shall perish" (Psalm 73:27). Your earnest prayers for that one may still be unanswered.

Yet God has ways of causing that person to change his thinking and to turn his will in the right direction. Years ago many farmers used mules in plowing and harvesting. Those big, stubborn beasts often refused to do what they were supposed to; no amount of whacking, pushing or pulling budged them even an inch. What happened then? A small fire was kindled on the ground beneath the mule and soon he was glad enough to get going. Sometimes God has to push, pull, or even to build a fire.

Three things hinder hearts from turning to God. They are self, sin and Satan. God may often have to let a person fail in many ways until he discovers that his own self is not to be trusted. God may have to let him go on in sin until, through suffering or great sorrow, he sees that sin has been the cause. Satan often uses worldly pleasures and success to keep a person from the Lord; a person is so satisfied with them he does not see his need of a Savior.

The Lord can quickly bring to Himself one whose heart is willing, but when He has much to do in a life, it will take time. Pray on; God uses prayer as a powerful, moving force against whatever is holding that person in bondage.

Remember God's power, love and promises. Remind Him of them. "Remember Thy Word to Thy servant, in which Thou hast made me hope" (Psalm 119:49). "It is good that one should wait quietly for the salvation of the Lord" (Lamentations 3:26). For "The Word of our God shall stand for ever" (Isaiah 40:8). "Continue steadfastly in prayer" (Colossians 4:2).

Whether the prayer is for yourself, for someone who is not a Christian, or for the blessings of God to be upon another Christian (they, too, may set their will against Him), remember that it often takes time for God to answer prayer.

For Thinking and Doing:

1. Read Matthew 7:13, 14, 21-27.
2. What way of life is represented by the wide gate and easy way?

3. Who does Matthew 7:24 say is the wise man?

4. If you are praying for someone who is not a Christian, keep on praying.

Difficulties Encountered

"Put on all the armor God gives you, so that you will stand up against the Devil's evil tricks" (Ephesians 6:11, TEV).

> True-hearted, whole-hearted, faithful and loyal,
> King of our lives, by Thy grace we will be;
> Under the standard exalted and royal,
> Strong in Thy strength we will battle for Thee.
> —F. R. Havergal

How does one do battle for the King? One way is by prayer. We don't get very far along before discovering that we must take into account someone else in this matter of prayer besides God, ourselves and the person or thing prayed for. The enemy of our souls is Satan, who is fighting against us. Satan is against prayer. He will do everything possible (and he can do a lot) to hinder God's work and will being done in another life or to get us to give up praying.

All Christians find it difficult to pray at times. When we start to pray God may seem unreal and far away. We may try a bit and then decide to wait until we feel that God is hearing. But is God real or unreal according to whatever we happen to feel about Him? Perhaps there has been too much work or play and a sleepy head or tired body gets us down. When there is no prayer someone misses the touch of God upon his life and some blessing of God fails to reach its mark—perhaps a blessing meant for you.

People are soul and spirit, mind and heart in a physical body. God's children always have their human nature as well as His nature within. Our new, Spirit-led nature has a desire to pray, yet our human minds are taken up with things of self and the world. Sometimes it is an effort to think about the things of God; we just don't want to.

We are like the three disciples whom Jesus asked to pray for Him when He was in a time of terrible agony. Instead of praying they went to sleep. From among hundreds of others, these three were chosen for this precious privilege, but they missed it. It was then that the Lord said to them, "Watch and pray that you may not enter into temptation; the spirit indeed is willing, but the flesh is weak" (Matthew 26:41). "Watch" means an enemy is near. "Pray" because the enemy will do everything to tire and discourage you and to tempt you to give up praying if only for a day.

It is part of the battle to stand against Satan who "trembles when he sees the weakest saint upon his knees." He knows it means his defeat when we pray. Don't just plan to pray—do it! Keep on praying no matter how you feel.

For Thinking and Doing:

1. Read Ephesians 6:10-18.
2. Name the parts of the armor given in this passage.
3. Which ones do you feel are the most important?
4. Are you keeping on in learning God's truth and in your praying?

133rd Day

Assured Answers

"Ask anything, using My name, and I will do it" (John 14:14, LNT).

Are you really wanting to have your prayer answered? If so, notice carefully the things in this verse where Jesus promises, "Whatever you ask in My name, I will do it, that the Father may be glorified in the Son" (John 14:13).

First we are to pray in Jesus' name. To ask in Jesus' name is not just saying those words at the end of a prayer. It is like your Mother sending you to her friend next door to say, "Mother wants to borrow a salad bowl, please." You are not requesting something you want or asking in your own name. You use your Mother's name to ask for something she wants, and for her sake it is given. You see, to truly ask in Christ's name means that we really want His will to be done and that when we pray our desires are exactly the same as His. In heaven the Lord Jesus Himself joins with us, saying, "Father, this is what I want too." Our living Savior is God's beloved Son and is most precious to the Father. So when we ask for that which will give joy and honor to His Son, God will gladly do it for His sake.

What are the things the Son wants done and for which we may pray and expect God to do? John 14:13 tells us we should pray "That the Father may be glorified." What is the meaning of "glory"? The glory of God is the excellence of all He is in His character and the wonder of what He does. Even His home is glorious and beautiful. No one is able to add anything to this glory which is God's. Then how can we glorify, that is give glory to, the Father? He is glorified when we believe in Him, in His wisdom, love, power and holiness, and in all He is and does.

God is glorified when we trust Him. Abraham "was strong in faith, (thus) giving glory to God" (Romans 4:20, KJV). Our lips glorify Him when we use them to praise and thank our Father for His kindnesses and to tell others about Him. "He who offers a sacrifice of praise honors Me" (Psalm 50:23, Berkeley). The Father is given glory when His children are like Christ and so speak, live and pray that others are led to love and trust Him. The Lord tells us, "By this My Father is glorified, that you bear much fruit" (John 15:8).

Will the answers to your prayers glorify the Father? If so, you have Christ's sure word that He will do it. For such praying we need the help of God and the control and leading of the Holy Spirit. "The Spirit helps us . . . for we do not know how to pray as we ought" (Romans 8:26).

For Thinking and Doing:

1. Read Psalms 41:4; 51:6, 10; 86:11; 119:18, 27, 29, 133; 139:23, 24; 143:8, 10.

2. Name all of the requests in the above verses which you could pray for in His name.

3. Will you bring to God those requests which you especially need to have Him grant?

4. Memorize the verse in today's reading which means the most to you.

Conditions to Answers

"Take care to live in Me, and let Me live in you" (John 15:4, LNT).

The Lord Jesus says, "If you abide in Me, and My words abide in you, ask whatever you will, and it shall be done for you"

(John 15:7). What does it mean to abide? It means to stay in a place, as the spokes of a wheel are fastened into the hub or center of the wheel. The whole power-driven wheel moves as its hub moves, always following the center.

You are really like a wheel. Your life is moved by whatever you choose to be the center of your life. If self is that center, you will want what brings you praise, comfort and pleasure. But is that human self good enough to satisfy God, or even to satisfy you? Surely you must want someone you can always trust—someone noble, true, kind and great—to be the moving force of your life. Only Christ is worthy of that central place. Have you given it to Him?

The promise of answered prayer is given to those who have made Christ the center of their lives and who abide in Him. You may think that is too great a cost to pay for answered prayer. One cannot buy a Cadillac for the price of a bicycle, and the wonderful answers God gives to prayer are worth all they cost.

This is what it means to abide: "He who says he abides in Him ought to walk in the same way in which He walked" (I John 2:6). It is to live as Christ lived. He could say, "I always do what is pleasing to Him" (John 8:29). "All who keep His commandments abide in Him" (I John 3:24). The abiding one studies God's Word to discover His commands and does them. He gives up his own life of self-pleasing and lets the Lord Jesus take over; he does nothing independently of his Lord. His believing, obeying, praying, thinking and planning are all through Christ.

Your heavenly Father wants to bless you and, through you, to bless others. He, the Almighty One, waits to make you an instrument of power—prayer power. While you are praying God will be doing what you ask if your life is Christ-centered rather than self-centered. Is He your Lord and on the throne of your life? Is your life centered around Him or only around yourself?

For Thinking and Doing:

1. Read Jeremiah 29:12, 13; John 12:24-26; I John 3:24.

2. How does Jeremiah 29:13 fit in with the teaching in today's reading?

3. What does John 12:24-26 teach you about living for self?

4. How can we know we are abiding in Him and He in us according to I John 3:24?

Prayer Champions

"We receive from Him whatever we ask, because . . . " (I John 3:22).

A basketball coach knows that the members of his team want to win no matter what it takes. So he keeps teaching and training them how to better their play, not to discourage, but to make them champions. Our heavenly Coach wants each of His own to be prayer champions. So He also teaches us the rules and trains us in the ways of miracle-working prayer.

He seems to say, "I long that you will do and be all that I ask of you so that I can do and give all that you ask of Me. Come, let us together do the mighty works of God." Then He tells us still another thing which is needed for the answers of our prayers. "We receive from Him whatever we ask because we keep His commandments and do what pleases Him" (I John 3:22).

What are His commandments? They are like the rules of the game. Here are some of them:

1. "This is My commandment, that you love one another, as I have loved you" (John 15:12). Have love in your heart, kindness in your thoughts or words, and a desire to love and help others. Have no impatience, no jealousies, but only that which will help another person.

2. "When you are praying, first forgive anyone you are holding a grudge against" (Mark 11:25, LNT). Have no desire to get even for some real or imagined unkindness. Ask the Lord to help you to forgive and forget what was said or done.

3. "If . . . you remember that your brother (this means anyone) has something against you . . . go and make peace with your brother first (Matthew 5:23, 24, Phillips). Make things right between you and others. Some people are not big enough to say, "I'm sorry."

4. "Don't tell lies to each other; it was your old life . . . that did that sort of thing; now it is dead and gone" (Colossians 3:9, LNT). "Instead we will lovingly follow the truth at all times—speaking truly, dealing truly, living truly" (Ephesians 4:15, LNT).

5. "Stay away from sin" (I John 2:1, LNT). This includes unbelief, gossip, unclean thoughts or ways.

6. "Don't worry about anything" (Philippians 4:6, LNT). Don't worry! If we have given ourselves and our affairs to God, it is wrong to doubt His love and care for us.

7. "Do those things which are pleasing in His sight" (I John 3:22, KJV). Just as you can please a friend by doing things you know he will like, we can please God in the same way. "That your daily lives . . . should bring joy to Him who invited you into His kingdom to share His glory" (I Thessalonians 2:12, LNT).

Don't be discouraged when you fail to live up to all the rules at once. Basketball champions are not made in a day and neither are God's. Confess your failure and let Him teach you the better way. He sees the desire of your heart. Keep on trying, trusting and praying. He will help you win the victories.

For Thinking and Doing:

1. Read Psalm 119:10, 11, 32-37; Colossians 1:9, 10.
2. What requests does the psalmist make in these verses from Psalm 119?
3. Do you think God longs to answer such prayers?
4. What does Paul pray for that you will pray for today? See Colossians 1:9, 10.

136th Day

A Great Adventure

"The Lord is your keeper . . . He will keep your life" (Psalm 121:5, 7).

Robin Lee Graham, the young teen-ager who sailed the world alone, has captured the imagination of all those who love adventure. An article with photographs in the National Geographic Magazine tells some of his exciting experiences. His love for sailing began at age 13 when he sailed through the South Seas with his parents and an older brother. On his 16th birthday Robin first revealed his dream of sailing alone from Los Angeles to Honolulu. Some months later, when he had accomplished this safely, he decided to continue and circle the globe.

How could a young lad make such a venture alone? His first sailing experience gave him confidence as his father taught him to navigate by sun and stars with a sextant. The summer before he started out he pored over charts and books with his father to learn the trade winds, ocean currents and weather patterns in order to choose the most favorable route. All across the vast expanse of ocean he would steer a true course with his navigational aids. His father provided for him all the things he would need.

Not many people have the opportunity for such a remarkable adventure, but everyone of us must learn to steer our course in the most thrilling adventure of all—on the sea of life. Like Robin, we need charts and some way to steer a safe course; we must have our needs supplied along the way and have a goal toward which we strive to travel.

God, our heavenly Father, provides the charts and He can help us find the route that will bring us to the goals we seek. The great principles and truths of His Word are charts by which the Christian can choose the right course. His Son is our Pilot who can teach us how to navigate, help us through every mishap, and bring us through rough seas and storms in safety. Unlike Robin, who traveled alone and experienced great loneliness at times, we need never be alone; we have our Pilot with us. "The Lord . . . goes with you, He will not fail you or forsake you" (Deuteronomy 31:6).

Just as there is guidance for the navigator in the stars, so there is guidance for the Christian in God's Word. "Thy Word is a lamp to my feet and a light to my path" (Psalm 119:105). This is one of the ways God leads His children. Two other ways are by the voice of the Holy Spirit speaking within your heart and through the circumstances in your life.

Often when you have a difficult decision to make, you will read some verse of Scripture which almost stands out on the page because it applies so directly to your situation. Again, when you must choose one path or another, you may have a deep impression within you which is the right way. Sometimes God brings circumstances about in our lives or some open door of opportunity that helps to assure us of His leading. But you must remember to ask God to guide you, and then trust Him to do it.

For Thinking and Doing:

1. Read Psalm 107:23-32.
2. Name some of the dangers Robin faced in sailing alone.
3. Compare Robin's need for charts to our own need for the Bible.
4. How important is your familiarity with God's Word?

His Plan

"God is our Maker, and . . . He has created us for a life of good works, which He has already prepared for us to do" (Ephesians 2:10, TEV).

You remember we talked on the 12th day of our readings about the fact that God has a plan for your life, a plan more wonderful than you have ever dreamed. You want your life to count for something and to be the very best.

The greatest thing you can be is what God wants you to be!

You can only reach that best as you allow the Lord to take you there. "I know, O Lord, that the way of man is not in himself, that it is not in man who walks to direct his steps" (Jeremiah 10:23). We cannot know by ourselves whether or not our own plans are the right ones, but "As for God, His way is perfect" (Psalm 18:30, KJV).

Before any of us were born, the Lord knew about our coming, and as He looked into the future He saw just the very place and way in which each of us would be happiest and could serve Him best. Like map makers mark out the road for every mile, God has planned the right way for every step of our lives. Just as a map guides a traveler to a definite place, so the Lord's guidance leads to the fulfillment of His plan.

Before starting to follow a guide one usually wants to know where he is going. At times our Guide tells His children something of His wonderful final plan for them. He told the teen-age Joseph that some day he would be a mighty ruler and He told Paul, the young Jew, that he would be a missionary, yet they knew nothing of the many experiences that lay ahead. But "He led them forth by the right way" (Psalm 107:7, KJV). "He led them in safety, so that they were not afraid" (Psalm 78:53).

Are you truly God's child, that is, born again? Are you trying to please Him? If so, He may have already spoken to your heart about some special work, but if not, it does not mean there is none for you. Jesus is waiting for you to tell Him that you choose His plan for your life and that you give yourself entirely over to Him so that His will can be made plain and you can do it. No one can guide a person who stalks off in the opposite direction. So keep close to your Guide and choose His way, not yours. As you find His plan, He can bring your life and your personality to their greatest fulfillment.

Paul has said in Ephesians 2:10 that God has created His children for a life of good works—works which He has already prepared for us to do. Not just any good works will bring us to the fulfillment, but those that He has chosen for us will.

For Thinking and Doing:

1. Reread all the Scripture verses in today's reading.
2. What reasons can you think of for choosing His plan for your life?
3. What thought in today's reading means the most to you?
4. Choose a favorite verse in today's reading and memorize it.

138th Day

His Way

"Make Thy way straight before me" (Psalm 5:8).

David, the king of Israel, prayed that he would be led in God's paths. Solomon, renowned as the wisest man, wrote in Proverbs 3:5, 6: "Trust in the Lord with all your heart, and do not rely on your own insight. In all your ways acknowledge Him, and He will make straight your paths." The King James Version gives the promise, "He will direct thy paths."

You may say, "How can we know God's plan for our lives and His way in some of the difficult decisions we must make?" We have mentioned in the reading for the 136th day that God leads His children in three ways: through His Word, through the voice of the Holy Spirit speaking to your heart, and through circumstances in your life. You can safely go ahead if all three of these ways are clear and sometimes if only two of them are clear. However, depending upon circumstances alone is unwise.

Jonah had a clear word from the Lord that he was to go to Nineveh, but he chose instead to go in the opposite direction to

Tarshish. Circumstances were favorable: there was a ship going to Tarshish, and he had the fare to pay for the trip. But God had told him to go to Nineveh, and he was running away from God's plan. It is a fascinating story how God brought him to Nineveh in the end, after he had been in the belly of the great fish for three days and three nights. (Incidentally, if you have a friend who can't believe this story, you can tell him there are historical cases on record in the Encyclopedia Brittanica of men who have had the experience of being swallowed by a whale and who lived to tell about it.)

God often leads His children by a clear word from the Bible. It may be a verse you have previously memorized which He will bring back to your remembrance. It may be that some verse will impress you in a special way in your reading of a passage of Scripture or in some message or sermon you hear.

When you have a difficult choice to make in your life, turn first to God's Word and let Him speak to you through it. "Thy Word is a lamp to my feet, and a light to my path" (Psalm 119:105). The light will usually not shine far out ahead, but it will make plain each next step "When you walk, your step will not be hampered" (Proverbs 4:12). Your way will be opened up before you step by step. Just keep on obeying and the path will be made clear as you go forward. "Your path will be clear and open," is the promise of Proverbs 4:12 according to the Amplified Old Testament.

Somewhere in the Scripture there is just the right word to guide you. Ask the Lord to give it to you, but do not flip the pages of the Bible and take the first verse you happen to see. Be sure to ask the Lord to put the very verse of His choosing into your heart and then trust Him to do it. Often one must not only pray about the matter, but wait in quietness before the Lord until He makes His will known. It will not be a waste of time; it is the only safe thing to do. "Commit thy way unto the Lord. Trust also in Him, and He shall bring it to pass" (Psalm 37:5, KJV).

For Thinking and Doing:

1. Read the story of Jonah in Jonah 1; 2:1, 2, 10; 3:1-3.

2. Why did Jonah get into trouble and when did he begin to get out of it?

3. What three things does Proverbs 3:5, 6 tell us are necessary if the Lord is to direct our paths? Memorize verse 6.

4. Pray today for God's guidance for special needs in your daily life.

His Voice

"O that today you would hearken to His voice!" (Psalm 95:7).

Has there ever lived a person who did not need God's guidance? You may reply, "Just one: Jesus, the Son of God." Yet His every act and word was controlled by His Father. He tells us, "The Father . . . has Himself given Me commandment what to say and what to speak" (John 12:49) and, "The works which the Father hath given Me to finish . . . I do" (John 5:36, KJV). As the Father guided the Son in every detail of His life, so will He also teach us by the Holy Spirit.

Because the Holy Spirit lives within each true believer, it is He who reveals God's will. He chooses the very Scripture verse we need for guidance and puts it within our heart. Often the Spirit will press upon us a feeling that we ought to do or say a certain thing. It may sometimes seem that down deep inside we hear words which tell us what to do. It is the Holy Spirit urging, speaking. "Your ears shall hear a word behind you, saying, 'This is the way, walk in it,' when you turn to the right or when you turn to the left" (Isaiah 30:21). What a wonderful promise this is for God's children.

There is something to remember here: the Spirit never shouts. His voice is a sound of gentle stillness. Those who will quiet their own thoughts and wishes and will listen carefully can hear what the Spirit says. Now comes the question, "How can the Spirit's voice be known, recognized and understood?" That takes practice, for the more often we let Him speak to us, the more easily we will know His voice. It is the same way you have learned to know your mother's voice: you've heard it many, many times. Remember to listen as you pray.

In John 10:3, 4, Jesus speaks of the way sheep follow their shepherd. "The sheep hear his voice . . . follow him, for they know his voice." In John 10:27 He says, "My sheep hear My voice, and I know them, and they follow Me." When Christ dwells in our hearts His Holy Spirit speaks to us and we know His voice.

"Be not wise in thine own eyes" (Proverbs 3:7). That means don't trust your own ideas. Instead, "Trust in the Lord with all thine heart. In all thy ways acknowledge Him (allow Him to guide, and then) He shall direct (point out) thy paths" (Proverbs 3:5, 6, KJV). He has promised and He will do it; there is no doubt about it.

A light cannot be seen nor can a gentle voice be heard through a thick wall. Neither can a wall of sin or doubt be allowed to stand between the Holy Spirit and our hearts.

For Thinking and Doing:

1. Read Deuteronomy 15:5, 6; 28:1, 2; 30:9, 10; Psalm 95:6, 7; Matthew 22:37-40.

2. What reason does the psalmist give in Psalm 95 for listening to God's voice?

3. What promise is connected with obeying His voice according to the verses in Deuteronomy?

4. What is the greatest commandment? See Matthew 22:37.

140th Day

His Signs

"I will guide thee with mine eye" (Psalm 32:8, KJV).

In the days of David, servants waiting upon their master watched every moment for the slightest glance or sign which would indicate some service he desired; they were guided by his eyes and hands. In seeking God's will we should look to Him for some sign of His leading. "As the eyes of servants look to the hand of their master, as the eyes of a maid to the hand of her mistress, so our eyes look to the Lord our God" (Psalm 123:2).

We have already seen that His sign may be a verse of Scripture or the leading of His Spirit within our hearts. Besides these, He often gives us some confirming circumstance in our lives.

Our heavenly Father makes use of many things to guide His children. The wise men were led to the baby Jesus by a star; God led an army of David's to victory by the "sound of marching" in the wind-blown tops of the trees (II Samuel 5:24). On a missionary journey Paul was prevented by the leading of the Holy Spirit from going to preach in Asia; God used a vision of a man calling him to come to Macedonia to lead him to go and help them (Acts 16:9).

Today God does not speak to us through visions because we have the Bible. We always need to test a circumstance which appears to be His leading by the principles of His Word.

A young Christian who was working in a bank was praying that she might meet the one God had chosen to be her life partner. One day a very handsome young man, who was new at her bank, began paying special attention to her. Several days later he asked her for a date. Was this the one for whom she had been praying?

During the friendship that developed she realized he was not a Christian, for he scorned the teachings of the Bible and did not go to church. He was not even open to talk about the spiritual things which meant most to her, and he did not honor the One who was her Lord. Remembering God's clear word to all believers in II Corinthians 6:14, "Do not be mismated with unbelievers . . . what has a believer in common with an unbeliever?" she broke off their relationship before they became serious.

Just as Jonah had the opportunity to go to another place than where God intended, so we cannot count on a circumstance alone to guide us; we must look to Him and to His Word.

God not only guides us through open doors of opportunity, but also by closed doors as He did for Paul on his missionary journey. Even a disappointment can turn out to be His appointment. He may lead us to give up some friendship that would hinder our spiritual development in order to bring to us another which will enrich all our lives.

"I will lead the blind in a way that they know not, in paths that they have not known. I will guide them. I will turn the darkness before them into light, the rough places into level ground" (Isaiah 42:16). Our way will be made clear and safe as we trust our Guide and look to Him.

For Thinking and Doing:

1. Read I Thessalonians 5:21; Ephesians 5:17; II Corinthians 6:14-18.

2. How did the girl in today's reading follow the signs of God's Word in the verses above?

3. Why is it important to ask God for His leading about your choice of friends?

4. Will you ask Him today to help you find friendships that will enrich your life, and not hinder you?

Walking Safely

"The Lord alone did lead him . . . cared for him" (Deuteronomy 32:12, 10).

For most of us the days are much alike. Because today will be spent with the same family, the same school, and the same friends, we feel we can get along without God's help. We may think His guidance is needed only in the very important things. But is this true? Suppose that on the walk to school one morning a car suddenly swings around the corner and knocks you down or you slip on the school steps and break an ankle. Then you need help badly. If you had known these things would happen, you would have gone down the steps more carefully. But you didn't.

It was just one little step which caused a fall and a broken ankle. Just so, one wrong choice or one step out of God's way can lead into deep trouble. Perhaps you are invited to a party that promises to be lots of fun, and instead of waiting to answer until you are sure the Lord would want you to go, you say at once, "Yes, I'll come. Thanks." But at that party you may begin a friendship which will finally turn your heart away from the Lord.

Whenever possible we should take time to discover God's will before deciding what to do: what invitations to accept, whether or not to join some club at school, what friends to make. Often one needs to decide a matter at once; then within your heart speak quickly to Him, "Lord, guide me now."

God will often use another person as a messenger or guide to help us find His way. You will have great comfort in talking with someone else about the things which trouble you, but be most careful to whom you talk. You would not ask directions from a traveler who did not know the way himself. So when wanting help and advice, be sure to go to a Christian who really knows the Lord and lives in obedience to His Word—one who will also pray for and with you.

Do you want to go safely; Then as you begin the day in prayer, put yourself and your affairs into God's keeping and ask Him to lead you in His way through the moments and hours and to turn you aside from anything that would cause you harm or be wrong in His sight.

"Teach me Thy way, O Lord, and lead me in a plain path" (Psalm 27:11, KJV).

For Thinking and Doing:

1. Read Psalm 91:9-16.
2. What does verse 9 promise and to whom?
3. Why are we protected and delivered according to verse 14?
4. Name the promises given in verses 15 and 16.

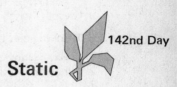

Static

"And the Lord will guide you continually" (Isaiah 58:11).

Sometimes other people try to keep us from going the way we know God would lead us. We also have hindrances from the enemy of our souls. Satan never is concerned about our travelling a road of our own choosing, but He does try to hinder our going God's way.

What will the enemy do to keep the believer from going the way God guides him, that is, the way of blessing and reward? He will try to keep him from choosing to follow the Lord in the first place. If this fails, the next move will be to hinder him from following God's guidance.

Through the broadcast, "Voice of America," messages of a better way of life were radioed to countries under communist control, but the angered Russians created so much static that the words of the broadcast could not be clearly heard by the listeners. Similarly, when the believer prays for guidance, Satan produces so much static that it becomes very difficult to hear and understand what God says. Satan slips confusing thoughts into our minds, makes us doubt God's leading, or causes our wills to influence us. He also uses other people to give us wrong advice. Expect such hindrances, but don't let them confuse you. Guidance is promised for those who really want it; God will not fail.

Satan never gives up; even when guidance comes he interferes. Once God's will is known he tries to keep us from doing it. He will try to hurry us into some impulsive decision or to keep us from acting by suggesting that it will be impossible to do what is asked of us. He tries to scare us by telling us of the problems we'll get into if we obey.

Satan may so stir things up to confuse the situation that you wonder whether or not you really have received guidance. Even when you follow God's leading you may wonder if you are really doing the right thing. When things seem to go all wrong when you obey, it is the enemy at work. Keep steady; your faith in God is being tested but He will see you though. Never go back on your guidance. When you are sure God is leading press right on through difficulties.

"Thanks be to God, which giveth us the victory through our Lord Jesus Christ" (I Corinthians 15:57, KJV).

For Thinking and Doing:

1. Read Psalms 32:8; 78:70-72; 48:14.
2. What does Psalm 32:8 promise the one who looks to God for guidance?
3. What people were guided by the skillfulness of God's hands according to Psalm 78?
4. Memorize Psalm 32:8.

143rd Day

Something Nobody Wants

"Man is born to trouble" (Job 5:7).

Today we'll talk about something everybody has and nobody wants. We think that our lives should be forever happy. Instead all sorts of troublesome things come upon us: pain which hurts our bodies, sadness or disappointments that bring suffering to our hearts and minds. These are the things we have but do not want.

Why doesn't God so manage that everyone can be happy all the time? That is not possible as long as sin and selfishness are in the world. For instance, a fellow might steal your car and enjoy riding in it. The very thing which gave him pleasure made you unhappy. Or turn that idea the other way around. Have you ever done some selfish thing which got you what you wanted but brought unhappiness to others? So you see, it is impossible to keep everybody happy all the time.

It would be neither fair nor kind of the Lord to keep every person happy all the time. What about the boy who took your car? It is only fair that he should have to suffer in some way for his wrongdoing. God is fair and He is also kind. When people set themselves to go on in sin and sinful pleasures, God often lets them go through loss, pain and trouble. It may be the only way to turn them to the Lord for forgiveness. Such trouble is God's love in action as He rescues them from a life which would end in eternal death. "Some were sick through their sinful ways and suffered affliction. For they had rebelled against the words of God and spurned the counsel of the Most High . . . Then they cried to the Lord . . . and He delivered them from their distress" (Psalm 107:17, 11, 13).

You might think that some people who are really wicked have everything they wish for: health, friends and riches. This question bothered the psalmist who wrote Psalm 73. He confessed that he was envious when he saw the prosperity of the wicked (verse 3), their health (verse 4), and their freedom from trouble (verse 5). As he pondered this question he sought God's answer (verses 16, 17). "Then," he said, "I perceived their end . . . how they are destroyed in a moment" (verses 17, 19). "For lo, those who are far from Thee shall perish" (verse 27).

Trouble does not only come as a result of sin. Christians suffer in many ways also, and in the following days we will be thinking about some of the reasons.

For Thinking and Doing:

1. Read Psalm 73:1-6, 12-13, 16-19, 23-28.

2. What benefit did those described in Psalm 107 have from their trouble? See verse 13.

3. As the life of the good and of the wicked are compared in Psalm 73, what advantages did the psalmist believe he had? See verses 23-28.

4. Which verse in Psalm 73 would you choose as a favorite verse?

144th Day

Blessing in Disguise

"For He will hide me in His shelter in the day of trouble" (Psalm 27:5).

Christians do strange things sometimes. When everything goes our way we say, "Oh, God is so good!" But when any trouble comes we change our minds. It is like saying, "I will trust God and believe in His love and promises only while things are going my way." This is stupid of us, isn't it? For often God's most priceless gifts come to us in the ugly wrappings of suffering.

203

Some years ago the boll weevil swept across one of the southern States, and those hungry beetles destroyed almost the entire cotton crop. Many cotton growers were frantic because it meant their ruin. Desperately they turned to raising peanuts. The result was that soon they were making much more money than by raising cotton.

God sometimes works like this with us. Not that troubles are good in themselves, but He brings blessings to us by them. "All things work together for good to them that love God" (Romans 8:28, KJV). This is one of the most wonderful promises of God.

"All things" means even trouble. He promises it will work together for good to those who belong to Him. Notice that this promise does not apply to everyone. While you keep on loving and trusting God, He works to make even difficult things bring you happiness and blessing. You may not discover the blessing all at once, but be patient. It takes time for the working together.

Trouble has many uses. It may be like the warning sign at a railroad crossing. Then the speeding auto must slow down as the great express train roars past across the highway. Sometimes it is like the spanking my neighbor gave to her tiny daughter. It was the only way to stop her from running into the street among swiftly moving cars. A sickness, a disappointment, that girl or fellow who failed you, these may be keeping you out of serious danger or from a harmful friendship. God knows.

The Lord may let you have much wealth, health and honor, or His love might deny you these if He knows they would draw your heart away from Him. Would this not be the kindest thing for you in the end? "Better is a little with the fear of the Lord than great treasure and trouble with it" (Proverbs 15:16).

"I am the Lord your God who teaches you to profit" (Isaiah 48:17). To profit means to gain, to get something of greater value. If our Lord allows suffering, it is so that our lives will be made richer by it. If He takes away one thing, it is only to give us something better. We can trust Him.

For Thinking and Doing:

1. Read Psalm 91.

2. Can you give three truths which the verses quoted in today's reading tell you about trouble?

3. Does Psalm 91 promise freedom to the believer from all trouble? What does it promise?

4. Memorize Romans 8:28.

For Our Good

"We know that all that happens to us is working for our good if we love God and are fitting into His plans" (Romans 8:28, LNT).

Perhaps you've been in real trouble lately, and it was not your fault. Why did it happen? You may feel mistreated or be almost cross or disappointed with the Lord. It's easy to see the reason bad people, and even some "good" ones, have trouble. But Christians are God's own children. Why does He allow them to suffer? The answer to this big question is that God never promised that Christians would not suffer; instead He said they would suffer. "In the world ye shall have tribulation" (John 16:33, KJV).

Why is this? We suffer because we are in human bodies that can become ill and be hurt in different ways. We all make many mistakes and bring trouble on ourselves. We are still in a world where there is unkindness and misunderstanding and where things and people disappoint us. God allows it for our good. Is that hard to believe?

God's sinless, glorious Son suffered. The Lord Jesus was a "man of sorrows" in His earthly life (Isaiah 53:3). He was made "perfect through suffering" (Hebrews 2:10). He "learned obedience through what He suffered" (Hebrews 5:8). Because Jesus suffered, He is able to perfectly understand how we feel when we suffer and He knows how to help. He learned by experience how even obedience to the Father will sometimes bring trouble upon us. Satan, God's enemy, works against us. As it was for Christ, suffering may be in God's will. "Let those who are suffering in line with the will of God entrust (trust the keeping of) their souls unto God" (I Peter 4:19, Berkeley).

Certain religions teach that troubles and sufferings of any kind are never God's will and that they should be refused. Everyone, they say, should claim and expect from God the health, riches and happiness which is his by right. It sounds wonderful, doesn't it? The only mistake is that our Lord does not say that. However, Christians often suffer troubles which God never wants them to have. They bring trouble upon themselves through their own wrongdoing. We need to ask ourselves, "Is my present trouble my own fault or something God has allowed for a special purpose of His own?''

For Thinking and Doing:

1. Read I Peter 4:12-19.
2. What kind of trial is Peter talking about in verses 12-14, 16?
3. What kind is he talking about in verse 15?
4. How would you explain verses 13 and 14?

For Training

"Let God train you, for He is doing what any loving father does for his children" (Hebrews 12:7, LNT).

Missionaries working among jungle tribes in Africa took into their homes some of the poor, filthy jungle children whose bodies were diseased and covered with sores. These girls and boys were always lying, stealing and doing all sorts of wrong things. They couldn't understand that they were dirty, mean and bad. It was the only kind of life they knew.

Yet the missionaries knew a better way. They bathed and cared for them, and in patient love taught the children how to keep clean and well, to choose the right, and to do it. At first the boys and girls fought against these things. Which do you think would be most kind: to let them go on living in sickness, dirt and sin, or to train them into a better way of life?

Compared with the holy, loving Lord, the nature of each of us is like those dirty, rebellious youngsters. Would you want your children to be like that? God doesn't either. That is why He has to change us, both for His sake and ours. His scrubbings, medicines and teachings are usually uncomfortable; we don't like them. Someone makes fun of us and the Lord uses that to scrub away a bit of our pride. Those lies we told got us into deep trouble; it was the medicine we needed to cure us of that subtle sin. Perhaps Mother's illness taught us to be more helpful at home.

Our Father God knows that in the end we will be far happier and safer in His way for us. Through different kinds of trouble, great or small, He carefully trains. Sometimes He has to punish those He loves. There is a wonderful reason why we must not fight against this. He does it for our good, in order that we may share in

His holy character. Those who learn God's lessons, though they may seem hard, will grow in their inner lives.

God's Word tells us, "Don't be discouraged when He has to show you where you are wrong" (Hebrews 12:5, LNT). Don't think it's no use trying, and let's not shrug it off. Ask God what He is trying to teach you so that you can learn it and grow to be more like your Lord.

For Thinking and Doing:

1. Read Hebrews 12:5-11.
2. What does Hebrews 12:5-9 teach you about discipline?
3. What is God's purpose according to Hebrews 12:10?
4. What is the result given in Hebrews 12:11?

147th Day

For a Higher Purpose

"As the heavens are higher than the earth, so are My ways higher than your ways" (Isaiah 55:9).

Have you ever seen a large diamond just out of the mine? It is just a dirty, rounded stone with no light or sparkle. You probably wouldn't give five cents for it. However, there is a great difference between what happens to a diamond and what happens to an ordinary stone.

The plain rock may border a flower bed or, after being cut, used to help build a house. A diamond doesn't have such an easy time. The workman cuts it with sharp tools. Again and again he slices until all that spoils its beauty is cut away. Then the precious stone is pressed against a whirling wheel which grinds the entire surface. Over and over the diamond has to endure the polishing and grinding until not one flaw remains. Now it is a priceless, beautiful gem.

Most Christians are content to be ordinary rocks, comfortably filling a useful place. But if we long to be of utmost value to

God and to the world, we must expect the grinding and the polishing. This is the way the Master Workman frees us from the ugly things of our human nature. The polishing process can be a painful thing, and the Lord uses difficulties in our lives in many and unexpected ways.

Perhaps He is already working on you. Some of your polishing may be an answer to your prayer. You may pray for patience, and God might answer by putting you with a slow, stubborn person. Instead of exploding you will have to look to Jesus to keep you kind and quiet. Perhaps you pray to become unselfish, and others seem to be more grabby than usual. These are some of the ways God works to make us more like our lovely Lord.

You may want to take yourself out of the Workman's hands, thinking that to grow in the Christian life isn't worth the cost. But God and the world needs diamond Christians. God is fitting you for a place of honor. The time is surely coming when Christ will reign as King over the universe. "That at the name of Jesus every knee should bow" (Philippians 2:10). "If we endure, we shall also reign with Him" (II Timothy 2:12).

Above all, keep "looking unto Jesus" (Hebrews 12:2). How does one look unto Jesus? With the eyes of his mind and heart. Think of Him, Who He is, and what He has promised. Think of His power and His love for you. "Look . . . to the things that are unseen" (II Corinthians 4:18) as yet, but which are everlasting.

Remember that Jesus did not come to make life easy, but to make us strong. "Take your share of suffering as a good soldier of Christ Jesus" (II Timothy 2:3). "Your sorrow will turn into joy" (John 16:20). "Be strong and of good courage, do not fear . . . for it is the Lord your God who goes with you; He will not fail you" (Deuteronomy 31:6).

Difficulties which God allows to come can work to fulfill His higher purposes for us. When they come, look to Him for His purpose and count on Him to bring you through them.

For Thinking and Doing:

1. Read II Timothy 1:8, 9; II Timothy 2:1-5, 12.
2. What kind of suffering was Timothy talking about in the above verses?
3. Do Christians have this kind of suffering today?
4. Can you see some difficulty or trouble in your life as God's polishing process?

He Delivers

"God is our refuge and strength, a very present help in trouble" (Psalm 46:1).

When a person who cannot swim falls into deep water he screams for help. Most Christians start begging the Lord to get them out of trouble the moment they get into it. Sometimes we do need help at once. But actually there are two things we should do before we pray to God for His help and deliverance.

First, "Offer to God a sacrifice of thanksgiving" (Psalm 50:14). This takes real faith and courage. It is so much easier to drop down into the dumps. Thank Him for what? For the many good things you have, for His promises to help, and for the way He is going to turn this trouble into a blessing. Thank Him that He has promised to be a refuge and strength to you.

Second, "Pay your vows to the most High" (Psalm 50:14). A vow is a solemn promise. Did you promise God to pray and study His Word or do some other thing, but you failed? Confess your failure and start at once to be obedient. Then expect Him to keep His promise to you. "Call upon Me in the day of trouble; I will deliver you, and you shall glorify Me" (Psalm 50:15). When the help comes we must praise God.

"Deliver" has two meanings: 1) to set entirely free, and 2) to fit a person to go through the hard thing. So pray about every need. Usually the Lord lifts us out of the trouble at the right time or He changes things. However, if that would not be best, He will take us through in triumph.

The apostle Paul had wonderful deliverances: out of the hands of murderers, out of a dark prison, out of the sea where he almost drowned, and many others. Yet Paul (probably the bravest and most Christlike Christian) had a kind of suffering which, like a sharp thorn deep in his flesh, never ceased to prick. Three times he begged for its removal, but the Lord said "No." God said that it was better for Paul to have the thorn because it would make him live entirely by the Lord's strength, and God's grace would be enough for Paul's every need. See II Corinthians 12:7-9.

When Paul realized the thorn would bring an extra blessing, he exclaimed, "I am happy to boast in my weaknesses, so that the power of Christ may abide upon me. I delight, therefore . . . in insults . . . in persecutions" (II Corinthians 12:10, Berkeley).

For Thinking and Doing:

1. Read II Corinthians 11:23-28, 32, 33.

2. Think about all the wonderful deliverances God gave to Paul in his missionary service. Do you believe He can deliver you out of trouble?

3. Explain what you think Paul meant in II Corinthians 12:10.

4. Will you follow Psalm 50:14, 15 when in trouble?

149th Day

Trouble and Fear

"Fear not . . . I will help you" (Isaiah 41:10).

Trouble often brings fear to our hearts. Are you afraid? Everyone is at times. There is the fear of what might happen or of a very real trouble that is present. All sorts of fears can pile up. We might be afraid of losing a friend or failing an exam. We may dread to tell the truth or fear what others may say or do.

Fear never comes alone but always drags along its twin, worry. Fear and worry weaken our minds and act like a poison in the bloodstream of our bodies. It is sin for a Christian to harbor fear and worry in his heart. They will turn his faith into doubt and weaken him. They will spoil his witness for the Lord.

We are helpless against fear, but God is not. He understands. He knows that often there is a reason for our human nature to be afraid. So again and again He tells His own to "Fear not." Why? Because "with us is the Lord our God, to help us" (II Chronicles 32:8). He is with you every moment, today and in every tomorrow. He always knows just what to do. Nothing takes Him by surprise. Even now the living Lord is planning how to help you if a trouble comes. Yet He cannot help unless you do your part.

Someone has said, "If your knees tremble, kneel on them." Tell your heavenly Father of each fear, small or big. Confess, "I am afraid." God dearly loves His children and His comforting answer is, "Fear not, for I am with you . . . I will strengthen you, I will help you" (Isaiah 41:10). Pray to Him as David did, "Make haste to help me, O Lord!" (Psalm 38:22).

Take a good look at the thing you fear. Is it too big for the Almighty God to work out? Of course it isn't. So hand it all over to Him—the whoever or whatever that is making you afraid. "Let Him have all your worries and cares" (I Peter 5:7, LNT), and don't hang onto it when once you've given it to God to manage.

Then "trust in the Lord" (Proverbs 3:5). Think about Who it is that promises to help you. "With God nothing will be impossible" (Luke 1:37). "According to your faith be it done to you" (Matthew 9:29. It is as you keep on believing Him that the Lord will help.

For Thinking and Doing:

1. Read Psalm 62:8; II Chronicles 20:17; I Peter 1:6, 7; Psalm 27:1.

2. What should we do in trouble according to Psalm 62:8?

3. Who will bring you through according to II Chronicles 20:17?

4. Memorize Psalm 27:1.

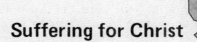

150th Day

Suffering for Christ

"It is no shame to suffer for being a Christian" (I Peter 4:16, LNT).

On a hillside the Lord Jesus sat with His disciples. They had gone with Him from town to town. They had seen His miracles and heard His truthful, loving words. Some of those whom Christ helped and healed believed and loved Him. Many others hated Him or were indifferent and turned away. Remembering these things the disciples may have asked, "Lord, if we live for You, will we be treated as You are?"

Christ told them, "If they have persecuted Me, they will also persecute you" (John 15:20). Then did He say, "It's not fair, but try to bear it bravely"? No, He said just the opposite. "Blessed (given special favor) are you when men hate you, and when they exclude you (from their company) . . . on account of the Son of Man! Rejoice in that day . . . your reward is great in heaven" (Luke 6:22).

When anyone does wrong, it is his fault if people do not like him. But if they make fun of you, dislike you, or even hate you for being true to Christ in act and word, do not be upset and, "Don't be surprised . . . instead be really glad because these trials will make you partners with Christ" (I Peter 4:12, 13, LNT).

What must one do at such times? It is natural for our old human nature to want to fight back, but we are to meet all these things in our new nature—by Christ's nature which is in us. He "never answered back when He was insulted; when He suffered He did not threaten to get even" (I Peter 2:23, LNT). "See that no one pays back evil for evil, but always try to do good to each other" (I Thessalonians 5:15, LNT).

Christ has said, "Love your enemies. Do good to those who hate you" (Luke 6:27, LNT). Many Christians today suffer persecution for their Lord behind the iron and the bamboo curtains. The book, Christ in a Communist Prison, by Richard Wurmbrand is the story of terrible cruelty Christians have suffered at the hands of Christ's enemies. It is also a wonderful story of Christ's love in a Christian's heart, reaching out in blessing to his persecutors.

You may not experience physical suffering and persecution, but somewhere your loyalty to Christ will cost you something. The true Christian is different and he faces opposition. When it comes, look to your Lord. He will not only be your Shield and your Defense, but He will also be your Reward. "Your reward from heaven will be very great, and you will truly be acting as sons of God, for He is kind to the unthankful, and to those who are very wicked" (Luke 6:35, LNT).

For Thinking and Doing:
1. Read Luke 6:27-37.
2. Apply Luke 6:31 to some situation in your own life today.
3. Explain in your own words the teaching of Luke 6:32-36.
4. Can you think of illustrations of the truth of Luke 6:38?

Living Together

"God places the solitary in families" (Psalm 68:6, Amplified).

You are a very special person. No one has ever been exactly like you; no one ever will be. You have a personality distinct from any other. Although the Lord made everyone separate from everybody else, He did not put each of us in a hole by himself like so many telephone poles. We began life in one of the most important groups, the family, made up of parents and children in a home. It is God's plan that we live, work, play and worship Him in groups and that we love and help one another.

Much of your success or failure in life will depend upon how well you learn to live in a group and get along with all sorts of people. This is especially important if you are a Christian. However, to live happily with others is often very difficult, as it is at home for instance. Is that where you have the most trouble? Many of us do, but it is right there that we can learn best how to fit our lives in with others, with their rough edges of irritation or selfishness. Besides it's the best place to get our own unpleasant bumps smoothed off.

What is home to you? It is more than a place where you live, work, hang your coat, and are always welcome. It is being with your family and where you stop pretending and are just yourself. The others do that too, and this is partly the reason it is often hard to get along at home though you love your family dearly.

Home could be happier if we were more alike. Maybe your parents do not feel the need of many friends as you do. You may be full of fun and energy, but they might not like to do the things you enjoy. Perhaps you are unlike anyone in the family, and you sometimes can't understand your family nor can they understand you.

There has always been a generation gap or a feeling in youth that older people do not understand them. However, trying to understand one another is the basis for learning to get along with people. The Lord made no mistake when He made families and put you in one. We shall see some of the reasons in the readings of the following days.

For Thinking and Doing:

1. Read Psalm 139:1-6, 13-18.

2. Give David's reasons from the above verses for feeling the Lord knew all about him.

3. What seems to you to be the most important benefits that being a member of a family brings?

4. Name some things you learn in family living that will prepare you for getting along with people in other groups.

152nd Day

Common Complaints

"Let everyone see that you are unselfish and considerate in all you do" (Philippians 4:5, LNT).

Let's face it: there are problems for young people growing up in a family. Do any of these common complaints of young people sound like your own?

"My parents want me to be happy, but to always follow their way."

"I am not allowed to decide things for myself; my parents want to choose my friends."

"I cannot entertain my friends at home."

"My parents expect too much of me at home; I have no time to myself."

"My parents want to know about everything I do."

"Mother and Dad nag at me about things they don't want me to do."

"My parents are not really interested in me or my problems."

"I hardly know my parents; they are seldom home."

There may be other problems you have, but they all add up to this: "My parents don't see my side. What can I do?"

Will you let God tell you what to do? Perhaps you can't hear Him because there are so many voices speaking in your heart, such as the noisy voices of anger, criticism, resentment and unforgiveness. By an act of your will these must all be gathered up and put aside as you take time and get quiet before God in prayer. Then listen to His Word to you, "Be kind to one another, tenderhearted, forgiving one another, as God in Christ forgave you. Let all

214

bitterness . . . and anger . . . be put away from you" (Ephesians 4:32, 31).

, The Child Jesus grew up in a human family. Suppose He were a young person in your home, faced with your problems. How would He behave? You may say, "Oh, but He was God." If that is so, Who has been living in your heart since you were born again? "No longer I who live, but Christ who lives in me" (Galatians 2:20). "I can do everything God asks me to with the help of Christ who gives me the strength and power" (Philippians 4:13, LNT).

There would be no problem if you and your parents could agree. So you need to talk matters over with them in order to let Mother and Dad see your side. You may have tried to do this and it only made matters worse. But how did you do it? Was it in anger or rebellion, putting the blame on them? Read carefully I Corinthians 13:4-7. Before talking with your parents, talk much with the Lord. Ask Him to put His thoughts into your heart and theirs.

Write a list of the important reasons you have for wanting to do certain things. It will help you to think things through. Also write a list of reasons why your Mother and Dad might feel as they do. "May our Lord Jesus Christ Himself . . . Who has loved us . . . encourage your hearts and strengthen you in every good thing you do or say" (II Thessalonians 2:16, 17, Williams).

For Thinking and Doing:

1. Read Romans 12:9, 10, 16-19, 21.

2. What is your part in living in harmony with others according to Romans 12:18?

3. What depends on you in your own problems of living with others? Name specific things.

4. Think of illustrations from your own relationships of how to apply Romans 12:21 to them.

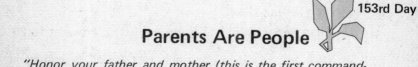 **153rd Day**

Parents Are People

"Honor your father and mother (this is the first commandment with a promise), that it may be well with you and that you may live long on the earth" (Ephesians 6:2).

"How does it feel to be a parent?"

"I don't know. I've never been one!"

That's quite true! Yet you cannot decide fairly about your home problems unless you see both sides of the matter. We need to take a thoughtful look at Mother and Dad. We see they make mistakes. Of course they do; only God is perfect. They are people. They are often tired and discouraged and have disappointments and heartaches. They, too, long to be understood and loved.

You owe your parents much. Think of those years when you depended on them for almost everything you had and did? They sacrificed time, money and comforts to take care of you, and they are probably still doing this. Think of the good things and many advantages you have from your parents and in your home. Are you forgetting these by building up a great pile of the few things you wish were different?

Do you thoughtlessly ignore your parents, as though you said, "I'll take all you will give me, but I don't want you!" So Dad, home from a hard day's work, sighs as you go whistling out of the house and slam the door behind you. "Len only wants the use of my car and the money I give him. He doesn't care for me," he may think. And Mother, after a similar brush-off, may say, "Gail just wants to use the house as a place to eat, sleep and telephone. I am simply someone to wait on her. She acts as though it is a boring thing to have to spend a little time with the family now and then." Are you like that? Would you like your children to treat you like that?

The Lord says, "You must honor your father and mother," that is to give them their proper place in your heart. Be thoughtful, try to communicate with them, and share your interests with them. And "follow God's example in everything you do just as a much loved child imitates his father. Be full of love for others, following the example of Christ who loved you" (Ephesians 5:1, 2, LNT). Is it sometimes hard to respect and love your parents? Neither are you or I worthy of God's love for us. As a Christian are you making it easier for your family to see what Christ is like?

For Thinking and Doing:

1. Read Ephesains 6:1, 2; Ephesians 5:1, 2; Proverbs 16:20, 21, 24, 32.

2. Give reasons which you think are back of the commands of Ephesians 6:1, 2.

3. Name ways in which you think young people can honor their parents.

4. What do you learn from the verses in Proverbs that would help relationships with others?

Obeying Parents

"Children, obey your parents in everything, for this pleases the Lord" (Colossians 3:20).

You are young, with all the zip and zing of a 200 horsepower engine. That's fine; but a powerful engine is not enough. A car also needs brakes and a steering wheel with a hand upon it. God expects your Father and Mother to be the brakes and the hand upon the wheel. He tells them this. "Train up a child in the way he (or she) should go" (Proverbs 22:6). "Bring them up (your children) tenderly with true Christian . . . advice" (Ephesians 6:4, Williams).

Just as we have driving rules and curbs to keep cars in the road for safety's sake, wise and loving parents must have rules and curbs to keep their children from harm and evil, even though the children sometimes rebel.

God's Word is, "Children, obey your parents in everything" (Colossians 3:20). Obey only when we understand the reason why? Obey some times and in some things? No, that's not what it says. "But," you may say, "God doesn't know my parents. They are not always fair or kind. They expect too much." Oh yes, God knows these things and He knows your parents even though they may not know Him. And that command is still in the Bible.

You may think, "It doesn't touch me. I'm no longer a child." "Children" means sons and daughters; not just the very young. As long as our parents supply our food, clothes and home and while we are still in our teens, we are to obey. Is God asking too much? It all depends on what place He has in our hearts. He says that to obey is right.

To obey one's parents greatly pleases the Lord. You may long to do some special thing for the Lord who has done so much for you. You might even be willing to go to some far-off land to preach and even die for Him. Yet you can do something for Him right at home. If you will let the Holy Spirit keep your old human nature dead, so it will not fight against Mother's and Dad's instructions, you will be living to please Him every day of your life.

When we obey our parents we also obey the Lord. Jesus says of the obedient Christian, "The one who obeys Me is the one who

217

loves Me; and because he loves Me, My Father will love him; and I will too, and I will reveal Myself to him" (John 14:21, LNT).

For Thinking and Doing:

1. Read Proverbs 1:7-8; 15:31-33; Ephesians 6:1-4.

2. What does Solomon, the wisest man of his time, advise his son in Proverbs 1:8?

3. What reasons does Paul give for children obeying their parents in Ephesians 6:1-3?

4. What advice does he give parents about bringing up their children in Ephesians 6:4?

155th Day

Problems About Parents

"Thus says the Lord . . . I have loved you with an everlasting love" (Jeremiah 31:2, 3).

Perhaps you do have some very real or unusual problems with your parents. They may seem not to love you or never want to do things with you. They may not be interested in you or your friends, in your problems, or in what you do. You may feel unwanted and alone. There may be no one to turn to for encouragement and guidance, whose strong understanding love stands ready to help in all the hard places. If this is so, it would be easy to let yourself become involved with the wrong crowd since you can do as you please. You could even wreck your life. Instead you may face your situation and ask the Lord to help you in it.

Some grown-ups do not understand young people. Perhaps this is true of your parents, and so they feel uncomfortable with you and your friends. There are other mothers and fathers who cannot believe they are not perfect parents. They have each other and are satisfied with just providing you with things you need. "We give our children everything possible to make them happy," some parents say. "What more can we do?" They do not dream you have problems.

Very few parents are really "without natural affection" (Romans 1:31, KJV), having no real love even for their own children. Yet some are. Sometimes a parent seems unable to be close to one child, but favors another. Perhaps there is serious and constant quarreling in your home; it may even be on the verge of breaking up. Some of you have parents that are already separated

218

or divorced. You may have real emotional problems, being torn between them because you love them both. You may have parents who do not know the Lord, who oppose your becoming a Christian, and make your commitment to Christ very difficult for you.

Is there any help for you with these problems? Indeed there is. These may be big troubles, but you have a very great God. He promises, "I will be a father to you, and you shall be my sons and daughters, says the Lord Almighty" (II Corinthians 6:18). "For my father and mother have forsaken me, but the Lord will take me up" (Psalm 27:10).

Often a close relative or friend, a school counselor or a pastor can give young people who have serious home problems wise counsel and real help. However, the One who is always by our side to help and who never fails you is your Resource in whatever your circumstance may be. He will comfort you as He has promised. "As one whom his mother comforts, so will I comfort you" (Isaiah 66:13).

For Thinking and Doing:

1. Read John 14:18, 21, 23, 27; John 15:13-15.
2. What promises does Christ give His own in John 14:18?
3. What is the proof of our love to Him according to John 14:21?
4. What comfort does the Lord give us in John 14:27; John 15:13-15?

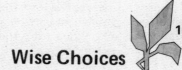

156th Day

Wise Choices

"The beginning of wisdom is this: Get wisdom" (Proverbs 4:7).

There is a tingling something in the air. When you are in your teens you want somehow to take hold of life, to feel it and enjoy it. You want to be part of all that is going on around you, to go places and do things. You are sure life has many interesting and exciting people and things for you to know and do. Right now you feel quite able to take on anything.

It was not like this a few years ago. Life was pleasant enough when you were younger, but it was different. Mother and Dad planned everything and you were satisfied to let them. Now that is past; you are growing up and feel that you can think for yourself. You suddenly want to live your own life and to make your own choices. However, it is God's plan that now, while you can have your parents' help, you gradually learn to make your own decisions so that you develop into a person who will make wise choices.

Although you long to be independent of your mother and dad, you still need what only they can do or give. While still at home you can have their suggestions as you learn by experience how to think things through and make wise choices for yourself. Otherwise you will be unable to meet problems and people with wisdom and good judgment as a grown-up person. It is better to make some less important mistakes now than to make big ones later. As your parents let you start making some of your own decisions, you will gain valuable experiences. However, this involves your being responsible; you will need to show them you can be trusted.

The three most important choices for your future are: 1) your choice of friends, 2) your choice of a career, and 3) your choice of a mate.

Your choice of friends now can affect the other two choices for good or for bad. Although you want to be friendly with everyone, your close friends will influence your life in many ways. First ask the Lord for His leading about the friends you make. Then you will be wise to heed your parents' advice about your friends, for they understand people better than you do, having had more experience. As a Christian you want to find other Christians to be your closest friends. A true friendship in Christ can be one of the most enriching experiences in your life. On the other hand, one wrong friendship can destroy some of the best things your parents have tried to give you, or it might lead you away from the Lord.

God expects fathers and mothers to guard their young people from making serious mistakes. They have to know what their children are doing and with whom. The right kind of friend will never try to get you to deceive your parents in any way. As you look to the Lord for His leading and accept your parents' advice, you will learn to make wise choices.

It was said of King Hezekiah: "He did that which was right in the eyes of the Lord. And the Lord was with him" (II Kings 18:3, 7).

For Thinking and Doing:

1. Read Proverbs 6:20-23; 17:17; 18:24; 27:6.

2. Name some examples of times when you think parents' advice can be a real help.

3. Give reasons why you think the choice of your friends is so important.

4. What thought from the references in Proverbs seems valuable to you?

157th Day

Love One Another

"Let us practice loving each other, for love comes from God" (I John 4:7, LNT).

In I Corinthians 13 God gives us a list of the ways in which we are to think and act toward others. They are the ways of love. We truly want to do as our heavenly Father asks but often it seems impossible. We may try to be patient with one person, but the next minute we may be rude or angry with another. It is most discouraging, isn't it? The trouble is that we are looking for this love in the wrong place—in our natural hearts—and we will never find it there.

All these different qualities of love are found in just one Person. Only our Lord Jesus is perfect Love. But in letting Him live out His life in us and asking and expecting Him to do it, we can grow in love to others. From Him we can learn the real secret of living together and getting along with our families, friends, and other people in our world.

Does it matter if we love or not? God says that love is the greatest thing in earth and in heaven. The word of Jesus is, "This is My commandment, that you love one another as I have loved you" (John 15:12). "By this all men will know that you are my disciples" (John 13:35). "Love does no wrong to a neighbor; therefore love is the fulfilling of the law" (Romans 13:10). It is complete obedience to God's law which tells us not to lie, steal, etc. For you see, when we love another, we will not want to deceive him or do him any wrong.

Love is described in I Corinthians 13:4-7, LNT, in this way:

"Love is very patient and kind" (verse 4). It quietly and patiently bears unkindness and keeps kind and gentle.

Love is "never jealous or envious" (verse 4). It does not envy, but is glad when others have good things which it does not have.

It is "never boastful or proud" (verse 4). Love will care too much for others and think too little of self to show off or brag. It is too big and fine for that.

It is "never haughty or selfish or rude. Love does not demand its own way. It is not irritable or touchy. It does not hold grudges and will hardly even notice when others do it wrong" (verse 5). Love is always thoughtful of others, willing to give up its own way; it does not become angry. Love will not remember unkind things or try to get even.

"It is never glad about injustice (when wrong is done), but rejoices whenever truth wins out" (verse 6). It is made happy by goodness.

"If you love someone you will be loyal to him no matter what the cost. You will always believe in him, always expect the best of him, and always stand your ground in defending him" (verse 7).

Because love is so important, "Let us practice loving each other, for love comes from God and those who are loving and kind show that they are the children of God . . . for God is love" (I John 4:7, 8, LNT).

For Thinking and Doing:

1. Read John 13:35; I Corinthians 13.

2. Since love for others is the mark of a Christian, how do you score on the points described in today's reading?

3. What reason does Paul give concerning the importance of love?

4. Ask the Lord to teach you how to truly love others.

158th Day

Dating

"Do not be mismated with unbelievers" (II Corinthians 6:14).

The day before yesterday we read about the importance of choosing the right friends. Perhaps at no time in your life will they influence you more than when you are in your teens. In

222

these years you also begin to be interested in the opposite sex, and problems of boy-girl relationships arise. Dating brings one of the first questions: will you go steady or not?

Your classmates at school take different attitudes about going steady. Those who do usually say something like this, "Going steady means I will never be left out; I can always count on having a date. Doing things together with someone I know well, someone who really cares about me and likes me best, is much more fun."

Those who prefer not to go steady like to have different dates. "It's more fun this way; you get to know different people. You get too serious when you go steady."

Which is the wise choice? Certainly having dates with different friends will widen your experience with people and give you a better background of knowledge of the opposite sex. This will be of value in your later choice of a life partner. Around you, you see fellows and girls who go steady and who are getting too serious. Absorbed in one another, grades in school suffer. Sometimes an early marriage results and educational plans for one or both must be changed. Did you know that statistics show that teen-age marriages fail more often? Half of them go on the rocks, usually because of financial problems and immaturity.

But you may say, "I'm not thinking of marriage yet, but only of having a good time." Yet dating is your first step in association with the opposite sex which will eventually lead to courtship and marriage for most young people.

The Bible has a principle about the choice of all your close friends, in fact it is a command which applies especially to marriage. "Be ye not unequally yoked together with unbelievers" II Corinthians 6:14, KJV). You will be friendly with those who do not know your Lord, but what if you should fall in love with someone you have been dating who was not His? Then you would have a real conflict over obeying this command. Ask the Lord to guide you in your decisions about dating. He alone knows the end from the beginning and He is by your side, ready to help you.

For Thinking and Doing:

1. Read II Corinthians 6:14-18.

2. The Living New Testament translates verse 6: "Don't be teamed with those who do not love the Lord, for what do the people of God have in common with the people of sin? How can light live with darkness?" Give some reasons you can think of for this command.

223

3. Give reasons for observing this command even when you are only in the dating period of your life.

4. Pray for the Lord's leading in your dating.

The "New" Morality

"You are not your own" (I Corinthians 6:19).

In school and everywhere around you are young people with low standards about relationships with the opposite sex. You want to be popular, but you can't go along with the crowd. You ask, "How can I be popular and not compromise my standards?"

Those in positions of leadership among young people see good answers to this question in individual lives. Some boys and girls develop most interesting personalities with their hobbies and wide interests. One girl may be a good conversationalist, and another such a good listener and so truly interested in others that they love to be with her. Such girls do not need to depend upon their physical charms to attract admirers. Young people with real goals will keep their standards high.

In these days of freedom concerning sex, young people are bombarded from all sides with unwholesome ideas about it. Is the "New Morality" really new, or is it only a new upsurge of the age-old problems of immorality?

A little paperback book, *It All Depends,* by F. Ridenour gives the Christian answer to the current ideas about morality which perplex young people today. After discussing some of the problems of the new morality, the author concludes that the answer to being moral for the Christian is found in Romans 12:1-2. He uses a combination of the Phillips and Living New Testament translations: "As an act of intelligent worship . . . give . . . your bodies (to God), as a living sacrifice, consecrated to Him and acceptable by Him. Don't let the world around you squeeze you into its own mold, but let God remold your minds from within, so you will learn from you own experience how His ways will really satisfy you."

God has His answer to those who argue for sexual freedom, which is really sexual license: "Do you not know that your body is a temple of the Holy Spirit within you, which you have from God? You are not your own; you were bought with a price. So glorify God in your body" (I Corinthians 6:19, 20).

In other areas of life also, young people are faced with great pressures to relax their standards. Smoking, drinking, marijuana and drugs, these habit-forming temptations which can damage body and mind, surround them. One drink can start some people on the road to being alcoholics and one experiment with a drug can lead to addiction.

Those who belong to the Lord have His Word in Romans 12:1 to guide them. Anything that would harm the body, which is the temple of His Holy Spirit, would grieve Him. He is the One who can help overcome temptation and who is by your side to counsel and to guide you. "You are not your own," this is His reminder for every temptation. He stands with you to overcome it. Not your trying, but His strength will win out. "For I can do everything God asks me to with the help of Christ who gives me the strength and power" (Philippians 4:13, LNT).

For Thinking and Doing:

1. Read James 1:13-15.
2. What part do you think your thoughts have in temptation according to James 1:14?
3. In what other ways can we play with temptation or bring it into our lives?
4. The Living New Testament translation of I Corinthians 10:13 reads, "But remember this—the wrong desires (temptations) that come into your life aren't anything new and different . . . and no temptation is irresistible. You can trust God to keep the temptation from becoming so strong that you can't stand up against it, for He has promised this and will do what He says. He will show you how to escape temptation's power so that you can bear up patiently against it." What is your part, and what is God's part according to this verse?

160th Day

Love Not the World

"Stop loving this evil world and all that it offers you, for when you love these things you show that you do not really love God" (I John 2:15, LNT).

While athletes are in training they have to deny themselves many pleasant things. Nor does God train His heroes by feeding them compliments and candy. God's champions are never softies. They are willing to do and bear the hard things and to side with God and right. The Bible teaches us that there are three things which weaken and defeat the Christian: 1) the world, 2) the flesh, and 3) the devil.

We have learned that the way of victory over the flesh, our sinful human nature, is to keep from yielding to it, to treat it as dead, and to let the Lord Jesus live out His life in us.

We are told about the hindrance of the world, "Love not the world, neither the things that are in the world" (I John 2:15, KJV). What is the world and its things that we are not to love? It is not the earth, for God has filled the earth with beautiful and useful things for man's happiness and good. Instead it is those things, plans and people that do not give God His rightful place.

Christians have to live in the world as a fish lives in the water. We are surrounded by it as we swim in it. We can enjoy many of the things other people enjoy. But just as the water does not soak into the fish, so we are not to allow anything of the world to enter into our lives and take God's place in our hearts. "All these worldly things, these evil desires—the craze for sex, the ambition to buy everything that appeals to you, and the pride that comes from wealth and importance—these are not from God. They are from this evil world itself" (I John 2:16, LNT).

The world is like a beautiful, great ship which, unknown to the passengers, is slowly sinking. So although we are not to love the ways of the world, yet we should have God's kind of love for its millions of people who are in danger of perishing because they have rejected God and chosen the world and its ways. May our Lord give you and me understanding hearts so that we will not want to climb aboard the sinking ship, but that we will do our utmost to save some out of it before it is too late.

"The whole world is in the power of the evil one" (I John 5:19). "The prince of this world," the devil, will use all the pleasures of his world to draw the Christian away from Christ. We need to keep close to the Lord through study of His Word and through prayer, faith and obedience. Jesus says that you "are not of the world even as I am not of the world" (John 17:16). "We are the children of God" (Romans 8:16, KJV).

For Thinking and Doing:

1. Read John 17:9-20.

2. In Jesus' prayer for His disciples, what are the two or three main requests of His prayer in the above verses?

3. Are we included in His prayer? See John 17:20.

4. Name some of the things of the world which you think would hinder your Christian life.

Wings of Power

"Resist the devil and he will flee from you" (James 4:7).

It is a grim sight: A single fighter plane is being attacked by one of the enemy. It seems to have no chance! Suddenly the fighter plane breaks away and zooms up into the great blue yonder, above and beyond the power of the enemy craft to follow. Now the young pilot looks down upon his destroyer. His pulse quiets; he sees clearly and flies steadily. He is safe.

Sometimes we are hard pressed by the attacks of our enemy, Satan. He is the third of the trio, "the world, the flesh and the devil," which can hinder our Christian life. When the Lord asks you to put Him first and your heart has responded to Him, you can count on a pull in the other direction from Satan. Sometimes he works through the pull of the alluring temptations of the world, or he may use the pull of other young people saying to you, "People will think you're odd if you live for the Lord. Don't be different. Follow the crowd."

Yes, there is the crowd and most of us want to be popular. Yet you can't be popular with the crowd unless you go along with them. Some of the things they do are often questionable and sometimes quite wrong. How can you or I go along with them and be true to the One we follow? Some of the crowd may be scornful of God and the teachings of the Bible.

When you put your Lord first even some of your friends may turn away. It is not that they don't like you, but they do not want to follow your Lord. Never mind. He will bring you wonderful friends if you ask Him. You never can give up anything for Him that you are not rewarded for many times over. Trust Him to bring you Christian friends who will mean more to you than the crowd ever could.

Just as the pilot soared above the attack of the enemy plane, you can rise above the attacks of your enemy, Satan. As the pilot had the needed power, in Christ you have it also. "You are of God, and have overcome them; for He who is in you is greater than he who is in the world" (I John 4:4). With Him you can rise above the remarks of the crowd and resist the pull of the things which may look so attractive, but are so destructive.

227

"They who wait for the Lord . . . shall mount up with wings like eagles" (Isaiah 40:31). We shall mount up with wings—one wing is God's Word and the other is prayer. Are you using your wings and counting on His power within?

For Thinking and Doing:

1. Read Ephesians 4:27; 6:13-17; I Peter 5:8; II Corinthians 11:14, 15.

2. How do we sometimes give Satan an opportunity to attack us?

3. What is our armor according to Ephesians 6:13-17?

4. Can you think of ways Satan appears to us as an angel of light?

Living in Danger

"Now it is high time to awake out of sleep" (Romans 13:11, KJV).

A few years ago some houses were built over an old, unused coal mine. Those who lived in them were warned of their danger but the warnings were laughed off. Everything seemed safe and peaceful, so work and play went on as usual. One night the ground beneath those homes slipped a bit, but not enough to disturb the sleepers. Then suddenly there was a mighty roar as the upper earth caved in. People and collapsing houses were hurled into the empty spaces below. Not one life was saved. "How terrible," you say. Yes, yet the people of the entire world, some living on your street, are in far greater danger.

God planned that men should build their lives upon the solid, safe foundation of the teachings of His Word. Instead they have gone on building their lives and their nations on material things, secular interests, and empty pleasures. They are filled with pride, self-will and godlessness; they have rejected God's safe foundation. "Woe to him who builds . . . by unrighteousness"

(Jeremiah 22:13). "They shall be destroyed forever" (Psalm 92:7, KJV).

Today the world seems on the brink of disaster. Our scientific knowledge, which can bring great blessing, has also brought nuclear power which threatens the destruction of civilization. Scientists and thoughtful men everywhere warn us of our danger. Love of money corrupts governments and fosters crime which has so increased that the streets of our cities are unsafe. Rebellious attitudes and hatred flare into violence and riots.

There are signs of the collapse of right standards and true values in many areas of life. American and other so-called Christian nations have left God out of their national life and these results have followed. Someone has said, "If we do not have Christ, we will have chaos." What men say about these conditions is important, but what God says is most important. "Such are the paths of all who forget God; the hope of the godless man (the man without God) shall perish" (Job 8:13). Throughout the Bible the ultimate destruction of evil men is taught.

"No one who denies (who will not have) the Son has the Father" (I John 2:23). "You will die in your sins unless you believe that I am He (the Messiah)" (John 8:24). The Bible teaches that those who reject Christ as their Savior and Lord are in terrible danger; they face an eternity without God in everlasting punishment. In Christ's teaching He warned us about this danger. "These shall go away into everlasting punishment" (Matthew 25:46, KJV). If you were passing a burning house would you just hurry by because you didn't wish to think of the danger of those who lived there or would you ring the doorbell and warn them?

How many people we all know do not want Christ Jesus as their Savior and as the Lord of their lives. These people, as well as nations which do not worship God, are living in danger. God wants each of us who know Him to help others see their danger. He calls to us, "Whom shall I send?" It is the privilege of every Christian to respond, "Here am I! Send me" (Isaiah 6:8).

For Thinking and Doing:

1. Read II Timothy 3:1-4; II Thessalonians 1:7-9.

2. Which of the descriptions given in the II Timothy verses fits conditions today?

3. Throughout the Bible the destruction of the wicked is predicted. Would heaven be heaven if they were there? What kinds of people are described in II Thessalonians 1:8?

4. Will you say, "Here am I. Send me" if there is someone you can help?

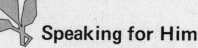

Speaking for Him

"Let him who has My Word (in his heart) speak My Word" (Jeremiah 23:28).

Do you know that God is always speaking to people's hearts? He wants them to know He loves them and wants to save them, but so often their hearts are not tuned in to God. He seems unreal and far away. They do not read the Bible so they cannot know all He would say to them. You and I have to speak for Him and tell them what He wants them to know and how He loves them. We can be witnesses for Him.

What shall we say? God says, "Speak My Words to them" (Ezekiel 2:7). Knowing certain Bible verses will help. The Bible teaches that God is a living Person though He does not live in a body like ours (Hebrews 11:6), and that He lives in a glorious, sinless place called heaven. He wants everyone to trust Him, to know Him now, and to live with Him forever.

However, we cannot know or please God or ever see His heavenly home unless He gives us a new kind of nature: a new nature that cannot sin (John 3:3). The Bible teaches that no sinner could ever be in heaven and that "all have sinned" (Romans 3:23). The punishment for our sin is the death of our souls—never to have that wonderful, everlasting life that only God can give (Romans 6:23).

Jesus, God's own dear Son, came from heaven, lived on earth in a human body, and took all the punishment for our sins as He was dying on the cross (I Peter 2:24). To anyone who will believe this, who doesn't want to go on sinning, and who will take the Lord Jesus into his heart, God will give everlasting life (John 3:16). His sins will be forgiven and He will be God's own loved child forever (John 1:12; I John 5:11, 12).

Write out the verses in the preceding paragraph on a card and try to memorize at least some of them. They will help you to share with someone else what God has done for them.

For Thinking and Doing:

1. Read through again the above verses which you have written out.

2. Choose one today to memorize. Try to learn all of them as you can.

3. In Matthew 28:19-20, what were Jesus' parting words to His disciples?

4. You probably know a number of other young people who do not seem to know Jesus. Begin to pray now that you will want to share with them what you have learned of Him.

Seed and Soil

"He that goes forth weeping, bearing the seed for sowing, shall come home with shouts of joy" (Psalm 126:6).

In witnessing to someone about Christ you need first to win his trust and friendship in order to show that you are sincere in all you do and say. If you are and if you let the Lord Jesus live out His life through you, this in itself will witness to others about Him.

Often you might have only a short time to speak to someone about Christ and to tell him what the Lord means to you and why you love Him. If he seems interested, ask if he would like to know what the Bible says about our Savior. He may answer that he does not believe the Bible or what it teaches. Let him talk. Then if you can, explain the reason you believe as you do, but never try to make anyone listen who does not want to. Wait for another time. Meanwhile you could invite him to your Sunday school, church or a special program at your young people's meeting.

Don't be discouraged if your friend does not respond as you think he should. When we speak to others about the things of God, it is like planting seeds in their hearts. All seeds need time to grow. They won't pop up from the ground at once. So be patient. You may have to plant many seeds before one takes root in the heart and begins to sprout. Above all else, pray. Only God can bring a person to open his heart to Him. Pray that He will do His wonderful work in the heart of the one to whom you have witnessed.

Continue to learn the verses you have written down so that you can use them in sharing with someone else what Jesus Christ came into our world to do for us. As a witness for Him, you can plant His Word as a seed; He alone can make it grow.

For Thinking and Doing:

1. Read Mark 5:19-20; Matthew 13:3-9.

2. What challenge do you find for yourself as you read about the healed man?

3. Describe the different kinds of soil given in Matthew 13:3-9.

4. Now see Matthew 13:18-23 for Jesus' explanation of the story He told. Which one of the soils best describes you?

165th Day

Life-Giving Water

"Rivers of living water shall flow from the inmost being of anyone who believes in Me" (John 7:38, LNT).

Part way up the mountains a circle of hills formed a bowl which became a shallow lake in rainy weather. A few trees and shrubs grew there but no water ever spilled over into the dry riverbed that sloped away through the valley. There were few signs of life or growth.

Then a marvelous change took place. Engineers uncovered a spring within the bowl. Soon the pure, life-giving waters filled the lake to overflowing and the stream went hurrying down along the old dry channel of the river. Around the lake and in the valley, grasses and flowers sprang up, trees put forth leaves, and children came to play. People in nearby towns used the water in their homes. Wherever the water flowed something good happened.

We Christians are too often like that parched, almost-empty lake. Like those few shrubs and trees, we are only showing a little of the life of Christ. What about our efforts to bring others to Him? We may talk to them and pray for them, yet sometimes very little happens. Nothing much will happen until we are filled with the life-giving water that only God can give and there is a spilling over into the lives of others. It is impossible for a river to flow out of a dry lake.

God says to each of His own, "Be filled with the Spirit" (Ephesians 5:18). This is a command. Jesus promises, "He who believes in Me, from within him . . . rivers of living waters shall flow. This He said about the Spirit which those who believed in Him were to receive" (John 7:38-39). Within the Christian is the mighty Holy Spirit who first fills his whole being and then overflows into others' lives like a life-giving river.

Even when we are filled with the Spirit, not everyone we try to lead to Jesus will turn to Him at once. But we will be able to fill the longings of those whose hearts are open to God and who thirst for Him. Others will see the beauty of our Lord in us and His life-giving water will come into our homes and into the homes of friends and neighbors.

"When the poor and needy seek water . . . I the Lord . . . will open rivers in high places . . . and (in) the dry land springs of water" (Isaiah 41:17, 18, KJV). Be God's lake. Never think you are too young or unimportant. A small lake can fill and overflow just as truly as a large one.

For Thinking and Doing:

1. Read John 15:14-16; John 4:14; John 7:37-39.
2. According to John 15:16, why did God choose you?
3. What two promises did Jesus give us in John 4:14?
4. What promise did He give in John 7:38, 39 for those who long to share the living water with others?

166th Day

Being Filled

"Blessed are they which do hunger and thirst after righteousness: for they shall be filled" (Matthew 5:6, KJV).

Out on a lonely, sun-baked desert a man was staggering across the sands. He was nearly dead from heat and thirst. Just a little way ahead he saw a clear pool of water and leafy trees. Hopefully he pushed on and on, but the lost wanderer never found that water. He died of thirst, for what he saw was a mirage: just the reflection of a real pool which lay many miles away.

Some people who profess to be Christians are like that mirage, they are not the real thing. "Be filled with the Spirit" (Ephesians 5:18). He will cause your life to put forth the beauties of the life of Jesus, for He is "the Spirit of Christ" (Romans 8:9). Only then will you have the living water to give those who the Bible teaches are lost and dying. Many of them thirst for God, but they do not know how to find the safety of the salvation which Jesus gives us unless someone tells them. How may one be filled? First ask God to perform this wonderful miracle in your life, and then make room for Him to do it. He cannot fill you if the channel of your life is choked with self or sin.

233

There are some who have no desire to be filled with the Holy Spirit. They are content with a little faith and a few good works that are just enough so that they look like Christians. Such people may really care nothing for those who are without God and lost. Are you one of these?

Earnestly ask God to give you His longing to help the lost and to make you willing for anything He would have you do. "He that winneth souls is wise" (Proverbs 11:30, KJV). "And those who are wise shall shine like the brightness of the firmament; and those who turn many to righteousness like the stars for ever and ever" (Daniel 12:3). Yet it is "not by might, nor by power, but by My Spirit, says the Lord" (Zechariah 4:6).

You do not know the deepest needs of other hearts and lives nor how to meet them. But all is known to the Spirit "of wisdom and understanding" (Isaiah 11:2). You do not always know what to say or do to help them or what Bible verse to use. But the Spirit of counsel can show you. You have no power to convince another of his need or to lead him to Christ; you are unable to make God's Word a living power in another's life. But the Spirit of might is well able. "Be filled with the Spirit" (Ephesians 5:18). Give all of yourself to the Holy Spirit so He can fill you.

For Thinking and Doing:

1. Read Luke 11:9-13, Matthew 18:12-14.

2. If a Christian asks to be filled with the Holy Spirit, what will God do according to Luke 11:13?

3. How concerned is God for each lost sheep according to Matthew 18:14?

4. As you pray today ask God to help you yield your life to Him so that He can fill you with His Holy Spirit.

167th Day

Wholly Yielded

"Give yourselves completely to God—every part of you . . . you want to be tools in the hands of God, to be used for His good purposes" (Romans 6:13, LNT).

Have you asked to be filled with the Holy Spirit? He will have to prepare you to receive the answer. No great jet plane roaring through space would be handed over to a boy. But when a young man has had enough training and experience, he can be

234

trusted to pilot that plane. God also has to teach and prepare His children before He can entrust them with this mighty power, the fulness of the Spirit. He must also be able to see that we want the power only for that which is holy, for the blessing of others, and to the praise of our Lord, and not for any selfish, personal reasons.

Our Father can only give the Spirit in fulness to those who are wholly yielded. All that they are and all they have must be turned over to Him in day-by-day obedience. Does that seem too big a price to pay? It costs much to be Spirit-filled, but you must be all for God in order to have God's all for you. Ours is the great honor of being filled by the Holy Spirit. Are you preparing your heart? Have you made room for the Lord to do this wondrous thing in you? If so, do not be discouraged if the answer does not come at once or in the way you thought it would. Expect God to answer. He will not fail the longing, obedient one who puts his trust in Him.

We cannot choose the manner of the Spirit's filling nor just how His fulness will show itself in us. The first result will be to bring forth in our own lives the precious fruit we read of in Galatians 5:22-23. The Holy Spirit "will guide you into all the truth" (John 16:13) and through you "He . . . will tell you all about Me (Christ)" (John 15:26, LNT). That is what He wants to do with you just now.

In His own time He will give you heavenly gifts to fit you for special kinds of work for God. "Now God gives us many kinds of special abilities, but it is the same Holy Spirit who is the source of them all. There are different kinds of service to God . . . There are many ways in which God works in our lives . . . The Holy Spirit displays God's power through each of us" (I Corinthians 12:4-7, LNT).

Our gift will be a gift of special power, understanding, faith, or for some special service. Read of the different gifts in I Corinthians 12:8-12. We know what happens to a lake when its spring waters no longer flow in. The lake is soon emptied. And unless we are very careful that will happen to us. We must be kept filled. Do not choke the spring. You will become like the thing which controls you. Is it self or God the Spirit?

What happens when the Holy Spirit is in full control of a life? There are many stories in the book of Acts which tell of men who were filled with the Holy Spirit. By His great power they were able to help many people find true purpose and direction for living by finding Jesus. The Holy Spirit cannot be simply a powerful influence from God or a good, religious feeling. For power has no wisdom and a religious feeling cannot be grieved. If He were just a feeling or a force, we might wonder whether that power would disappear, become weak or whether it was for us. No, the Spirit is God and He is unchangeable and everlasting. He waits for your earnest prayers and your whole obedience so that He can fill you.

For Thinking and Doing:

1. Read John 15:1-5, 16; Romans 6:13, 16-19; Galations 5:22, 23.

2. What do you learn from the illustration of the Vine and the branches?

3. What two choices are given in the Romans 6 passage? Which one have you made?

4. If you are filled with the Holy Spirit, what fruit will it bring into your life according to Galatians 5:22, 23?

168th Day

A Great Company

"The Lord gave the word: great was the company of those that published it" (Psalm 68:11, KJV).

In a South American jungle great trees shadowed the black waters of a deep and narrow river. Chattering monkeys leaped here and there. At times there came the scream of a frightened bird. No human beings lived in this dark tangle of palms, trees and ferns.

Into the dark river slipped a canoe with two Indian paddlers and a young American girl, Sophie Muller. Why had this American girl come to such a lonely, dangerous place? She was obeying the call of her Lord. At home in New York she had heard Him say, "You are to go into all the world and preach the Good News (the Gospel) to everyone, everywhere" (Mark 16:15, LNT). God had told her to go. "Yes, Lord, but where?" she asked.

Far away in the dense jungles of Columbia and Brazil lived thousands of Indians. Their languages were unwritten and unknown to any but themselves. They had never been told of God's love, that Jesus died for everyone, and that they might have a glorious home in heaven. Through the centuries they had lived in ignorance, fear and suffering.

236

Sophie Muller gave God what He needed—the love and trust of an utterly yielded heart. She was His messenger to those who were lost without Christ. To reach them there would be weariness and discouragements. Satan ruled among these people; he would fight against her. She would go alone, yet not alone for the Lord had promised, "I will be with you . . . I will not fail you or forsake you. Be strong and of good courage" (Joshua 1:5, 6).

So Sophie went on and on by truck or horse, by river boat and canoe until she reached the small heathen village of Sejal. Here she learned the Indian's language, put it into writing, and led many people to Jesus. But many more needed to hear of His salvation, so she moved on. Into her pack were put a Bible, native bread, powdered milk, a raincoat, a few clothes, a mosquito net and hammock, as well as all that would be needed to teach her pupils how to read and write. With two Indian guides Sophie pressed on.

Sophie Muller belongs to the great company of missionaries who have travelled afar to tell of God's love to others. Ever since the Apostle Paul began his first missionary journey, Christians have left their homes to spread the Good News of the Gospel to other lands.

For Thinking and Doing:

1. Read Jeremiah 1:4-9.
2. When the prophet Jeremiah was called of God, what excuses did he give?
3. What assurances did God give to him?
4. With what did God equip him? See verse 9.

169th Day

Faith Comes by Hearing

"How shall they ask Him to save them unless they believe in Him? How can they believe in Him if they have never heard about Him? And how can they hear about Him unless someone tells them?" (Romans 10:14, LNT).

It was hard going for the travelers. The river was racing now and any moment the canoe might be wrecked by unseen jagged trunks of trees which had fallen into the water. Sophie shivered in a cold rain which soaked her blouse and slacks. Finally they left the canoe and followed a trail leading up to the Cuyari River. At the top of the soggy bank the hammock was hung between two trees just as the blackness and loneliness of a jungle night closed in. "It's still raining," Sophie wrote in her diary. "My head aches. I've a fever, plus three big ulcers on my leg—all swollen up."

Sunshine came in the morning and back to the trail again they went. But it was really not a trail. Sophie wrote, "Twisted roots . . . knee-deep water, and mud, mud." Mile after mile they went on walking and stumbling. "In places like this," her diary says, "I like to sing 'He shall give His angels charge over thee . . . in all thy ways.' And then with the eyes of faith you can see them going on in the trail ahead."

Into the Rio Cuyari they came at last, and soon they reached the first of the Karom tribe. "Many bad people along here," Sophie's guides said. So as she struggled up the river bank her prayer was, "Help me, Lord, to find an open door." For if the Indians here turned her away, no other villages would let her in.

In the first hut she saw a group of queer-looking men with dark, stupid-looking faces; their dirty bodies were covered with purple blotches. Could they ever learn? "I have come to teach you about God," the white girl said, "and how to read and write." No one moved or spoke. They only laughed. But the Lord was working for His servant and it was decided she could stay; her pack and hammock were put into a tiny hut. Sophie knew that within those poor ugly bodies were unhappy, frightened hearts.

These Indians believed that there were cruel, evil spirits out beyond in the jungle who hated them, made them sick, and sent them every kind of suffering. Now, with Sophie's coming, night after night the whole village heard of the God who loved them and of the Savior, the Lord Jesus Christ. They learned that He was stronger than evil spirits and was ready to forgive their sins and make them free from fear and sin. Was all this really for them? It seemed too good to be true. Jesus had said, "Him who comes to Me I will not cast out" (John 6:37). Many came and were received into His kingdom.

After his conversion when Paul began to preach about Christ, he was in danger of his life from both the Jews and Greeks (Acts 9:23, 29). Yet he had been called by Christ Himself to serve Him. Danger and difficulties do not keep Christ's disciples from their service for Him. How could those without Christ "hear, unless someone told them?" "Faith cometh by hearing, and hearing by the Word of God" (Romans 10:17, KJV).

For Thinking and Doing:

238
1. Read Acts 16:9, 10, 16-34.

2. What impressed you most about this story of Paul?

3. What was he doing in prison when deliverance came?

4. Why do you think Paul did not hurry to escape from prison as soon as his chains were released?

Sharing His Longing

"The Son of Man came to seek and to save the lost" (Luke 19:10).

In Sophie's classroom hut there swarmed thousands of stinging gnats. Fighting dogs ran in and out. Little children seemed to be everywhere. Parrots flew and screamed. In spite of all this a number of people were learning about syllables and how to copy letters and words. How pleased they were with themselves. Sophie taught them hymns, too, and these they happily shouted as they tried to sing above the noise.

Through it all God was saving souls. Men and women were praying together to their new-found Father. Unpleasant things were forgotten, Sophie tells us, "and we entered into the joy of our victory with Christ, and we (by faith) beheld Him in all His resurrection glory." Yet only a short time before, these people had never even heard of Jesus Christ. So the first of the Karom tribe became children of the Lord of heaven and earth Who died that they might live.

Now that God was changing lives and many had learned to read, Sophie must push on to other villages along the river. So she moved from place to place. Usually there went on with her some who wanted to learn more of what she taught.

In her diary she wrote, "You meet group after group who know nothing of Him who is the Way, the Truth and the Life. As they listen to the story of Jesus and His love, you can't help but feel that you have ceased to exist. It seems like you are being borne along in the great tide of God's longing 'to seek and to save that which is lost.' The one thing you know is that you are one of those who knows the Way of life and there are many farther on who do not know." She had to go on and on. They had to be found and shown the Way before it was too late.

During the day Sophie gave her time to the Indians. But at night she would be in a small palm-leaf shelter alone with the

Lord. Her heart sang with the song of the wind as she remembered God's promises. "The darkness hideth not from Thee. If I . . . dwell in the uttermost parts . . . even there shall Thy hand lead me" (Psalm 139:12, 9, 10).

In telling the men of Athens of the living God, Paul said, "In Him we live and move and have our being" (Acts 17:28). His heart longed to tell more and more people of Christ who died to save them from their sin. Through the centuries since, countless missionaries have had the same longing and as a result, "The people who sat in darkness have seen a great light, and for those who sat in the region and shadows of death has the light dawned" (Matthew 4:16).

For Thinking and Doing:

1. Read Acts 17:18, 22-34.
2. Name some of the things Paul tells men about God in these verses.
3. Of Whom does Paul speak in verse 31, and of what proof does he speak?
4. Memorize Acts 17:27, 28; "Yet He is not far from each one of us, for in Him we live and move and have our being."

171st Day

Loss Becomes Gain

"Whatever gain I had, I counted as loss for the sake of Christ . . . For His sake I have suffered the loss of all things . . . in order that I may gain Christ" (Philippians 3:7, 8).

Month after month God's young servant followed the rivers and jungle trails. Home was wherever her hammock was hung. Food was usually whatever the Indians might give her, which was often very poor. She thanked God that her teeth were strong enough to chew the tough pieces of crocodile meat.

240

Christ has said, "In the world you have tribulation" (John 16:33). But with it was the promise that "If we endure, we shall also reign with Him" (II Timothy 2:12). There were days when the road ahead seemed endless, with the hundreds of unreached ones still waiting. There were blistering days of burning eyes and an aching head, the sun's rays cutting like a knife. In her diary we read, "I'll have to sing, 'Where Jesus is 'tis Heaven' in order to keep joyful. For I see so many dying. I'm tired of the filth and sickness, flies and biting dogs. I get tired of teaching day after day, night after night." It often seemed more than she could bear. One would cry out, "Lord, give me the faith that walks and does not faint!" Then as she looked up to the Mighty One who holds the universe, He brought quietness and rest. "Be of good comfort," the Lord would say, "thy faith hath made thee whole" (Matthew 9:22, KJV).

The Holy Spirit strengthens tired bodies. Sophie could forget the weariness in the joy of seeing the power of Christ at work in Indian hearts. They didn't want to be like dogs, they said. They wanted to have the Spirit of God. Now their hungry hearts were being fed the Living Bread. The Light from heaven was shining in hundreds of souls that were dark and dead before. How they prayed, coming to God with love and eager faith. And how they sang, meaning all the words of praise and thanks.

More and more, as the farther villages heard about the good news that was being told among the river people, they sent to beg Sophie to come to them. It was hard to leave behind those who needed so much more teaching from God's Word. But they were His children now and she must trust them to His care. Besides, many of the Indians she had taught went along with her for further study. They would return and teach the others.

The book, *Shadow of the Almighty,* tells of the life of Jim Elliot, one of the five missionaries killed by the Auca Indians in 1956. Were the lives of these five men lost? No. God reached those Auca tribesmen even through this seeming tragedy, and their story has inspired many young people to give their lives to service for Christ. As a college student Jim Elliot wrote, "He is no fool who gives what he cannot keep, to gain what he cannot lose."

For Thinking and Doing:

1. Read II Corinthians 11:22-33; 12:9, 10.
2. What kinds of dangers did Paul experience?
3. What do you think Paul meant when he said, "When I am weak, then I am strong" (II Corinthians 12:10)?
4. In spending his life for Christ, what did Jim Elliot gain?

Expendable Lives

"I will most gladly spend and be spent for your souls" (II Corinthians 12:15).

If the Christian Indians were to know Christ better, they must learn more about Him, His plans and His will. So Sophie returned Sejal and went busily to work preparing books for them, parts of Scripture, hymns and simple, helpful stories. All were written in their own languages.

Many messages reached her from the tribes. "We have left our sin since hearing God's Word." "We think of our Master, Jesus." "We want to see His face."

Soon she went back to them with the books, and what a welcome she received in the villages. Many more had turned to Christ. From all directions they came in from the jungles. "Tell us everything about God," they said. And Sophie did her best. Untaught Indians from farther on sent messengers to ask, "Come to our place and teach us about our Father, God." "Did you come from heaven?" they asked. "No," she would answer. Then she would go and tell them of the One who had come from heaven in love for their souls. Thus the Holy Spirit was gathering in the lost.

But all was not easy. There were the same dangerous, tiring trips and all the hindrances of the one who was against her work, Satan. One time Sophie spent five days and nights alone in the jungle, hearing the "ji, ji" night cry of the tiger and the wild screams of monkeys angered at her presence. She shook and groaned with weariness. Had God forgotten His child? No, the Lord does not forget and at last the Indian guides arrived. The next day they were once more canoeing down a dark river to another village.

Sophie knew that lives were slipping into eternity like water down the river. They were dying as they had lived—without God and hopeless. She wrote, "It is here that night still lingers on in the souls of men even though long since the Son of God has risen to light the whole, wide world." "I am the Light of the world," He said. "He who follows Me will not walk in darkness, but will have the Light of Life" (John 8:12). "Go ye into all the world and preach the Gospel to the whole creation" (Mark 16:15).

God led the Apostle Paul to go out into the far reaches of his world to tell others about Christ. His life was spent for his converts who became faithful followers of Christ. His epistles to his churches, Corinth, Rome, etc., tell of his deep love and concern for them that they stand fast in the faith. Acts 27 and 28 give the thrilling story of shipwreck and his experiences as a prisoner on the way to Rome. God used him to spread the Gospel there, and from Rome it has spread throughout the world. What if Paul had not been willing to spend his life for Christ? The Great Commission is given to all Christians: "Go therefore and make disciples of all nations" (Matthew 28:19).

For Thinking and Doing:

1. Read Acts 28:16-31.
2. To whom at Rome did Paul first bring the Good News of Christ and His resurrection?
3. Did they all believe?
4. Describe in your own words the great opportunity God gave Paul as a prisoner in Rome. See verses 30 and 31.

173rd Day

Their Only Help

"Jesus told him, 'I am the Way—yes, and the Truth and the Life. No one can get to the Father except by means of Me'" (John 14:6, LNT).

The Lord looks with sorrow upon the myriads of heathen peoples living in lonely jungles or crowding the great cities of pagan lands. He sees their sins, their misery, their Godlessness, and He longs to deliver them. The Lord also looks with deep sadness upon Christians who do not seem to care about the thousands of hopeless souls who daily slip away into the river of death and everlasting darkness, Christians who don't even seem to care enough to pray.

"He died for all" (II Corinthians 5:15). This even includes those who worship His great enemy, the devil. Christ died for the evil head-hunters and for the cruel tribes who send away their old sick men and women to starve or be eaten by wild animals. Christ suffered death to save the poor, ignorant people of India who horribly torture their bodies, thinking they can thus fit their souls for heaven.

243

In their desperate need, their only help is the Lord Jesus Christ. He is the only way to God and heaven. Jesus is all that is truth. They need Him who is Life and who shares His glorious life with others.

"God our Savior . . . wants all persons to be saved" (I Timothy 2:3, 4, Berkeley). "Everyone who calls upón the name of the Lord will be saved. But how are men to believe in Him whom they have never heard? And how are they to hear without a preacher? And how can men preach unless they are sent?" (Romans 10:13-15).

How may these far-off people be reached? They can be reached by radio, by tape recordings, and through the printed page of papers, books and Bibles. They can be reached by the Lord's missionary servants as we pray for them and give our money to support them in their work. What message shall they hear? God answers, "You shall speak My words to them" (Ezekiel 2:7). When? "Now is the accepted time; behold, now is the day of salvation" (II Corinthians 6:2, KJV).

The pagan world is under the power of the evil one. Their need is now. Your time to help is now.

For Thinking and Doing:

1. Read Luke 4:14-21.
2. Why did Christ say Isaiah's words were fulfilled as He read them?
3. How are people in pagan lands poor, captives and blind?
4. How can we take His Good News to them?

174th Day

Ripe for Harvest

"Pray therefore the Lord of the harvest to send out laborers into His harvest" (Matthew 9:38).

If you are a Christian and are not interested in lost souls around the world, there is something wrong. Even though you are young and may not yet know God's plan for your life, you can take part in foreign missionary work from where you are now.

A wheat rancher labors to have his barns filled with wheat. First he and his men plant seed. When the wheat is fully ripe he will send the reapers to gather in the crop. Which of the rancher's workers does the most important work: the ones who supply the seed, those who sow, or the reapers? All are equally important.

The Lord Jesus said that He is like a wheat rancher. He is "the Lord of the harvest" (Luke 10:2). "The field is the world" (Matthew 13:38). "The seed" which is sown "is the word of God" (Luke 8:11). This seed must be planted all over the world so that Christ will have much grain, precious souls, gathered into the barn of His heavenly home. Christians are His servants. Each has a work to do. All are equally important, but all must work where and as their Master directs—some sowing and others reaping.

Therefore, while you may not be called to work in far-off parts of the field, you can help to make it possible for others to go. You can give what is needed to carry on Christ's work of planting or reaping. Most important, you can pray. Ask God to protect His missionary servants, to guide and cheer them, and to send in all they need of helpers, money and supplies. Pray that the Lord Jesus will be very real and near to them. Ask that God will cause His Word, the planted seed, to take root in hearts so that there may be a great harvest for Him. Pray with other Christians as well as alone.

There are other things you can do. The missionary life is usually a lonely one. It is often very dangerous and difficult. How much pleasure it would give if you or perhaps your young people's group would write to some missionary or missionary's child. Let them tell you of their problems; then make their work your own special part of God's field for which you pray and work. Ask God to guide you in finding just where He would have you help in His great harvest field. Millions are living there without knowing, while millions are living here without going.

"Christ . . . loved . . . and gave Himself" (Ephesians 5:25). "God (the Father) so loved the world that He gave" (John 3:16). He gave His most precious treasure. It has been said, "We may give without loving, but we cannot love without giving." If we have love for the unsaved, we will, like Jesus, give our entire selves to God and to His work. We will, as God the Father, give of our treasures—plans, money, time and strength.

"Give, and it will be given to you; good measure, pressed down, shaken together, running over" (Luke 6:38). God will in some way make up to us for all we sacrifice for Him. He is no man's debtor; we can never outgive God.

For Thinking and Doing:
1. Read Matthew 13:24-30, 36-43.

2. Who does Jesus say are the good seed and who are the weeds or tares?

3. Who will destroy all evil doers at the end of the age?

4. Ask the Lord today to guide you to find some part in His great missionary task.

175th Day

So Send I You

"Here am I, send me" (Isaiah 6:8).

God gave the Apostle John a vision of heaven. He saw wonderful, beautiful things which he recorded in the book of Revelation. He heard the voices of countless myriads of angels worshiping God the Son. He heard heaven's songs sung by those from every tribe, tongue, people and nation as they praised Him who died for their salvation. Will some of those who sing be there because you answered God's call, "Yes, Lord. Here am I; send me"?

We cannot tell where or how God's special call will reach us if He should call us to go to the mission field. Isaiah heard it in the temple; Ezekiel heard it as he lay beside a river. It may reach you while you pray or read, or through a missionary message. But you must be sure it is a call from God. If part of your reason for wanting to be a missionary is because you think it would be exciting to travel to new places, then the desire is not from Him. His call only falls into hearts that feel a mighty urge that souls must be saved for His sake, that souls who know not God are lost, and that the joy of having Christ must be shared with others.

Jesus said, "As the Father has sent Me, even so I send you" (John 20:21): "The Father has sent His Son as the Savior of the world" (I John 4:14). For Christ it meant always doing the Father's will instead of His own, and in the place God chose. It meant doing it through loneliness, weariness and pain and going steadily on in spite of every attack by His enemies.

If we are called to a distant land, it will be the same for us as it was for our Master. Those that our Lord calls to His missionary task need to realize that theirs is a great and holy work. They must understand that their lives are wholly His and not their own. Nothing less will do because of the dangers and discouragements. Only when heathen people see the love of Christ in the missionary will they respond.

Do you long to be one of God's messengers? Do you feel that He has chosen and has called you? If so, you will want to get all the training you need for His work at some good Bible school. Remember your call must be from God. At every step look to Him for His leading.

Some countries no longer let missionaries in, but they will accept Christian carpenters, teachers, doctors, mechanics, farmers, nurses, etc. Perhaps to some of these places or in one of these ways the Lord Jesus will send you forth to win the lost to Him. "I chose you," Christ said, "and appointed you that you should go" (John 15:16). If this is His word to you, you could have no greater honor put upon you.

For Thinking and Doing:

1. Read John 4:31-38; Matthew 19:29.
2. What did Christ say was His food, that which sustained His life?
3. Where are the fields today which are white for harvest?
4. What promise is there in Matthew 19:29 for anyone who gives up home and loved ones for His service?

176th Day

Christ's Church

"I will build My Church" (Matthew 16:18).

Do you belong to a church; "Yes," you may reply, "I belong to the Baptist Church," or it may be the Presbyterian Church or some other one. You may say you belong to this church because your parents attend there or because you are a member yourself. Even then, you may not belong to the one true Church. For you can join any church and still not belong to God's true Church.

On the other hand, if you are a Christian, you could live alone on a desert and you would belong to God's one true Church. God's Church is not made up of those who call themselves by any special name, but is made up of everyone who has truly accepted the Lord Jesus as Savior. God's true Church is "the church of God, which He (Christ) hath purchased with His own blood" (Acts 20:28, KJV).

This Church was not formed by men, but by God. The Holy Spirit placed you in this Church when you were born again (I Corinthians 12:13). The true Church is both unseen and seen. It is

247

invisible or unseen because only God can see the souls and spirits of those who form this great Church. Its members are found in all lands and nations, yet they are all one church in Christ Jesus.

In another way, however, the Church can be seen, for a group of believers who gather together to pray and worship the Lord are called a church. Every true Christian should belong to a church, joining with others in carrying on the work of Christ in the world. "Let us not neglect our church duties and meetings" (Hebrews 10:25, LNT).

At the time when Jesus went back to heaven there were only a few Christians. They met in homes and God's Church was small. But as people in places farther away were won to Christ, other church groups were formed and so we read of "the church of God . . . at Corinth," or "the church in Jerusalem" (I Corinthians 1:2; Acts 8:1). Today God's children have divided into many groups and call themselves by different denominational names. But names do not matter; God looks at hearts. Either you belong to Christ and are in His much-loved Church, or you are not His and are outside the true Church.

Your name may be on a list of church members, but the important thing is that God shall have written your name as a member of His Church. No church can save us from God's judgment and bring us to heaven; only Christ can do that. If you have asked Christ to come into your heart as your Savior from sin, your name is written in the Book of Life. In the book of Revelation we are told that there is to be a final judgment for those who have rejected Christ and whose names are not in His Book of Life. "If any one's name was not found written in the book of life, he was thrown into the lake of fire" (Revelation 20:15).

Jesus is the "head over all things for the church, which is His body" (Ephesians 1:22, 23). Each member of the true Church, every born-again person, is joined to Christ, the head, because each one shares His life. This is why the Church is called Christ's spiritual body. "Christ is the head of the church, His body, and is Himself its Savior" (Ephesians 5:23).

Just as your head needs your body to carry out its plans, so Christ in heaven needs His spiritual body to carry out His purposes here on earth. Even as your head cares for the happiness and welfare of each part of your body, so Christ is always planning for the highest good and blessing of His own. "Just as the body is one and has many members, and all the members of the body, though many, are one body, so it is with Christ" (I Corinthians 12:12).

248

"God has so adjusted (fitted together) the body . . . that the members may have the same care for one another. If one member suffers, all suffer together; if one member is honored, all rejoice together" (I Corinthians 12:24-26).

For Thinking and Doing:

1. Read Matthew 16:12-18; Ephesians 1:22, 23.
2. What was Peter's answer to Christ's question in Matthew 16:16?
3. Who revealed this to him according to verse 17?
4. What confession must we make, like Peter, to become members of God's true Church?

True Teaching

"The Holy Spirit tells us clearly that in the last times some in the church will turn away from Christ" (I Timothy 4:1, LNT).

The Lord Jesus warns, "Take heed what you hear" (Mark 4:24). Be very careful what you listen to, for "there will be false teachers among you, who will secretly bring in destructive heresies (dangerous teachings), even denying the Master who bought them" (II Peter 2:1). "Some shall depart from the (Christian) faith" (I Timothy 4:1). They "speak evil of the things that they understand not; and shall utterly perish . . . And many shall follow" them (II Peter 2:12, 2, KJV).

God has shown us this picture of the days in which we are living. It tells of pastors and leaders in some churches who teach that the Bible does not always mean what it says and that certain parts of God's Book are not to be trusted. They use the Bible, but they "wrest (or twist) the scriptures" (II Peter 3:16) and pull God's truth out of shape to suit their own ideas.

For example, they may say that Jesus saves from sin, but they teach that we are saved from sin only by following the example of His holy life and being willing to suffer to help others. They deny that in death our Lord took the punishment of our sins upon Himself and that God gives eternal life to all who receive Christ as their Savior. They claim that man is accepted by God because of his own good works, but God says, "Not because of works" (Ephesians 2:9).

Again we are told that they will even be denying the Lord. These false teachers speak in a familiar way of "Jesus," but they refuse to believe the whole truth about Him, namely, that the Lord Jesus is truly God as the Father is God. Christ said, "I and the Father are one" (John 10:30).

They deny that Jesus was born into this world without a human father having any part in His birth, although the Scriptures say He was (Luke 1:30-35). Of course these false teachers were not there with the disciples who saw Christ after He arose from the dead, but that does not bother them. They simply say that His bodily resurrection can't be true. They deny other things also. How sure of themselves they are and how proud they are to set their own minds against the truth of God. Of all such God says, "Professing themselves to be wise, they became fools" (Romans 1:22, KJV) and "bringing upon themselves swift destruction" (II Peter 2:1).

When you choose the church you will join and attend, be sure its teaching is true. True teaching is centered upon Christ, that He is truly the Son of God, that He gave Himself on the cross to atone for our sin, that He is risen from the dead, that He is our living Savior, and that He is coming again.

You will meet false teaching in your school life also. Teachers will discredit the Bible, especially in your science courses where many statements are based on the theory of evolution. Remember there are outstanding scientists who do not accept this theory and who point out that scientific fact does not conflict with the Biblical story of creation.

Read your Bible and know what it teaches so that you may be able to see what is false teaching. "Study to show thyself approved unto God . . . rightly dividing the word of truth. Know what His Word says and means" (II Timothy 2:15, KJV & LNT).

For Thinking and Doing:

1. Read Matthew 7:15-20; I John 4:1-3.

2. How do the verses in Matthew tell us we can know false teachers?

3. Look at Galatians 5:22, 23 for the fruit of the Holy Spirit which should be seen in true teachers.

250   4. How does I John 4:2, 3 say we can know true teaching?

Worship

"It's not where we worship that counts, but how we worship. For God is Spirit, and we must have His help to worship as we should" (John 4:22, 24, LNT).

Every Sunday morning church doors are open and bells and chimes call Christians to come and worship God. It is really not the bells which call, but Christ Himself. "The Lord . . . hath spoken . . . Gather my saints together unto Me" (Psalm 50:1, 5, KJV). "Learn from Me" (Matthew 11:29). "Worship the Lord your God" (Luke 4:8). "Praise God in His sanctuary" (Psalm 150:1). "Not neglecting (failing) to meet together" (Hebrews 10:25).

The Church is on earth to make the Lord Jesus known, to speak forth God's Word, and to win hearts to Him. As members, by prayer and loving-kindness, we are to help one another be what God wants us to be. So we have Sunday services, prayer meeting, Sunday school, and all the different church activities. "Christ . . . loved the church, and gave Himself for it" (Ephesians 5:25, KJV). He loved it enough to die to bring it into being and He loves it now. We miss God's best if we remain away from church, for in church meetings we learn about the things of God and our Lord.

Should we attend church even if we can't always understand all of the sermon? Yes. Here are the answers given by young people: "I don't go to church only to hear the sermon, but because Jesus said, 'Where two or three are gathered together in My name, there am I in the midst of them!' (Matthew 18:20, KJV). It pleases my Lord to have me go to meet Him there." "I go because I love the Lord and want my neighbors and friends to see that I put Him first."

Suppose that the first person we should meet as we leave church next Sunday would be the Lord Jesus Christ. How wonderful would be the smile on that radiant, majestic face. He would talk with us as earnestly and kindly as to His dearest disciples. We would be thrilled to know that we are His. But what if He should speak with sadness, "I am sorry you were not in church today. I had planned a special blessing for you." "But Lord," you would reply, "I was there." "Yes, but only part of you was there," He could say, "Where were your ears, your heart and your mind?"

You go to church to worship and draw near to the Lord, yet do you sometimes find your heart and thoughts far from Him? Your lips may be singing hymns, your eyes may be upon the preacher, and your body may be sitting in the pew, but the real you may be elsewhere with your thoughts busy with other things.

Ask the Lord before you go to keep your mind from wandering and to help you to worship. As you sing the hymns concentrate on the meaning of the words, for the great hymns of the church will help you to worship as you do this. Have your Bible with you and open it to the Scripture passage, thinking about it as your pastor reads. As you grow in your spiritual life you will understand more and more of the sermons. Most important of all, you will be able to apply what is taught to your own life.

For Thinking and Doing:

1. Read Acts 17:22-28; Psalm 95:1-7.
2. Why does Paul say God has made us according to verse 27?
3. What are the reasons we should worship Him given in Psalm 95:1-7?
4. Will you ask Him to help you worship Him as you should?

179th Day

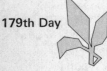

Service

"As servants of Christ . . . rendering service with a good will as to the Lord" (Ephesians 6:6, 7).

You may wonder, "What part do I have in the church?" God may use your lips to sing or speak for Him or your feet to do His errands. He may use your ears to listen to someone in trouble or your hands to give them help. Be sure of this: Our Lord has need for every member of His body; He has a place and plan for you in His church. We are to serve one another in love, for by doing this we serve the Lord.

We serve, but how? First ask the Lord what He wants of you. It may seem that you don't have much to offer. It is not what you have that matters, but what you do with what you have. The one little stone which sped from young David's slingshot was used by God to save a nation. Ask God to show you where you can serve Him best.

Can you play an instrument or sing? If so, use that lovely gift of music to touch others for Christ. "Sing unto Him" (Psalm 33:4, KJV). We should always sing words of praise and worship unto Him, not just to an audience. You may be asked to pray, lead a young people's meeting, or tell what Jesus means to you and how He has answered prayer. Your pastor may be able to use you in daily vacation Bible school or in teaching a class of little children. Some of your money could go toward carrying on God's work here at home and around the world. Do you know someone, a friend or neighbor, who does not attend church? An invitation to go with you to your church might bring him to know Christ.

Maybe you are afraid of failing or are unwilling to fill a small place of service. Not to try is the worst kind of failure. Never mind if others seem to have a more important work than yours. We all make mistakes, but by our failures we learn what not to do. We all grow discouraged at times and want to give up. But it is said, "a winner never quits, and a quitter never wins." So if God gives you a task, stay with it and let the Holy Spirit do His work through you. "Whatever you do, do it with all your heart, as work for the Lord and not for men, for you know that it is from the Lord that you are going to get your pay . . . so keep on serving Christ the Lord" (Colossians 3:23, 24, Williams).

There are lonely people in hospitals to whom a visit or a get well card would mean much. In far-off lands there are missionaries working alone for their Lord who would be greatly encouraged by letters from your Sunday school class or young people's group. You can have a vital part in the work of missionaries at home and abroad by praying for them. Choose some missionaries, perhaps supported by your church, for whom to pray and ask God what He would have you give toward their support.

Young people's organizations which work with all denominations offer many opportunities for service for Christ. Young Life Campaign and Youth for Christ have clubs in many cities for young people of high school age. Campus Crusade for Christ and Inter-Varsity Christian Fellowship have chapters on college campuses. Some friend of yours who does not know Christ might be reached if he goes with you to a meeting of one of these groups.

"Now glory be to God who by His mighty power at work within us is able to do far more than we ever dare to ask or even dream of—infinitely beyond our highest prayers, desires, thoughts, or hopes" (Ephesians 3:20, LNT).

For Thinking and Doing:

1. Read Matthew 25:31-46.

2. What kinds of service for others are mentioned in these verses?

3. For Whom does Christ say such service for others is really given?

4. How would you connect this teaching with the commandments of Matthew 22:37-40?

180th Day

In Remembrance of Him

"Do this in remembrance of Me" (I Corinthians 11:24).

The night before His crucifixion Christ was having supper with his disciples. He "took bread: and when He had given thanks, He broke it, and said, 'This is My body, which is (broken) for you. Do this in remembrance of Me" (I Corinthians 11:23, 24). "In the same way, He took a cup, and when He had given thanks, He gave it to them, and they all drank of it. And He said to them, 'This is My blood . . . which is poured out for many" (Mark 14:23, 24). "As often as ye eat this bread and drink the cup, you proclaim the Lord's death until He comes" (I Corinthians 11:26).

We are thankful that Christ was born, but above all, we are thankful for His death. For salvation and every Christian joy and blessing are ours only because the Savior died. God wants us to remember that, even as the loaf of bread was broken, so Jesus' body was broken as He hung upon the cross. As crushed grapes yield their life-giving juice, so the blood of our Lord flowed from His wounds in order that we might live. Without his death we would be forever lost. Jesus asks us to remember His death in this special way which is called the "Lord's Supper" or "Communion." It is not just for one group of Christians, but it is for every member of the true Church. When you belong to Him, you share in the right to remember His death in this way.

When Christ gave the bread to the disciples and said, "This is My body," and about the grape juice or wine, "This is My blood," of course He did not mean that His living flesh and blood really turned into bread and wine for the disciples to eat and drink. Christ meant that the bread and wine were symbols of His death;

254

things which are seen are used to teach us about things we do not see. They stood for or represented the broken body and shed blood of our Lord.

Certainly the death of God the Son is the most solemn, wonderful, yet most awful event that ever took place. If people make light of it and if they refuse to accept it as their only way of salvation, they have no right to take of the Lord's Supper. They would be acting out a lie by pretending to believe that Christ was bearing their sins as He died upon the cross. Of every such person God says, "Whoever, therefore, eats the bread or drinks the cup of the Lord in an unworthy manner will be guilty of profaning the body and blood of the Lord, and bring judgment upon himself. Let a man so examine himself and so eat of the bread and drink of the cup" (I Corinthians 11:27-29).

As you take of the Lord's Supper it will help if you will close your eyes and mind to other things and thoughts and think of Jesus, thanking Him and loving Him for all He has done for you. Confess to Him any known sin and ask Him to forgive and cleanse you. Then Christ Himself will draw very near and make Himself real to your quiet heart.

One more thing: those who are Christ's own are to keep on celebrating His death until He comes, for He is coming again. This is the great hope of every Christian. We shall see our Lord and Savior and "when He appears we shall be like Him" (I John 3:2). "Everyone who has this hope resting on Him purifies himself as He is pure" (I John 3:3, Berkeley). His Holy Spirit within your heart makes all this possible. What a glorious future God has planned for His own!

For Thinking and Doing:

1. Read I Corinthians 11:23-32, I John 3:1-3.
2. Why do you think Christ wants His followers to remember His death?
3. Why is it necessary to examine ourselves?
4. What does the promise "we shall be like Him" mean to you?